# Resistance and Emotions

This book discusses different ways in which the cross-roads between emotions and resistance can be theorised. While the sociological field focuses primarily on emotions that are entangled in the relationship between the individual and collective, the cultural studies field has recently started to emphasise affects as a 'rescue' from the deterministic aspect of the poststructuralist approach (in which language decides everything) (Hemmings 2005, 2014). Scholars promoting the 'affective turn' argue that affects and interpretations are inseparable. By taking affects as the point of departure, it is argued that it is possible to show how bodies move in their own ways, but still in relation to others. Departing from this, it becomes interesting to explore how emotions are involved in different power relations and how they feed resistance. If we accept that emotions and interpretations are entangled and inseparable then we must investigate emotions as powerful forces of resistance.

The chapters in this book were originally published in a special issue of the *Journal of Political Power*.

**Mikael Baaz** is an associate professor in International Law and an associate professor in Conflict and Society. He currently works as a senior lecturer in International Law at the Department of Law, University of Gothenburg, Sweden, and as an affiliated senior research fellow in Political Science at the Department of Social and Behavioural Studies, University West, Sweden.

**Satu Heikkinen** is a senior lecturer in Sociology at Karlstad University, Sweden. Heikkinen's research interests are ageing, power and categorisation among others. She is currently writing about ageism and age discrimination.

**Mona Lilja** is a Professor in Peace and Development Studies at the School of Global Studies, University of Gothenburg, Sweden. Lilja's area of interest is the linkages between resistance and social change as well as the particularities – the character and emergence – of various forms of resistance.

# Resistance and Emotions
Interrogating Crossroads and Social Change

*Edited by*
Mikael Baaz, Satu Heikkinen and Mona Lilja

LONDON AND NEW YORK

First published 2018
by Routledge
2 Park Square, Milton Park, Abingdon, Oxon, OX14 4RN, UK

and by Routledge
711 Third Avenue, New York, NY 10017, USA

*Routledge is an imprint of the Taylor & Francis Group, an informa business*

© 2018 Taylor & Francis

All rights reserved. No part of this book may be reprinted or reproduced or utilised in any form or by any electronic, mechanical, or other means, now known or hereafter invented, including photocopying and recording, or in any information storage or retrieval system, without permission in writing from the publishers.

*Trademark notice*: Product or corporate names may be trademarks or registered trademarks, and are used only for identification and explanation without intent to infringe.

*British Library Cataloguing in Publication Data*
A catalogue record for this book is available from the British Library

ISBN13: 978-1-138-48253-1

Typeset in MinionPro
by diacriTech, Chennai

**Publisher's Note**
The publisher accepts responsibility for any inconsistencies that may have arisen during the conversion of this book from journal articles to book chapters, namely the possible inclusion of journal terminology.

**Disclaimer**
Every effort has been made to contact copyright holders for their permission to reprint material in this book. The publishers would be grateful to hear from any copyright holder who is not here acknowledged and will undertake to rectify any errors or omissions in future editions of this book.

*This book is dedicated to Gerd Lindgren, for her inspiration and devotion, and for her endless support.*

# Contents

| | | |
|---|---|---|
| *Citation Information* | | ix |
| *Notes on Contributors* | | xi |
| 1 | Emotions and resistance: An introduction<br>*Mikael Baaz, Satu Heikkinen and Mona Lilja* | 1 |
| 2 | Exploring self-loyalty in the context of social acceleration:<br>theorising loyalties as emotions and resistance<br>*Markus Arvidson and Jonas Axelsson* | 7 |
| 3 | Norm-critical rationality: emotions and the institutional influence of<br>queer resistance<br>*Andreas Henriksson* | 23 |
| 4 | Resistance against material artefacts: university spaces,<br>administrative online systems and emotions<br>*Anna-Lena Haraldsson and Mona Lilja* | 40 |
| 5 | Martyrdom and emotional resistance in the case of Northern Kurdistan:<br>hidden and public emotional resistance<br>*Minoo Koefoed* | 58 |
| 6 | Everyday resistance in psychiatry through harbouring strategies<br>*Mona Lindqvist and Eva Olsson* | 74 |
| 7 | Frontstage and backstage emotion management in civil resistance<br>*Majken Jul Sørensen and Andrew Rigby* | 93 |

CONTENTS

8 Campaigning for cooperatives as resistance to neoliberal capitalism 110
*Kristin Wiksell*

9 Concluding remarks 129
*Mona Lilja, Mikael Baaz, Satu Heikkinen and Annika Jonsson*

*Index* 135

# Citation Information

The chapters in this book were originally published in the *Journal of Political Power*, volume 10, issue 2 (March–October 2017). When citing this material, please use the original page numbering for each article, as follows:

**Chapter 1**
*Emotions and resistance: An introduction*
Mikael Baaz, Satu Heikkinen and Mona Lilja
*Journal of Political Power*, volume 10, issue 2 (March–October 2017) pp. 127–132

**Chapter 2**
*Exploring self-loyalty in the context of social acceleration: theorising loyalties as emotions and resistance*
Markus Arvidson and Jonas Axelsson
*Journal of Political Power*, volume 10, issue 2 (March–October 2017) pp. 133–148

**Chapter 3**
*Norm-critical rationality: emotions and the institutional influence of queer resistance*
Andreas Henriksson
*Journal of Political Power*, volume 10, issue 2 (March–October 2017) pp. 149–165

**Chapter 4**
*Resistance against material artefacts: university spaces, administrative online systems and emotions*
Anna-Lena Haraldsson and Mona Lilja
*Journal of Political Power*, volume 10, issue 2 (March–October 2017) pp. 166–183

**Chapter 5**
*Martyrdom and emotional resistance in the case of Northern Kurdistan: hidden and public emotional resistance*
Minoo Koefoed
*Journal of Political Power*, volume 10, issue 2 (March–October 2017) pp. 184–199

# CITATION INFORMATION

**Chapter 6**
*Everyday resistance in psychiatry through harbouring strategies*
Mona Lindqvist and Eva Olsson
*Journal of Political Power*, volume 10, issue 2 (March–October 2017) pp. 200–218

**Chapter 7**
*Frontstage and backstage emotion management in civil resistance*
Majken Jul Sørensen and Andrew Rigby
*Journal of Political Power*, volume 10, issue 2 (March–October 2017) pp. 219–235

**Chapter 8**
*Campaigning for cooperatives as resistance to neoliberal capitalism*
Kristin Wiksell
*Journal of Political Power*, volume 10, issue 2 (March–October 2017) pp. 236–254

For any permission-related enquiries please visit:
http://www.tandfonline.com/page/help/permissions

# Notes on Contributors

**Markus Arvidson** is lecturer in Sociology at Karlstad University, Sweden. His main interest is in sociological and social psychological theory and themes including loyalty, deception and social solidarity.

**Jonas Axelsson** is lecturer in Working Life Science at Karlstad University, Sweden. His research interests include the concepts of loyalty, solidarity and trust. In connection to these three concepts, one special interest is the Norwegian sociologist Sverre Lysgaard and his theory of worker collectivity.

**Mikael Baaz** is an associate professor in International Law and an associate professor in Conflict and Society. He currently works as a senior lecturer in International Law at the Department of Law, University of Gothenburg, Sweden, and as an affiliated senior research fellow in Political Science at the Department of Social and Behavioural Studies, University West, Sweden.

**Anna-Lena Haraldsson** is a senior lecturer in the Department of Social and Psychological Studies, Karlstad University, Sweden. Her research centres on the use and conception of time.

**Satu Heikkinen** is a senior lecturer in Sociology at Karlstad University, Sweden. Heikkinen's research interests are ageing, power and categorisation among others. She is currently writing about ageism and age discrimination.

**Andreas Henriksson** is a senior lecturer in sociology. He completed his doctorate in 2014, with a dissertation on singledom and singles' activities. His current focuses are mainly on intimacy, gender and relationality. He is also interested in wider issues of emotions, social theory and social psychology.

**Annika Jonsson** works a senior lecturer in Sociology at the University of Karlstad, Sweden. Among other things she works within the inter/cross-disciplinary tradition of death Studies, which investigates death as multifaceted phenomenon, not only historically but also in various contemporary contexts.

# NOTES ON CONTRIBUTORS

**Minoo Koefoed** is a PhD candidate in Peace and Development research at the School of Global Studies, Gothenburg University, Sweden. She researches constructive resistance practices in the context of 'democratic autonomy' in the Kurdish Movement in Southeastern Turkey. Her research interests include resistance, social movements, radical alternatives, self-organisation, prefigurative politics, ethnic minorities and indigenous peoples.

**Mona Lilja** is a professor in Peace and Development Studies at the School of Global Studies, University of Gothenburg, Sweden. Lilja's area of interest is the linkages between resistance and social change as well as the particularities – the character and emergence – of various forms of resistance.

**Mona Lindqvist** has a PhD in Sociology from the University of Karlstad, Sweden. Previously she has been working on migrant women and, among other things, their perception about mental health. More in detail, Lindqvist has studied how these women perceive themselves, their obstacles and their possibilities as well as their position and situation.

**Eva Olsson** is a senior lecturer and PhD researcher in Sociology at the Faculty of Arts and Social Science, Karlstad University, Sweden. She has specific competence in the field of sociology of emotions, organisational theory and analysis, regional development, such as commuting/living conditions. At present, her work is primarily focused on emotional working conditions in human service organisations.

**Andrew Rigby** is emeritus professor of Peace Studies, Coventry University, UK. He was for many years a reader in Peace Studies at the Bradford University School of Peace Studies, UK, before leaving to become the founding director of the Centre for Peace and Reconciliation Studies at Coventry University. He has had a long-term interest and involvement with Palestinian unarmed resistance to occupation.

**Majken Jul Sørensen** is an honorary postdoctoral research associate at the University of Wollongong, Australia, and senior lecturer at Karlstad University, Sweden. She is the author of several books and articles on nonviolent action, with a special interest in strategies and the use of humour.

**Kristin Wiksell** is a PhD candidate in sociology and affiliated to the Centre for Regional Studies at Karlstad University, Sweden. Her research primarily concerns organisation, power and resistance from a sociological perspective, with a specific focus on how worker cooperatives in Sweden are being constructed in social interaction between the employees.

# Emotions and resistance: An introduction

> … all the poetics of the dispersed marginal sexual, ethnic, lifestyle, 'multitudes' (…) 'resisting' the mysterious central (capitalized) Power. Everyone 'resists' – from gays and lesbians to Rightist survivalists – so why not draw the logic conclusion that this discourse of 'resistance' is the norm today (…)? (Žižek 2002, p. 66).

From the quotation above, which occurs quite often in scholarly literature today, several conclusions could be made. One possible conclusion is simply that resistance matters. Another one is that resistance is an 'activity' that is performed in relation to power. To push it even further, it could be argued that power and resistance are entangled in different and intricate ways. A third conclusion that is possible to draw from the quotation, at least indirectly, is that if you are interested in understanding social change, then you have to try and understand the complex web of entanglements between power and resistance as well as, we would like to emphasize, resistance(see further Baaz *et al.* forthcoming). Moreover, another important dimension, which is elaborated in this editorial, and in the special issue at hand, is resistance at the crossroad of affects and emotions.

Conventionally power and the study of power has been associated with and focused on, respectively, the military power of states and/or the capacity by someone else or an act in accordance with its or his/her will. However, from the 1970s onwards, scholars such as Lukes (1974, 1986) and Bourdieu (1986), and above all Michel Foucault (see e.g. 1975/1991, 1976, 1978, 1982, 1986, 1988a, 1988b, 1994, 1997, 2001, 2009) contributed to profoundly challenging this traditional understanding by analysing power in relation to various practices. Over and above this, they changed the focus of analysis from what power is to the ways in which power is performed. In this, Foucault added to the concept of sovereign power by introducing ideas such as 'disciplinary', 'capillary power', 'biopower' and 'governmentality' to the discussion and analysis.

While, Foucault truly revolutionized our understanding of power, his work is less helpful in understanding resistance and, by consequence, social change. Foucault was primarily interested in and focused on power (with resistance in parentheses); and when he actually studied resistance, he did so from the perspective of power. In consequence, Foucault did not, at least not in any greater detail, outline what type of resistance (hidden/open, individual/collective, organized/everyday, conscious/unconscious, etc.) interacts with or would be possible counter-reactions to power (see further Baaz *et al.* forthcoming). Thereby, even though Foucault matters in seeking to understand resistance and the relationship between resistance and power, it is necessary to move beyond his work and the huge number of scholars who work in the wake of Foucault (Thompson 2003).

An early pioneer in focusing more explicitly on resistance and the role of resistance in understanding social change is Scott (1972, 1985, 1989, 1990). His seminal work spurred a lot of subsequent research and today resistance, as a key component for understanding social change, is increasingly acknowledged (see e.g. Butler 1995, 1997, 2015, Bayat 1997a, 1997b, 1997c, 2000, 2009, Hardt and Negri 2004). The potential of dissent against sovereignty, disciplinary practices as well as bio-political governing, are gradually becoming recognized, which makes the invisible visible. People raise their voices against economic exploitation and neoliberal forms of governing subjects, but also against gendered and racist norms and practices.

Previously, the political practices of protesting, revolting and occupying, have received scholarly attention (see e.g. Baaz and Lilja 2016a). However, lately, practices of resistance that are

# RESISTANCE AND EMOTIONS

less visible have also been put under the microscope (see e.g. Baaz and Lilja 2016b, Odysseos *et al.* 2016, Baaz *et al.* 2017, forthcoming). 'Resistance' challenges all forms of 'domination' – not just the particular configuration of power relations that we call 'the state', but also exploitative practices, social acceleration, commodification, fetishism, alienation and economic injustices of capitalism, discursive truth-regimes and normative orders of gender, race, status and caste hierarchies. Moreover, power is seldom singular – it simultaneously relates to other forms of power.

Due to its broad scope, resistance studies involve several theoretical traditions, including, for example, state-oriented, structuralist and social movement studies, revolution studies and studies on guerrilla warfare, civil warfare and terrorism. It also draws on many specialist fields that, at least tangentially, engage with it: gender studies and feminism, queer studies, peace (and conflict) studies, political science, sociology, critical race studies, anthropology, pedagogics, psychology, media and communication studies, law, in particular critical legal studies, heritage studies and design, just to mentioning a few (Baaz *et al.* forthcoming).

All in all, resistance studies is an ever expanding field, which is increasingly nuanced and multifaceted. Resistance studies embrace 'resistance' as a practice that might be played out by organized, large groups and movements, as well as individuals and subcultures. It might be articulated through or against power-relations or be inspired by other resisters (copy-cat resistance). Resistance is an act or patterns of actions, which might undermine or negotiate different power-relations, but sometimes ends up reproducing and strengthening relations of dominance (Lilja and Vinthagen 2009). Sometimes resistance is carried out with intent, and sometimes unintentionally. But as argued above, regardless of the type, resistance exists in relation to power (and/or violence or inspiring forms of resistance) and the type of power often affects the type of resistance that is employed, as well as the effectiveness of various resistance practices.

Resistance can be understood as subversive and/or challenging to different forms of power. However, while power and resistance are constituted together, they are not always in opposition. Sometimes resistance transcends the whole phenomenon of being against something; instead it constructs 'alternative' or 'prefigurative' social institutions or is practised in self-loyalty with oneself (Arvidson and Axelsson 2017). In addition, power is sometimes created or recreated exactly through the very same resistance that it provokes (Henriksson 2017).

Previous research on resistance has primarily focused on, on the one hand, practices of agitating, organizing and dissenting or, on the other hand, less visible practices of resistance that are enacted expressly outside political spaces. In both cases, 'affects' and 'emotions', have rarely been the main focus of the research, even though they have played a silent but fundamental role in many theories of resistance (e.g. Scott 1972, 1990). Based on the perception that this is an obstacle for the further theoretical understanding of the entanglements of power, resistance and, by extension, social change, the overall aim of this special issue is to critically examine and explore the ways in which different emotions are interrelated or intra-act with resistance and its 'generally 'less than tangible' entities such as texts, signs, symbols, identity and language' (Törnberg 2013). Thus, we seek to fill a knowledge gap in the current literature on resistance by displaying not only how emotions make resistance possible, but also how emotions orient, embody, construct, or are the product of, resistance. The collection of articles presented here provides a novel excursion towards an elaborated understanding of how emotions offer us an original and multi-disciplinary tool to further understand various resisting conducts and political subjectivities.

In the remainder of this editorial introduction, we will outline five analytical observations or themes that emerge from the attempts of the contributors to this volume to theoretically develop and refine the assemblage of resistance, affects and emotions. These theoretical considerations could, more generally, also serve as a point of departure for future research that seeks to understand the complex relations between emotions and resistance. The suggested themes/theoretical considerations are as follows:

(i) *Emotions translate into motivations and various resisting practices*. Emotions seem to create resistance, non-governable subjects and undermine the very core of various self-disciplinary systems. According to Hemmings (2005, 2014), however, affects should not only be seen as a 'rescue' from the deterministic aspects of power; for example, the post-structuralist approach in which language decides everything. Emotions can be emancipatory and create 'non-disciplinary' subjects, but they can also discipline bodies, form realities and stop bodies from expressing themselves.

Emotions as an engine of resistance, tangentially interact with other fields and aspects, such as space (loss of land, memorial places, etc.) or different temporal dimensions. For example, as outlined in Anna-Lena Haraldsson and Mona Lilja's article in this issue, there is sometimes a temporal aspect of 'emotional' resistance. Fear, is an emotion experienced in the face of something that threatens us in the future. According to Heidegger, fear relates 'as something that threatens us, is not yet within striking distance, but it is coming close' (Heidegger 1962, p. 180). Fear, then, moves between the present and the future; between the immediate experience and potential hurt (Ahmed 2004). The time-traveling between then, now and the future creates emotions, which also shape our practices and how we act in order to change the future. Resistance acts of the 'now' sometimes emerge from a fear of what will be played out later (i.e. forthcoming climate refugees, raised sea-level, abortion prohibitions). Resistance, here, is played out in order to change the future.

(ii) *Emotional management can be seen as a form of resistance*. Both Minoo Koefoed's article as well as Mona Lindqvist and Eva Olsson's article in this issue explore resistance through Hochshild's theories of emotional labor (1983). Identifying and managing emotions could, from their argumentations, be understood as resistance practices that mirror different forms of power. In her study on a resistance movement in Northern Kurdistan, Koefoed defines *emotional resistance* as 'a form of resistance with the explicit aim of undermining the psychological power of violent state activities' (p. X). Conscious attempts of maneuvering emotional expressions or reactions aim to challenge power in different forms. This kind of resistance, refers to emotions, expressed publicly as well as hidden, but as 'deep acting', through emotional work (or labor) of the individual to really feel what she strives to express. Koefoed illustrates the latter case through an example of an individual who, at her brother's funeral, actively strives to reduce inner feelings of grief as they represent, to her, the very power of the Turkish state. By avoiding emotions of sorrow, the psychological power of the Turkish state is thereby undermined. Putting on faces, and trying to 'feel' unexpected emotions, might thus, shake the discursive order and work subversively.

(iii) *Resistance as the non-conformity to emotion rules*. Emotions are powerful instruments in human relations, which conform and regulate our actions to norms by signaling approval and disapproval. There are many examples where resistance has been expressed by silence and 'non-emotional' expressions instead of happiness or applause at public meetings. An investigation of resistance could embrace the study of non-conformity to emotion rules. For example, angry bodies in public spaces are frightening and a threat to the nation state and the order of democratic states. The resisting bodies, and emotions expressed in the moment of resistance, are in themselves a representation of a vibrant, political sphere (Mouffe 2005), which is not the sphere of normalization, homogenization and discipline. Similarly, sudden happy, laughing 'flash mobs', which suddenly invade public spaces are a recurrent, but rather new, form of resistance. In addition, sexual desire, humor, joy and laugher can be used to negotiate stereotypes or gendered norms. Billingsley (2017) argues that, while humor often reinforces women's silence – by trivializing expressions of sexism – humor and laughing could also be seen as a means to point out the existence of patriarchal structures in society. Humor could break silences and allow women to do resistance by showing emotions that are 'inappropriate' for women (laughing too loudly, etc.). According to Dahl (2006), the femme movement also uses 'inappropriate' emotions as resistance. Women's sexual desires and sexual agents are in focus, and challenge dominant ideas about which bodies are allowed to display sexual cravings in public spaces.

(iv) *Emotions create communities (of resistance).* Another important aspect of the entanglement of emotions and resistance is how emotions create communities (of resistance). Emotions are at the very core of loyalties, attachments and bonds (see e.g. Scheff on social ties and Goodwin *et al.* 2001 on social movements) and consequently, emotions are central for organizing groups and resistance. Departing from Goffman's distinction of front stage and back stage, in this issue Majken Jul Sørensen and Andrew Rigby show the importance of management of emotions back stage for the creation and reproduction of cultures of resistance in social movements. Rituals, symbols, humor and different cultural activities back stage all strengthen group solidarity. However, these communities of resistance can also create ties to local communities, which can strive to empower the wider community. In addition, emotions are of importance front stage when activists are acting in public in order to influence the emotions of others, thus, mobilizing and organizing resistance. The concepts of 'back stage' and 'front stage' are elaborated in several articles of this issue (see also Lindqvist and Olsson; Koefoed), which perhaps illustrates the fruitfulness of connecting overt expressions of emotions in public to covert, hidden emotional acts.

Also in this special issue, Kristin Wiksell exemplifies how emotions contribute to emerging resisting communities by showing how a narrative of 'a loving we' is constructed as an alternative to dominant neoliberal conceptions of production. She focuses on cooperations that strive to incorporate social values (e.g. democracy, equality and solidarity) and by way of their very existence may be understood as resistance, illustrating alternatives to dominant forms of organizing production. However, in analysing a marketing campaign for cooperatives she displays the fine dividing line between resistance and power, and the danger of non-critical resistance, which ends in reproducing the dominant discourse of neo-liberal capitalism.

(v) *Emotional, devoted resistance as a productive/constructive form of non-oppositional resistance.* Enthusiasm and devotion for 'alternative' or 'prefigurative' social institutions, which challenge the existing social order (i.e. 'constructive resistance') prevail as an emotional form of resistance, which is played out without actively being in opposition to others. Emotions not only form bonds and outward loyalties to, for example, pre-figurative institutions, but they also form an important type of inward loyalty, which Markus Arvidson and Jonas Axelsson explore in this special issue and term 'self-loyalty'. This kind of loyalty, 'being true to oneself' or 'one's ideals' can be voluntary or involuntary. According to the authors, it is the voluntary form of self-loyalty that is of importance in relation to resistance. Dominant discourses can be handled by a strategy of distancing oneself from the discourse. While, being interpellated by the discourse to, for example, a sub-altern subject position, the strategy aims at autonomy and keeping an inner distance in order to avoid expected feelings of, for example, shame or subordination. Here too, resistance is played out to resist disciplinary practices, and to protect oneself rather than being in oppositions to others.

## Acknowledgements

The editors of this special issue would like to thank Mark Haugaard, the editor of *Journal of Political Power*, for, on the one hand, entrusting us to edit this special issue and, on the other hand, for providing very constructive feedback. We would also like express our profound gratitude to the scholars who have served as anonymous reviewers and shared their profound knowledge, thereby substantially contributing to the improvement the quality of these papers.

# References

Ackroyd, S. and Thompson, P., 1999. *Organizational misbehaviour*. London: Sage.

Ahmed, S., 2004. *Cultural politics of emotions*. New York: Routledge.

Arvidson, M. and Axelsson, J., 2017. Exploring self-loyalty in the context of social acceleration: theorising loyalties as emotions and resistance. *Journal of Political Power*, 10 (2), 133–148.

Baaz, M. and Lilja, M., 2016a. Using international criminal law to resist transitional justice: legal rupture in the extraordinary chambers in the courts of Cambodia. *Conflict and Society*, 2 (1), 142–159.

Baaz, M. and Lilja, M., 2016b. Resistance, rupture and repetition: civil society strategies against intimate partner violence in Cambodia. *Global Public Health: An International Journal for Research, Policy and Practice*, 11 (1–2), 95–107.

Baaz, M., Lilja, M., and Östlund, A., 2017. Legal pluralism, gendered discourses, and hybridity in land-titling practices in Cambodia. *Journal of Law and Society*, 44 (2), 200–227.

Baaz, M., Lilja, M., and Vinthagen, S., forthcoming. Researching resistance: a critical approach to theory and practice. New York: Rowman and Littlefield International.

Bayat, A., 1997a. *Cairo's poor: dilemmas of survival and solidarity. Middle East Report*, 2–12.

Bayat, A., 1997b. *Street politics: poor people's movements in Iran*. Cairo: The American University in Cairo Press.

Bayat, A., 1997c. Un-civil society: the politics of the 'informal people'. *Third World Quarterly*, 18, 53–72.

Bayat, A., 2000. From 'Dangerous Classes' to 'Quiet Rebels': politics of the urban subaltern in the global south. *International Sociology*, 15 (3), 533–557.

Bayat, A., 2009. *Life as politics: how ordinary people change the middle east*. Stanford, CA: Stanford University Press.

Billingsley, A., 2017. Laughing against patriarchy: humor, silence, and feminist resistance. Available from: http://pages.uoregon.edu/uophil/files/Philosophy_Matters_Submission_Marvin_Billingsley.pdf [Accessed 5 May 2017].

Bourdieu, P., 1986. *Distinction: a social critique of the judgement of taste*. London: Routledge and Kegan Paul.

Butler, J., 1995. Subjection, resistance, resignification. *In*: J. Rajchman, ed. *The identity in question*. New York: Routledge, 229–250.

Butler, J., 1997. *The psychic life of power: theories in subjection*. Stanford, CA: Stanford University Press.

Butler, J., 2015. *Notes toward a performative theory of assembly*. Cambridge, MA: Harvard University Press.

Dahl, U., 2006. FEMME-INISM. *Arena*. Available from: http://www.magasinetarena.se/2006/08/24/femme-inism/ [Accessed 5 May 2017].

Foucault, M., 1975/1991. Discipline and punish: the birth of the prison. Harmondsworth: Penguin.

Foucault, M., 1976. The history of sexuality, vol. 1: the will to knowledge. London: Penguin.

Foucault, M., 1978. The history of sexuality, vol. 1: an introduction. New York: Pantheon Books.

Foucault, M., 1982. The subject and power. *In*: H.L. Dreyfus and P. Rabinow, eds. *Beyond structuralism and hermeneutics*. Chicago, IL: University of Chicago, 208–226.

Foucault, M., 1986. Disciplinary power and subjection. *In*: S. Lukes, ed. *Power*. Oxford: Basil Blackwell and New York University Press, 229–242.

Foucault, M., 1988a. *The history of sexuality: the care of the self*. Vol 3. New York: Vintage Books.

Foucault, M., 1988b. Technologies of the self. *In*: Luther H. Martin, *et al.*, eds. *Technologies of the self: a seminar with Michel Foucault*. Amherst: The University of Massachusetts Press.

Foucault, M., 1993. *Diskursens Ordning: Installationsföreläsning vid Collège de France den 2 December 1970* [The order of discourse: inaugural lecture at the Collège de France, 2 December 1970], translated by M. Rosengren. Stockholm: Brutus Östlings bokförlag Symposion.

Foucault, M., 1994. Two lectures. *In*: M. Kelly, ed. *Critique and power: recasting the Foucault/Habermas Debate*. Cambridge, MA: MIT Press, 17–46.

Foucault, M., 1997. *Society must be defended: lectures at the Collège de France, 1975–1976*. London: Penguin.

Foucault, M., 2001. Power/knowledge. *In*: S. Seidman and J.C. Alexander, eds. *The new social theory reader: contemporary debates*. New York: Routledge, 69–75.

Foucault, M., 2009. *Security, territory, population: Lectures at the Collège de France 1977–1978* [Lectures at the College de France]. London: Picador Pan Macmillan.

Goodwin, J., Jasper, J.M., and Polletta, F., 2001. *Passionate politics: emotions and social movements*. Chicago, IL: The University of Chicago Press.

Hardt, M. and Negri, A., 2004. *Multitude: war and democracy in the age of empire*. New York: The Penguin Press.

Heidegger, M., 1962. *Being and time*, translated by J. Macquarrie and E. Robinson. London: SCM Press.

Hemmings, C., 2005. Invoking affect: cultural theory and the ontological turn. *Cultural Studies*, 19 (5), 548–567.

Hemmings, C., 2014. The materials of reparation. *Feminist Theory*, 15 (1), 27–30.

Henriksson, A., 2017. Norm-critical rationality: emotions and the institutional influence of queer resistance. *Journal of Political Power*, 10 (2), 149–166.

Lilja, M. and Vinthagen, S., eds., 2009. Motstånd (Resistance). Malmö: Liber. 352 pages.

# RESISTANCE AND EMOTIONS

Lukes, S., 1974. *Power: a radical view*. London: Macmillan.

Lukes, S., ed., 1986. *Power*. New York: NYU Press.

Mouffe, C., 2005. *On the political: thinking in action*. London: Routledge.

Odysseos, L., Death, C., and Malmvig, H., 2016. Interrogating Michel Foucault's counter-conduct: theorising the subjects and practices of resistance in global politics. *Global Society*, 30 (2), 151–156.

Rasmussen, B., 2004. Between endless needs and limited resources: the gendered construction of a greedy organization. *Gender, Work & Organization*, 11 (5), 506–525.

Scott, J.C., 1972. Patron-client politics and political change in Southeast Asia, *The American political science review*. pp. 91–113, Vol. 66, No. 1 (Mar., 1972), American Political Science Association.

Scott, J.C., 1985. *Weapons of the weak: everyday forms of peasant resistance*. New Haven, CT: Yale University Press.

Scott, J.C., 1989. Everyday forms of resistance. *Copenhagen Papers*, 4, 33–62.

Scott, J.C., 1990. *Domination and the arts of resistance: hidden transcripts*. London: Yale University Press.

Thompson, K., 2003. Forms of resistance: Foucault on tactical reversal and self-formation. *Continental Philosophy Review*, 36, 113–138.

Törnberg, A., 2013. Resistance matter(s) resistance studies and the material turn. *RSN (Now Journal of Resistance Studies)*. No. 1, http://www.rsmag.org,pagevisited1/3-17

Žižek, S., 2002. *Welcome to the desert of the real! Five essays on september 11 and related dates*. London: Verso.

Mikael Baaz, Satu Heikkinen, and Mona Lilja

# Exploring self-loyalty in the context of social acceleration: theorising loyalties as emotions and resistance

Markus Arvidson and Jonas Axelsson

**ABSTRACT**

This article is a theoretical exploration of a layer of loyalty called self-loyalty. We define self-loyalty as an emotion that is channelled through social forms. To show the usage and relevance of the concept we present social acceleration as a contextualisation. Two self-loyalty strategies in relation to acceleration are discussed: a voluntary form based on resistance and an involuntary form based on acceptance and 'playing the game'.

## 1. Introduction

In this article, we examine a new form of loyalty, self-loyalty, and how it can be explored as both voluntary and involuntary in relation to resistance strategies, individualisation and social acceleration.[1] Self-loyalty – developed according to Swedberg's (2014) processual method of theorising – is seen as an emotionally-based phenomenon. We argue that this form of loyalty is one of many layers of loyalty and can be analytically used as a special form of loyalty. Furthermore, it can also contribute conceptually, theoretically and empirically to a deeper knowledge of contemporary phenomena that have often previously been thematised as autonomy or self-discipline. The aim of the article is to theoretically develop the concept of self-loyalty. We will fulfil this aim with the help of the following research questions: (1) How is self-loyalty related to other forms of loyalty? (2) How is the concept of self-loyalty related to some relevant family resemblance concepts? (3) How can the concept of self-loyalty help us analyse resistance in social acceleration? The first two questions are rather abstract, while the third is more concrete. When we answer the third question we contextualise self-loyalty with the help of Hartmut Rosa's theoretical framework of social acceleration. Both resistance to and acceptance of social acceleration is highly relevant in our analysis because social acceleration has such pervasive societal effects.

We begin this article by discussing the prefix 'self' in order to defend the use of *self*-loyalty and discuss how loyalty has been defined and used in previous research. A methodological section follows, where we discuss our methodological stance – namely, theorising that is inspired by Richard Swedberg. After these presentations, the article consists of three main parts that are related to the research questions.

## 2. The prefix 'self' and the concept of loyalty

Today, the prefix 'self' is commonly used with more and more words and expressions, such as 'self-realisation' 'self-acceptance', 'self-definition ' and 'self-radicalisation'. In this article, we argue that self-loyalty is another of these 'self' prefix words, which illustrate how concepts that describe collective and social phenomena transform into a more individualistic approach. One example of this individualistic tendency is the phenomenon of selfies. Fifty years ago photography was clearly directed towards environments and other people around you. A photographer took pictures of relatives, friends and beautiful landscapes and surroundings. If you wanted a self-portrait you asked someone else to take the photo. To turn the camera on oneself was in itself technically possible but was probably not very common among photographers. It is different today – selfies are maybe the most popular form of photography with the aim of getting likes in social media, such as Facebook and Instagram (for an interesting discussion about the role of selfies in relation to 'self-definition', see Murray 2015). Photography as a more individualistic phenomenon seems to have changed in a similar way to the phenomenon of loyalty. In our previous research, we have argued that the phenomenon of loyalty has generally broadened throughout history; for example, the broadening from the vertical to both verticality and horizontality in modern times (Arvidson and Axelsson 2014). The emergence of self-loyalty is one part of this broadening. We think, in a metaphorical sense, that loyalty has its own selfie – self-loyalty.

Selfies as a form of self-loyalty have similarities to Foucault's notion of hermeneutics and techniques of the self (Foucault 1994). In what Foucault (1994, p. 227) calls 'the care of the self' which originates both from ancient philosophy and Christian asceticism, there is a focus both on the practice and the principle of knowing oneself. Further, in the culture of the care of self, it was encouraged to be reflective and writing personal notes and reports. Nowadays, this occurs for example in taking selfies and posting personal reflections on social media. In sum, the 'care of the self' can be seen as an essential aspect of self-loyalty.

Accordingly, techniques of the self in the Foucauldian sense are themes that are new in the context of loyalty and can contribute to refining the concept. We think self-loyalty contains techniques similar to those described by Foucault in the way that people can alternate between voluntary and involuntary self-loyalty. These options are discussed later in this article.

Loyalty is a concept that is defined in a number of different ways and used in different contexts with different purposes. The concept has been discussed from different philosophical approaches (Ladd 1967, Royce 1995, Kirkeby 2002, Kleinig 2014) as a type of rational choice (Hirschman 1970, Fletcher 1995), as a concept based on the sociology of emotions (Connor 2007) and has also been used in empirically-based organisation and workplace studies (see for example Lysgaard 2001). The most sophisticated theoretical discussion on the concept of loyalty currently appears to be in business ethics journals like *Business Ethics Quarterly* and *Journal of Business Ethics* in which in-depth discussions of the concept of loyalty frequently occur (see e.g. Mele 2001, Randels 2001, Schrag 2001, Corvino 2002, Vandekerckhove and Commers 2004, Hajdin 2005, Provis 2005, Hart and Thompson 2007, Varelius 2009, Elegido 2013). But although in these, and similar, contexts there are some discussions about the self and its relation to loyalty the analysis and discussion are insufficient. Therefore this form of loyalty can fill a missing gap for understanding other forms of loyalty beyond the traditional views.

## 3. Methodological approach

In his book, *The Art of Social Theory* Richard Swedberg encourages social scientists to see theorising as a craft of its own that can be used in many ways. Swedberg emphasises a non-dramatic and practical approach for developing concepts and theorising, which is something that we do more or less consciously on a daily basis:

> The skillful use of existing concepts as well as the creation of new ones are both essential parts of theorizing. They are also activities that people engage in all the time, more or less automatically. In this they are just as much part of human existence as thinking in general. And again it is important to learn how to use and further develop this common capacity in a conscious way for purposes of social science theorizing. (Swedberg 2014, p. 58)

Thus, in the social science context, theorising as capacity and activity is neither worse nor better than, for example, collecting and analysing interviews or observations. Theorising can be a craft, as we already mentioned, where one can develop their competence in the same way as skilful interviewers. In theorising over and over again, it is possible to get better at it and thus be more experienced in the field. Theorising is mostly a matter of hard work and also a methodology of its own, which is described further in a clear and concrete way by Karlsson and Bergman:

> Social researchers try out, experiment with and play about with different concepts, relations between concepts and data, between concepts and other concepts, and between concepts and terms. (Karlsson and Bergman 2017, p. 9).

A perspective that Swedberg highlights, which originally comes from Georg Simmel, is the idea not to define a concept too narrowly. Instead, it is important to provide several examples where the concept can be used. We can identify at least two advantages of this. Firstly, it makes it easier for different social science researchers to use the concept from their own starting points. Secondly, it opens up for exploration of other concepts with a family resemblance to the chosen concept. As Swedberg suggests:

> …you can run through a number of potential new names in your mind, not just in an effort to find the right one, but also to discover something new about the phenomenon you are interested in. […] Each name has a series of meaning and associations; and these can be interesting to explore. (Swedberg 2014, p. 58).

The meaning and association between names and how names can be analysed and developed into rational and more abstract concepts, described by Swedberg (2014), resonates with Wittgenstein's notion of family resemblance concepts. What Wittgenstein means is that words can be similar, like members of a human family 'build, features, colour of eyes, gait, temperament, etc., overlap and criss-cross in the same way' (Wittgenstein 1958, p. 32). In the next section, we discuss self-loyalty in relation to other family resemblance concepts.

Another useful insight from Wittgenstein is the famous duck–rabbit example, which shows how the same image can be seen either as a rabbit or a duck depending on how the image is perceived (Wittgenstein 1958). Wittgenstein emphasises how the views of the duck-rabbit image can be changed. It is possible to imagine that a person has perceived only the rabbit in the picture throughout their entire lifetime because no one explained, to the person, that there is a different way of seeing it. In a similar way people can neglect the 'self' aspect of loyalty and just perceive loyalty in its previous uses with its focus on obligations to other persons, often in hierarchical relations (Arvidson and Axelsson 2014). This means that we have to move away from aspect blindness and instead open up to the approach of aspect changes in order to understand the multi-faceted concept of loyalty.

An important part of the change of aspect is that two or more aspects exist simultaneously; in the duck–rabbit image, both perspectives exist at the same time. This is similar to how we understand self-loyalty – it doesn't exist independently of how loyalty has been used in previous research; instead, it is another aspect or layer of loyalty. We do not deny that other types of loyalties play an important role today, but the focus on self-loyalty makes the picture of loyalty even more comprehensive. And with the help of the concept, we can probably see that sometimes a specific loyalty, which is *prima facie* seen as traditional and interpersonal, can actually be best described as self-loyalty. A loyalty to one's conscience, which will be discussed in the next chapter, is one example. Wittgenstein illustrates the ingenious idea of aspect change by telling a little story:

> I meet someone whom I have not seen for years; I see him clearly, but fail to know him. Suddenly I know him, I see the old face in the altered one. I believe that I should do a different portrait of him now if I could paint. (Wittgenstein 1958, p. 197)

The analytical approach in this article is inspired by this idea that in the 'altered face' of self-loyalty, it is possible to recognise the old 'face' of loyalties you have seen before. The painting of a different portrait could be to assimilate new perspectives on loyalties thanks to the concept of self-loyalty.

## 4. Self-loyalty in relation to other loyalties

Our point of departure is that loyalty is an emotion that is channelled in social forms. We largely agree with Connor (2007) in this respect. He writes about loyalty as an emotion intermingled with other emotions, such as pride, joy and anger and as an emotion, it is affected by social actions and social structures. In other words, Connor argues that loyalty is a complex emotional and social phenomenon layered in society. There is always a plurality of loyalties and conflicts among them are common. About the layered reality of loyalty he writes:

> The concept of layering can be considered a useful heuristic device with which to explore how an actor negotiates the range of competing loyalties that they will inevitably experience by being part of a social structure. Layering also highlights how loyalty operates across a range of social sites, spanning micro- and macro- sociological interactions. I defined layering as referring to the multiple types of loyalty that operate on the individual, spanning the micro to the macro levels of social structure. The concept of layering also gives an insight into how and why conflict ensues when multiple loyalties are called upon. (Connor 2007, p. 130)

In previous research, we have thematised the plurality of loyalties with the help of Simmel's idea of social forms (Simmel 2009, Arvidson and Axelsson 2014). As Simmel explains, just as there are different geometrical figures in mathematics there are also various social constellations and figures in social life that can be studied both in their form and in their content. Loyalty relations can vary; for example, in a workplace they can be both vertical and horizontal, and they can be voluntary or involuntary, and even alter depending on the context. We argue that this idea of social forms of loyalties is similar to Connor's reasoning about layered loyalty.

We define self-loyalty as an emotion of loyalty directed towards oneself that is channelled through social forms. We can see it as one of the layers of loyalty in society, which can be in different relations to other loyalties. It has seldom been used as a theoretical concept in academic contexts, but the idea is not new. A kind of self-loyalty can be traced back to how the concept of loyalty has been used in Japan and China. In Japan, loyalty in Confucianism often has the meaning of the servant's loyalty to his master. In China, however, the significance of the word instead points to the individual: loyalty means that persons are true to their own conscience (Morishima 1982, pp. 9–10). The basic Chinese meaning of loyalty includes the aspects of loyalty that we want to emphasise within the concept of self-loyalty. In other words, in addition to loyalty towards others in an *altercentric* way it is also important to characterise loyalty as truth against one's own self in a more *egocentric* way.

Among the more academic and theoretical discussions about loyalty, the contribution from Raz (1986) is closest to the approach to loyalty in this article. Raz argues, in the context of political philosophy, that loyalty and integrity are closely related. He writes: 'Loyalty to one's pursuits and relationships is a condition of integrity. A person of integrity is loyal to his commitments.' (Raz 1986, p. 355). This quotation from Raz shows an illuminative and fruitful way of presenting an approach to loyalty where integrity plays an important role, and the description fits in well with how self-loyalty is presented in this article.

As mentioned, loyalty can be vertical or horizontal, and voluntary or involuntary (Arvidson and Axelsson 2014). We want to transfer the second dimension – voluntariness and involuntariness – to self-loyalty. Our distinction between voluntariness and involuntariness here is only based on the experience – do we experience the self-loyalty as voluntary or not? We are aware of the philosophical problems related to voluntariness and involuntariness and the vast discussions concerning free will, unfreedom, the actor/structure-debate and the like. For pragmatic reasons, we have nevertheless chosen to use these concepts with a focus on the *experiences* of voluntariness and involuntariness. More precise definitions are worth developing in future empirical studies with the aim of exploring the concept further.

Self-loyalty is channelled through social forms. Therefore, the Simmelian analogy of geometrical forms also works in this case, where this form is one of several social geometrical forms of loyalty. Another argumentation from Simmel that supports self-loyalty is his notion of isolation and loneliness. Even these conditions constitute relations and society:

> …isolation, insofar as it is important to the individual, refers by no means only to the absence of society. On the contrary, the idea involves the somehow imagined, but then rejected, existence of society. (Simmel 2009, pp. 118–119)

In line with Simmel, we mean that self-loyalty, although it is the self that is emphasised, is not absent from relations and society. Even without physical and concrete interactions, other people are present in one's own mental and emotional world and consequently, loyalty is also present in this context.

In passing, we would like to add that we also believe that the individual – and hence self-loyalty – has some limited non-social and pre-social aspects, but we leave this discussion aside in this article.[2]

As an example of how self-loyalty can shed new light on past loyalty discussions, we now discuss some aspects from Hirschman's classic and well-known study *Exit, Voice and Loyalty* (Hirschman 1970). Hirschman presents two options for dealing with internal dissatisfaction in an organisation or in the case of a customer's dissatisfaction with a product: either the dissatisfied person leaves the organisation or the customer stops buying the product (exit); or the person stays in the organisation but voices dissatisfaction by protesting or the costumer continues to buy the item but complains about the products (voice). For Hirschman, the voice option is a sign of loyalty and the exit option is a sign of disloyalty. From an organisational perspective, the person who leaves the organisation, or stops buying their favourite product is obviously disloyal. However, by using the concept of self-loyalty we argue that instead of disloyalty it can be a question of a different loyalty strategy, where the priority could be loyalty to the self. It need not be a lack of loyalty that allows a person to leave an organisation, or start buying another product; instead, it may be another layer and another kind of loyalty that is at hand. In the next section, we develop this notion at length when we discuss loyalty and resistance. The dichotomy of loyalty/disloyalty is questioned; it can be replaced by different layers of loyalty instead, for example self-loyalty.[3]

Another interpretation and further development of Hirschman's exit/voice alternatives is that the options not only occur in the relation between individuals and organisations but also in people's own selves. Persons have exit/voice deliberation within themselves, as for example: shall I be true to myself, despite doubts (voice) or will l 'betray my ideals' and my own self-loyalty (exit)? [4]

## 5. Self-loyalty and family resemblance concepts

When it comes to working with family resemblance we are inspired by Haugaard's analysis of concepts of power as characterised by family resemblance and his way of contrasting language games that are either normative – what a concept *ought* to be – or analytical – to understand the concept in a sociological sense (Haugaard 2010). Regarding family resemblance, we see self-discipline and autonomy as two family resemblance concepts in connection to self-loyalty. Furthermore, we see the concept of self-loyalty as an analytical tool for sociological interpretation – and as a layer of loyalty – and we leave the normative aspects aside.

To use Swedberg's phrase, self-discipline and autonomy have a 'series of meaning and associations' (Swedberg 2014, p. 58), which differ from potential meaning and associations related to self-loyalty. We suggest that self-loyalty can be like an unexplored middle ground between the concepts of self-discipline and autonomy.

The theme of self-discipline developed by Foucault (1991) is well-known and plays an important role in social science. In the light of Foucault's work, phenomena that on the surface look like freedom and individualism, have been thematised as repressive self-discipline. Hence, concerning self-discipline, the meaning and associations tend to be 'too hard' and one can easily imagine a very repressive person. We suggest that many of the topics that are actually discussed with the help of the (Foucauldian) concept of self-discipline cannot easily fit in with this 'hardness'. With the help of self-loyalty, we can capture the devotion that often appears when people are struggling to get control over themselves and their everyday lives. We can catch sight of the more 'soft' and emotional side of self-discipline that is directed towards self-love.[5]

When it comes to personal freedom and autonomy, it is important to understand the practices and the ideals that characterise these in today's modern world (see Franck 1997)

The term autonomy exists in many formations and there are profound philosophical discussions about the concept (see e.g. Christman 2015). Here, we quote the following definition:

> ...the capacity to be one's own person, to live one's life according to reasons and motives that are taken as one's own and not the product of manipulative or distorting external forces. (Christman 2015)

In a Foucauldian discussion on autonomy, Nikolas Rose argues for confession as a way to constitute self and autonomy:

> In confessing, one is subjectified by another, for one confesses in the actual or imagined presence of a figure who prescribes the form of the confession, the words and rituals through which it should be made, who appreciates, judges, consoles, or understands. But in confessing, one also constitutes oneself. In the act of speaking, through the obligation to produce words that are true to an inner reality, through the self-examination that precedes and accompanies speech, one becomes a subject for oneself. (Rose 1989, p. 244)

But the concept of autonomy may also be of a practical nature, which, for example, becomes clear by the socio-technical use of it (Trist and Bamforth 1951). With the creativity and playfulness that Swedberg's (2014) theorising method opens up for, we can see the family resemblance between the words autonomy and self-loyalty. Autonomy comes from the Greek words for self: *auto* and law: *nomos*. Autonomy has parallels with following laws and norms that persons are setting up for their own life.

In contrast to the concept of self-discipline, the common meaning and associations related to the concept of autonomy tends to be to 'too soft'. The association can be to a freedom 'to do what one wants to do'. The regulating aspects – the connections to *nomos/law* are not clear. The concept of self-loyalty can help us see the regulating and ordering aspects, which were originally an important part of the concept of autonomy.

Also, loyalty like autonomy is etymologically linked to the word 'law' – namely the French word *loi* (Bryant 1915, Kleinig 2014) Strict etymological loyalty can be seen as synonymous with 'lawfulness;' thereby, self-loyalty can also mean lawfulness for oneself. What are we able to see if we theorise in this direction? Which aspects appear when the prefix 'self' is used in relation to lawfulness? Maybe some lack in the concept of autonomy is then visible. Perhaps self-loyalty in the context of autonomy describes the persistent pursuit, the patience, and the internal order that an individual's autonomy requires more clearly. Reasoning of this kind shows how changes in the nuances of words and exploring the family resemblance of words can lead to the development of new concepts. This approach can be linked to both Swedberg's (2014) method of theorising and Wittgenstein's notion of aspect change in the duck-rabbit example (Wittgenstein 1958).

## 6. Social acceleration: self-loyalty contextualised

With the aim of contextualising our discussion further, we relate to Hartmut Rosa's theoretical framework of social acceleration and how he uses it as a key element for understanding contemporary society (Rosa 2013). Self-loyalty can be both voluntary and involuntary in the light of social acceleration, which is shown in forthcoming sections of the article.

To motivate the centrality of social acceleration, Rosa uses many different sources, including both classical and contemporary thinkers. A quotation from Gundolf S. Freyermuth can summarise Rosa's overall view: 'We are contemporaries of a phase of acceleration that is unique in the history of humankind – and makes industrialization look cozy in hindsight'

(Freyermuth in Rosa 2013, p. 14). The concept of acceleration, which is crucial to his analysis, is described with the help of Helga Nowotny's definition of the concept that, in summary, describes acceleration as a social norm:

> ...goods, human beings, energy, money and information should change their locations *with increasing frequency* in order to circulate in a comprehensive sense, both economically and culturally. (Nowotny quoted in Rosa 2013, p. 64)

Rosa develops a framework of acceleration by drawing on social thinkers such as Simmel, Beck, Sennett and Foucault. One illuminative example that Rosa uses is Simmel's metaphorical explanation of the rounding of coins – they are round so they can roll faster in an economy.

Rosa identifies three main dimensions in social acceleration. Firstly, *technical acceleration*, where different technical inventions contribute to the increasing speed of both travelling and producing goods and services. Secondly, *acceleration of social change*, which argues that acceleration affects many spheres in society and in many cases, leads to a 'contraction of the present'. The third dimension, *acceleration of the pace of life*, illustrates how life has increased in tempo, both *objectively*, since research has shown that everyday activities such as mealtimes have become shorter and that people get less sleep, and *subjectively* in people's own experience of stress and feelings that they lack time. According to Rosa, social acceleration also has implications for identity formation thus self-thematising is expected from people in order to get acceptance in different contexts and they are also expected to be like 'time-juggling' players (Rosa 2013, p. 236).

After this brief introduction of the framework of social acceleration, we will, in the next sections, describe two variations of loyalty in relation to social acceleration. The first one can be seen as a resistance to social acceleration. We call it voluntary self-loyalty. The second one can be seen as an acceptance of social acceleration 'playing the game by its own rules'. We call it involuntary self-loyalty.

### 6.1. Voluntary self-loyalty as resistance in social acceleration

Rosa discusses examples of resistance to acceleration and calls this 'deceleration as ideology'. In this article, we interpret that ideology as voluntary self-loyalty. By sticking to one's own goals and visions people can become self-loyal instead of loyal to a workplace or acceleration in society. As is thematised in this article, self-loyalty creates different kinds of emotions like pride, anger and sadness. By extension, the emotions that this kind of loyalty creates can lead to actions of resistance as described in this section. Firstly, we present some reflections on loyalty and resistance.

The relationship between loyalty and resistance seems to be a rather unexplored conceptual terrain. Not even in very ambitious studies of loyalty (see Kleinig 2014) are these connections between concepts developed. Hence, much needs to be done in this area. The concept of self-loyalty can be of help for connecting loyalty and resistance. Often, especially in common-sense discussions, resistance means dismissing loyalty, for example, to a state or a company. We suggest that an alternative to using *disloyalty* to describe resistance is to conceptualise it as another social form of *loyalty* to other persons or objects or to oneself – self-loyalty. Dismissing one form of loyalty seems to imply a shift to other layers of loyalty. That is: the act of resistance can also be an act of loyalty. In this section, we discuss this at length and begin with a definition of resistance.

## RESISTANCE AND EMOTIONS

In Hollander's and Einwohner's (2004) rigorous discussion of the concept of resistance, 'action' and 'opposition' are described as two 'core elements' in nearly all definitions of resistance. Concerning the element of opposition, Hollanders and Einwohner write:

> A second element common to nearly all uses is a sense of *opposition* (…) this sense appears in the use of the words 'counter,' 'contradict,' 'social change,' 'reject,' 'challenge,' 'opposition,' 'subversive,' and 'damage and/or disrupt.' (2004, p. 538)

We think Hollander's and Einwohner's results are interesting, but we interpret the quotation in the following word-playing way: is opposition (nearly) always an alternative *position*? Can one be in opposition without taking an alternative position? We think not. To continue our play with words: resistance requires stance. In order to argue for this, we want to introduce some ideas from the discussion about 'organisational misbehaviour' in the sociology of work, which can be seen as similar to a general discussion about resistance.

One aspect of organisational misbehaviour, which has been theorised in an interesting way by Kirchhoff and Karlsson (2009), is rule breaking in the workplace. According to Kirchhoff and Karlsson, systematically breaking rules in a workplace means that *other* rules are necessary. In other words: rule breaking does not mean that some chaotic tendencies are set free – instead rules stand against rules and order stands against a different order. Rule breaking can be called the following of alternative rules. As Kirchhoff and Karlsson put it:

> In order to consciously break one rule, you follow another – there is no such thing as rule-free rule-breaking. Deliberately breaking a rule involves the rulebreaker drawing on a rule that he or she thinks overrides the first one. (Kirchhoff and Karlsson 2009, p. 457)

Now we have returned to the initial discussion in this section where breaking a loyalty is not only disloyalty but instead loyalty to something or someone else. In this view of loyalty and self-loyalty, we have applied similar thoughts that Kirchhoff and Karlsson have on opposition: if one is against something, they are probably for something else. We therefore, mean that opposition must be conceptualised as striving for an alternative position – not only as a striving against something that is not specified.

And *prima facie* it does not seem problematic to connect the two concepts – resistance and loyalty. If we think of the clearest examples of resistance – for example, in radical political activism – it is not hard to see links to strong personal political views and hence, our definition of loyalty as an emotion directed towards oneself that is channelled through social forms. Furthermore, self-loyalty that motivates resistance is in line with the Chinese definition of loyalty that we presented in the introduction: loyalty is all about being true to one's conscience: 'I regret nothing. One must be able to see oneself in the mirror' says the consultant who exposed the corruption and fiddling at Gothenburg Energy in 2010 (Sjögren 2010, our translation). In this example, the whistle-blower acted in a self-loyal way as an act of resistance against corruption and fiddling. What stands out in clear examples of resistance is not only opposition but a devotion *to* something – and that could be one's own life-projects or own values. Additionally, to take an alternative position/stance or following alternative rules, and do it over time, continuously takes time and needs disciplined, continuous efforts – and then it seems like self-loyalty is necessary.

The strategy of self-binding – i.e. limiting oneself in some way – can be a way of carrying out resistance and also gaining control over a situation; for example, starting a hunger strike for political aims. The classic example of self-binding is taken from the ancient Greek drama of Homer's Ulysses (discussed by, for example, Elster 1984, 2000, 2003), Ulysses is, when he is on his way with his ship to Ithaca, lured by the sirens' song. To avoid being tempted by the sirens, he asks his men to tie him to a mast so that he would be prevented from the temptations of the sirens' singing. He also says to his men that if he, during the journey as they pass the sirens, asks his men to loosen the straps, they should instead tie him up even more. Ulysses uses the strategy of binding himself to avoid being tempted by the sirens' song. Ulysses' strategy can be interpreted as a form of resistance towards the sirens' songs.[6] Self-binding is mentioned here because it can be seen as a form of self-loyalty that is worth further examination in another context.

In a study on young unemployed people in Sweden and how they handle the discourse of individualistic responsibility that affects societal understanding of the unemployed, three strategies appear: conformity to the discourse, distance from the discourse and resistance to the discourse (Hobbins 2015). Two of the strategies fit the argument here: distance and resistance. Distance from norms about work can be interpreted as a voluntary strategy of self-loyalty. Additionally, in this strategy the pressure from others was more or less ignored. The strategy of resistance can also be interpreted as a voluntary strategy of self-loyalty. This strategy has the aim of keeping autonomy (autonomy is closely linked to self-loyalty as we described earlier) and avoiding blaming oneself and avoiding social stigmatisations. Even if the emotional aspects of these strategies are not analysed by Hobbins, the strategy of distance can be interpreted as a sign of pride and as a way of ignoring feelings of shame from others because of unemployment. The strategy of resistance can be interpreted as anger against the discourse and work norms of society. In this way, these two strategies can be seen as emotionally linked to this form of loyalty and also linked to how we define the concept as an emotion.

Many examples of what we interpret as voluntary self-loyalty are presented in Lars Ivarsson's study on people in sports and music who are driven by their passion (Ivarsson 2014). Many autobiographical and biographical material by successful musicians and athletes concerns sticking to one's own dreams despite social pressure from parents and societal values. A key notion is 'to do your own thing', which Ivarsson calls passion, and in our context it parallels the characteristics of self-loyalty as an emotion, where passion and strong beliefs play a crucial role in succeeding in music, business or sport. Here is an extract from an autobiography by a member of the band The Eagles, Don Felder, which shows how he questioned his own self-loyalty when he was in a sad mood – in this case he stuck to his music career, in relation to his father's different opinions, which then led to a loyalty-conflict:

> I sank to an all-time low over the next few months and began to wonder if my father was right. I was married, nearly twenty-five, and if I hadn't made it by now, I probably never would. Maybe there was no future for me in music, and maybe I should have gone to college as Dad had always wanted. At least I have had something to fall back on. (Felder and Holden 2008, p. 78, see also Ivarsson 2014, p. 101)

The quotation shows how self-loyalty as an emotion creates sadness and maybe frustration when it is in conflict with other layers of loyalty.

Yet another example of resistance to social acceleration and change is whistle-blowing (see e.g. Ahlstrand *et al.* 2017). The accelerating exchanges between people, money and goods can lead to misconduct in workplaces, corruption and companies making poor decisions. A famous example of whistle-blowing in Sweden is the so-called Bofors-affair (see Haglunds 2009). Bofors is an armament factory in the town Karlskoga. In 1983, it was revealed that Bofors exported missile robots to countries that were banned from export trade. This example shows how global capitalism and its acceleration in exchange of goods, for example, enables problematic events to happen. Ingvar Bratt, who was working as an engineer at Bofors admitted to a journalist in 1983, that robots were exported to banned countries. He continued to give media more information about the affair and eventually left the company on 1 July 1984. Bratt's whistle-blowing was perceived negatively by citizens in Karlskoga. In their eyes, he was a traitor destroying the 'Karlskoga-spirit' – a mentality where all citizens should stick together – and the citizens also worried that the 'affair' would cause unemployment in Karlskoga, given that Bofors was an important employer in the town.

Some years later, Ingvar Bratt was interviewed in a radio programme about the affair. He had intended to be a person who carried out an appropriate act of resistance against the company's breaches of the law and a loyal person to society. Instead, the action was interpreted as betrayal and disloyalty to the town of Karlskoga:

> I had no clue about how it would end, how it would be received by the people in Karlskoga, if it would be successful...I would say that the crisis arrived when things did not make sense. When the reactions around me were not like I had expected. When a lot of people in my immediate surroundings, depreciated what I had done. And when I, one terrible night, actually realised that I – in the eyes of the people of Karlskoga – was an evil man. Me, who wanted to be the good person; other people were evil, and suddenly I understood that I was the evil man. And it was frightful and shocking to find out. (Bratt quoted in Haglunds 2009, p. 207)

The quotation shows how Ingvar Bratt felt strong emotions of fright and shock because of the different layers of loyalty that were in conflict: the choice of self-loyalty instead of loyalty to the organisation. This example shows how resistance against an organisation can lead to conflicts of loyalty and create strong emotions when having to choose between self-loyalty and loyalty to an organisation.

### 6.2. Involuntary self-loyalty as accepting and 'playing the game' social acceleration

As we discussed earlier, social accelerations require strategies on the individual level. Foucault's descriptions of techniques of the self, and self-discipline have many similarities with involuntary self-loyalty, which is presented in this section (see Foucault 1991, 1994).

In order to contextualise our discussion, the academic world can serve as an illustrative example (see Vostal 2016). With increased demands on competitiveness, academics have to build their own 'brand' and create an interesting research profile in order to compete for research funds. It is clear, in our point of view, that these demands are centred around the researchers' own competence and career, therefore the concept of self-loyalty can be applied here, because competition and pressure can be more intense in relation to those who are at the same level. This is a well-known fact from previous work-life studies (see e.g. Lysgaard 2001). Continual comparisons with colleagues at the same status level can be an experience of stressful pressure, and consequently we interpret such situations as an example of involuntary self-loyalty. Discourse theorist Norman Fairclough has been reflecting on this issue in relation to himself; he analysed his own CV and reflected on the 'game' he knows he himself is part of. There is an involuntary self-loyalty included in the academic game that has also become a part of self-identity:

> Doing one's job entails 'playing the game' (or various connected games), and what may feel like a mere rhetoric to get things done quickly and easily becomes a part of one's professional

identity. Self-promotion is perhaps becoming a routine, naturalised strand of various academic activities, and of academic identities. (Fairclough 1993, p. 153)

If we expand the discussion to labour, more generally, involuntary self-loyalty can be largely linked to the frequent requirements of 'employability' (see e.g. Garsten and Jacobsson 2004). Gillberg (2015) analyses 'fosterage to employability' in interesting ways. When Gillberg discusses policy measures for activating unemployed young adults, he describes the following examples:

Individual action plans, to write attractive CVs, presentation skills, to train for job interviews, measures to increase social skills, enhance self-confidence, etc. are common activities. The goal is to sell yourself as employable. It is not just the cognitive abilities that are trained but also other abilities and qualities. (Gillberg 2015, p. 48, our translation)

These abilities and qualities can be interpreted as including self-loyalty. Persons have to invest in themselves and be true to their self-realisation process. The presentation of merits in a CV should be summarised in a neat and comprehensible way – in some ways contradictory to the common description of societies and globalisation as fragmented and complex (see e.g. Urry 2003). To conclude, the demands and norms of society concerning employment can, without a doubt, lead to strategies in line with involuntary self-loyalty (cf. Hobbins 2015).

On a more general level, involuntary self-loyalty can be linked to social acceleration in different ways. Especially the subjective experience of social change as presented by Rosa that can lead to experiencing demands on effectiveness that affect people's identity and identity-formations. As Rosa argues, 'forced self-thematising' is a consequence of social acceleration where we, in many areas, are forced to reflect, present and talk about ourselves, and hence we become 'self-workers' (Rosa 2012). Such work involves a constant ambition to improve personality, self-development and marketing much like the development of a business. This can be done, as we mentioned earlier, in the form of presenting an attractive CV and trying to make oneself as employable as possible. One can formulate this as being a 'self-worker', who works in a company that is oneself.[7]

Research has shown, in the case of aviation service work and office work, the empirical anchor of Rosa's theoretical framework (Ulferts *et al.* 2013). The researchers state the following:

Data clearly show that work intensification is related to increases in work strain, which, at least in the long run, leads to reduced health. Thus, while we are forced to live with acceleration, it is important to know what may help to reduce the consequences. (Ulfert *et al.* 2013, p. 180)

The context described, that 'we are forced to live with acceleration', is in line with Rosa's arguments on different forces that emerge from social acceleration, and as a consequence people are forced to think more about their own loyalty rather than other layers of loyalty; for example, of being loyal to others. Hence, this experience of force can be described as involuntary self-loyalty.


## 7. Concluding remarks

The aim of the article was to theoretically explore the concept of self-loyalty. We wanted to fulfil this aim with the help of the following research questions.

(1) How is self-loyalty related to other forms of loyalties? Like other loyalties, this form is an emotion directed to the individual that is channelled through social forms. Here, we are inspired by Connor's reasoning about loyalty as an emotion and his idea that loyalties are layered. When it comes to social forms we also find inspiration in Simmel's notion of sociology as 'social geometry'. Like other loyalties, self-loyalty exists in voluntary and involuntary forms.

(2) How is the concept of self-loyalty related to some relevant family resemblance concepts? As with family resemblance concepts, we have discussed self-discipline and autonomy. We argue that self-loyalty can fill a gap, or a middle ground, between the two mentioned concepts. The problem with self-discipline is its 'hard' connotations. Many of the themes that are handled in regard to the concept are not so 'hard' or repressive against the self, as the word connotes – sometimes self-loyalty is then a more appropriate word. In contrast, the problem with the concept of autonomy is its connotation of 'softness'. The concept can connote 'free-wheeling' freedom, and the more regulating aspects of the phenomenon become overshadowed. This form of loyalty can help us in the method of theorising by focusing on law/*nomos*, which the concept of autonomy no longer easily connotes.

(3) How can the concept of self-loyalty help us to analyse resistance in social acceleration? It is voluntary self-loyalty that can help us to analyse this form of resistance. We could, for example, see this strategy among some unemployed people who instead of feeling ashamed in the perspective of work ethics, distance themselves from work as a core value. Loyal to themselves, they create alternative identities around values other than work.

To sum up, in starting with the analytical approach of Swedberg's theorising and Wittgenstein's notion of family resemblance concepts, we see potential in developing the concept of loyalty since new conditions in society need new conceptualisation in order for concepts to be relevant. We argue that self-loyalty and its relation to family resemblance concepts, such as self-discipline and autonomy, can be used as an analytical tool for phenomena and situations that the traditional concept of loyalty misses. In times of social acceleration, as described by Rosa, we think forms of loyalty and self-techniques in the Foucauldian sense have changed; hence, new forms must be added to the old ones. Another way to argue this could be that loyalty in itself is an irrelevant concept in contemporary society. One can claim that the concept is dead or at least in bad shape. In academia, in business and other contexts it is sometimes claimed that loyalty has been exposed to corrosion (Sennett 1998) and business gurus have announced that 'loyalty is dead' (Sennett 2006). We disagree, as we don't think loyalty is dead and maybe it is not even corroded. Maybe it has just changed form. And the main theme of this article is to show one of its new shapes. This is in line with Simmel's notion of sociology as the geometry of sociality and the importance of identifying and discussing new geometrical forms. Self-loyalty can be seen as one of many geometrical forms in the context of social acceleration.

## Notes

1. To our knowledge the term self-loyalty is hitherto very seldom used in a scientific context. One exception we have found is the psychodynamic use in Wurmser (2000).
2. See Archer (2000, 2003) for discussions on non-social and pre-social aspects of the self.

## RESISTANCE AND EMOTIONS

3. Another logical possibility that is not considered in this article is that a person can be totally disconnected to other persons or organisations, as in the state of anomie (Durkheim 2002). One characteristic of the state of anomie is the lack of loyalties.
4. There is a similarity here with the social psychologist Mead's (1934) division of the self in the spontaneous part 'I' and the reflecting part 'me'. In the context of this article, we leave aside further discussions about how Mead fits in and can be linked to our discussions.
5. For a discussion on self-love see Frankfurt (2004).
6. Another interesting discussion is if this can be defined as a rational or irrational resistance, for a discussion on rational or irrational resistance see Lilja *et al.* (2013).
7. For a discussion about marketing yourself as if you were a company see Persson (2003).

## Acknowledgement

The authors wish to thank Mona Lilja, Satu Heikkinen, Mikael Baaz and two anonymous referees, for important comments on the paper.

## Disclosure statement

No potential conflict of interest was reported by the authors.

## References

Ahlstrand, R., Arvidson, M., and Axelsson, J., 2017. Protest, tystnad och partiskhet: Replik på en teori om lojalitet och whistleblowing. *Norsk sosiologisk tidsskrift*, 24 (3), 257–265.

Archer, M.S., 2000. *Being human: the problem of agency*. Cambridge: Cambridge University Press.

Archer, M.S., 2003. *Structure, agency and the internal conversation*. Cambridge: Cambridge University Press.

Arvidson, M. and Axelsson, J., 2014. Lojalitetens sociala former – om lojalitet och arbetsliv. *Arbetsmarknad & Arbetsliv*, 20 (1), 55–64.

Bryant, S., 1914. Loyalty. *In*: J. Hasting, ed. *Encyclopædia of religion and ethics*. Edingburgh: T. and T. Clarke, 183–188.

Christman, J., 2015. Autonomy in moral and political philosophy. *In*: N.Z. Edward, ed. *The Stanford encyclopedia of philosophy* (Spring 2015 Edition). Available from: http://plato.stanford.edu/archives/spr2015/entries/autonomy-moral/ [Accessed 3 May 2017].

Connor, J., 2007. *The sociology of loyalty*. New York: Springer.

Corvino, J., 2002. Loyalty in business? *Journal of Business Ethics*, 41 (1–2), 179–185.

Durkheim, É., 2002. *Suicide: a study in sociology*. London: Routledge.

Elegido, J.M., 2013. Does it make sense to be a loyal employee? *Journal of Business Ethics*, 116, 495–511.

Elster, J., 1984. *Ulysses and the Sirens: studies in rationality and irrationality*. Cambridge: Cambridge University Press.

Elster, J., 2000. *Ulysses unbound: studies in rationality, precommitment, and constraints*. Cambridge: Cambridge University Press.

Elster, J., 2003. Don't burn your bridge before you come to it: some ambiguities and complexities of precommitment. *Texas Law Review*, 817, 1751.

Fairclough, N., 1993. Critical discourse analysis and the marketisation of public discourse: The Universities. *Discourse & Society*, 4 (2), 133–168.

Felder, D. and Holden, W., 2008. *Heaven and hell: my life as an Eagle, 1974–2001*. Hoboken, NJ: Wiley.

Fletcher, G.P., 1995. *Loyalty*. Oxford: Oxford University Press.

Foucault, M., 1991. *Discipline and punish: the birth of the prison*. Harmondsworth: Penguin.

Foucault, M., 1994. Technologies of the self. *In*: P. Rainbow, ed. *Ethics, subjecitivity, and truth*. New York: New Press, 225–251.

Franck, T.M., 1997. Is personal freedom a western value? *The American Journal of International Law*, 91 (4), 593–627.

Frankfurt, H.G., 2004. *The reasons of love*. Princeton, NJ: Princeton University Press.

Garsten, C. and Jacobsson, K., eds., 2004. *Learning to be employable: new agendas on work, responsibility and learning in a globalising world*. Basingstoke: Palgrave Macmillan.

Gillberg, G., 2015. Fostran till anställningsbarhet – tankar om ungas villkor på arbetsmarknaden. *In*: A. Bergman, G. Gillberg and L. Ivarsson, eds. *Tankar om arbete: 17 texter om arbete, arbetsliv och samhällsförändring*. Stockholm: Premiss, 38–54.

Haglunds, M., 2009. *Enemies of the people: whistle-blowing and the sociology of tragedy*. Doktorsavhandling. Stockholm: Stockholms universitet.

Hajdin, M., 2005. Employee loyalty: an examination. *Journal of Business Ethics*, 593, 263–275.

Haugaard, M., 2010. Power: A 'family resemblance' concept. *European Journal of Cultural Studies*, 13 (4), 419–438.

Hart, D.W. and Thompson, J.A., 2007. Untangling employee loyalty: a psychological contract perspective. *Business Ethics Quarterly*, 17 (2), 297–323.

Hirschman, A.O., 1970. *Exit, voice, and loyalty: responses to decline in firms, organisations, and states*. Cambridge, MA: Harvard University Press.

Hobbins, J., 2015. Unga långtidsarbetslösa och det individualiserade ansvaret. *Arbetsmarknad & Arbetsliv*, 21 (2), 58–72.

Hollander, J.A. and Einwohner, R.L., 2004. Conceptualising resistance. *Sociological Forum*, 19 (4), 533–554.

Ivarsson, L., 2014. *Att förena passion med försörjning: en diskussion om hobby och arbete i det senmoderna samhället*. Karlstad: Fakulteten för humaniora och samhällsvetenskap, Arbetsvetenskap, Karlstads universitet.

Karlsson, J.C. and Bergman, A., 2017. *Methods for social theory: analytical tools for theorising and writing*. London: Routledge.

Kirchhoff, J.W. and Karlsson, J.C., 2009. Rationales for breaking management rules – the case of health care workers. *Journal of Workplace Rights*, 14, 457–479.

Kirkeby, O.F., 2002. *Loyalitet. Udfordringen for ledere og medarbejdere*. København: Samfundslitteratur.

Kleinig, J., 2014. *On loyalty and loyalties: the contours of a problematic virtue*. Oxford: Oxford University Press.

Ladd, J., 1967. Loyalty. *In*: P. Edwards, ed. The encyclopedia of philosophy, Vol. V. New York: Macmillan & The Free Press, 97–98.

Lilja, M., Baaz, M. and Vinthagen, S., 2013. Exploring 'irrational resistance'. *Journal of Political Power*, 6 (2), 201–217.

Lysgaard, S., 2001. *Arbeiderkollektivet: en studie i de underordnedes sosiologi*. Oslo: Universitetsforlaget.

Mead, G.H., 1934. *Mind, self and society: from the standpoint of a social behaviorist*. Chicago, IL: University of Chicago Press.

Mele, D., 2001. Loyalty in business: Subversive doctrine or real need?. *Business Ethics Quarterly*, 11, 11–26.

Morishima, M., 1982. *Why has Japan 'succeeded'?*. Cambridge: Cambridge University Press.

Murray, D.C., 2015. Notes to self: the visual culture of selfies in the age of social media. *Consumption Markets & Culture*, 18 (6), 490–516.

Persson, A., 2003. *Social kompetens: när individen, de andra och samhället möts*. Lund: Studentlitteratur.

Provis, C., 2005. Dirty Hands and loyalty in organisational politics. *Business Ethics Quarterly*, 15, 283–298.

Randels, G.D. Jr., 2001. Loyalty, corporations, and community. *Business Ethics Quarterly*, 11, 27–39.

Raz, J., 1986. *The morality of freedom*. Oxford: Clarendon Press.

Rosa, H., 2012. *Weltbeziehungen im Zeitalter der Beschleunigung: Umrisse einer neuen Gesellschaftskritik*. Erste Auflage.

Rosa, H., 2013. *Social acceleration: a new theory of modernity*. New York: Columbia University Press.

Rose, N., 1989. *Governing the soul: the shaping of the private self*. London: Routledge.

Royce, J., 1995. *The philosophy of loyalty*. Nashville, TN: Vanderbilt University Press.

Schrag, B., 2001. The moral significance of employee loyalty. *Business Ethics Quarterly*, 11, 41–66.

Sennett, R., 1998. *The corrosion of character: the personal consequences of work in the new capitalism*. New York: W.W. Norton.

Sennett, R., 2006. *The culture of the new capitalism*. New Haven, CT: Yale University Press.

Simmel, G., 2009. *Sociology: inquiries into the construction of social forms*. Leiden: Brill.

Sjögren, K., 2010. Karin avslöjade mutskandalen. *Värmlands Folkblad*, 29 Nov, p. 7.

Swedberg, R., 2014. *The art of social theory*. Princeton: Princeton University Press.

Trist, E. and Bamforth, K., 1951. Some social and psychological consequences of the longwall method of coal-getting. *Human Relations*, 4, 3–38.

Ulferts, H., Korunka, C. and Kubicek, B., 2013. Acceleration in working life: An empirical test of a sociological framework. *Time & Society*, 22 (2), 161–185.

Urry, J., 2003. *Global complexity*. Cambridge: Polity.

Vandekerckhove, W. and Commers, M.S.R., 2004. Whistle blowing and rational loyalty. *Journal of Business Ethics*, 53 (1/2), 263–275.

Varelius, J., 2009. Is Whistle-blowing compatible with employee loyalty? *Journal of Business Ethics*, 85 (2), 263–275.

Vostal, F., 2016. *Accelerating academia: the changing structure of academic time*. Basingstoke: Palgrave Macmillan.

Wittgenstein, L., 1958. *Philosophical investigations = Philosophische Untersuchungen*. 2nd ed. Oxford: B. Blackwell.

Wurmser, L., 2000. *The power of the inner judge: psychodynamic treatment of severe neuroses*. Northvale, NJ: Jason Aronson Inc.

# Norm-critical rationality: emotions and the institutional influence of queer resistance

Andreas Henriksson

**ABSTRACT**
Norm critique is a recent discourse and practice in Sweden that is associated with queer resistance. It is taken up as a mode of governance in several Swedish institutions and companies. At face value, norm critique allows queer resistance to have a direct impact on institutional sources of norms in society. However, this article argues that such a shift in queer resistance replaces the queer emotionally overt subject with a rationalist style of emoting. It also argues that norm critique (re)institutes a subject position that paradoxically sides with contemporary forms of power and its demands for emotional competence.

## 1. Introduction[1]

Norm critique is a discourse and practice that has developed in Sweden over the last decade (Bromseth and Darj 2010, p. 13). Originally coined 'norm-critical pedagogy' by a group of academics and practitioners in the late 2000s, it springs in part from queer pedagogy, which was developed in the US, but also from queer theory more generally. Queer theory and resistance have figured in Swedish political, academic and cultural debates and social movements since the late 1990s (Rosenberg 2002). Norm critique thus represents a recent development in queer resistance that challenges norms from within institutions of power themselves. Lately, it has been taken up as a mode of governance in a number of Swedish public institutions and companies; for example, in a large public research foundation (Vinnova 2016), the Swedish Lutheran Church and in a forestry company (Nygren *et al.* 2012, pp. 25, 27).[2]

My aim in this article is to problematise norm critique by analysing the emotional regime that is discursively prescribed for the norm-critical subject in two important Swedish policy documents. I will argue that with norm critique, queer resistance has ostensibly turned away from overt expressions of emotions and has now embraced a rationalist mode of handling emotions. On the one hand, this move allows queer resistance to influence mainstream institutions that are an important source of norms in society. On the other, I will argue that this new mode of handling emotions also configures the norm-critical subject in ways that may play into the hands of power relations in contemporary society.

The shift away from overt emotional expression towards an apparently more rational discourse has marked the entrance of other social movements into mainstream institutions and politics. Studies have shown similar trajectories for certain feminist and leftist movements in the twentieth century (Hercus 1999, Polletta and Jasper 2001, Cossu 2010).[3] In this respect, norm critique is analogous to the ambition of other social resistance movements that seek to broaden legitimacy by adopting a more rationalist subject position. In short, it illustrates the adaptation of social resistance to a given institutional emotional regime in the name of institutional influence.

From its inception, queer resistance has levelled much of its critique at norms. The norm-critical discourse inherits this focus. Critics of this stance in queer theory have, however, argued that although critical of norms, antinormativity may inadvertently introduce new implicit norms that can be even harder to detect and resist, since they are introduced in the name of resistance (Jagose 2015, Wiegman and Wilson 2015). In this article, I will show how this is the case for norm critique, which not least assumes extensive emotional competence in its subjects.

My mode of analysis is inspired by Michel Foucault's understanding of enunciative modalities, and focuses on the norm-critical subject (Foucault 1972). It can answer the question; in what ways is the discursively speaking subject positioned, located and related to objects in the norm-critical discourse? It can also be used to answer: what emotions and emotional competence is the norm-critical discourse demanding of this subject? The norm critique encountered in the analysed documents presents itself foremost as a discourse that is offered to various institutions. It empowers members of these institutions to speak its critique. This is, as it were, the point at which queer resistance lends its voice to non-queer subjects, a moment that I think Foucault's focus on the subject of discourse is suited to capturing.

I have analysed two norm-critical documents that are co-written by representatives from social movements and institutions in Sweden. The social movements are RFSL [Sw. Riksförbundet för homosexuellas, bisexuellas, transpersoners och queeras rättigheter; Eng. Swedish Federation for Lesbian, Gay, Bisexual, Transgender and Queer Rights] and RFSL Ungdom, and the institutions Tema Likabehandling and Ungdomsstyrelsen; I will describe these texts, the movements and institutions below. Although emotions are not mentioned in the documents other than very fleetingly, it is possible to describe the emotional capacity required by the norm-critical subject that they construct. To uncover the emotionality of rationalist subjectivity is a mode of analysis consonant with the reasoning of sociologists who question the distinction between rationality and emotion, and seek the emotions associated with a certain rational style (Barbalet 2001).

I begin by orienting the reader to the relationship between emotions in social resistance and in institutions, as well as to the problems of antinormativity. A shorter section on method, discussing Foucault's analysis of enunciative modalities, is followed by empirical analysis. The analysis is divided into three sections, corresponding to the three aspects of enunciative modalities: position, site and relation to object. I then conclude the article and set the results against the context of the emotionality of institutions and of queer resistance.

## 2. Social movements and the emotions of rationality

In 2010, the group that coined the phrase 'norm-critical pedagogy' was surprised by the rapid institutionalisation of their discourse:

> Perhaps it is a Swedish phenomenon that truly radical perspectives that are critical of power, such as queer and norm-critical pedagogy, are embraced by state institutions at breakneck speed. (Bromseth and Darj 2010, p. 14; my translation)

Norm critique is said to partly spring from queer theory (Bromseth and Darj 2010, Kalonaityté 2014). Queer theory became a significant source of inspiration at Swedish universities and in Swedish social and cultural debates in the late 1990s. One of the early Swedish texts on queer theory was Tiina Rosenberg's *Queer feminist agenda* from 2002. Rosenberg is a professor of gender and performance studies, and her book has been republished several times. In her book, Rosenberg included the American 'Queer nation manifesto' from 1990 (Rosenberg 2002). It is a text noticeably full of emotions; it talks about anger, fear, terrorising straight people, hate, outrage, bitterness, happiness and suffering. For example:

> I hate every sector of the straight establishment in this country – the worst of whom actively want all queers dead, the best of whom never stick their necks out to keep us alive. (ACT UP 1990)

This outburst of emotions has parallels in a Swedish queer activist context. Cathrin Wasshede, for example, writes about the strategic display of hatred as part of queer resistance in Gothenburg during the 'hate straights day' proclaimed by the activists (Wasshede 2013). More generally, Sara Ahmed argues that queers often experience emotions other than those whose lives fit better with heteronormative ideals (Ahmed 2014). In particular, she points to the relative comfort that can be experienced by living a life closer to norms, and a corresponding discomfort experienced by queers.

If we compare these queer emotions with the lack of emotions in norm-critical texts (I will describe that lack below), we recognise a significant difference that needs to be understood in light of the emotional changes in queer resistance that its institutionalisation in Sweden has brought.

Emotional regimes can be described as the informal norms, specific to given activities and situations, that regulate which emotions are expected, acceptable and not acceptable (Hochschild 2003b). There has long been a recognition in philosophy and sociology of an institutional divide between rationality and emotion in the West (Barbalet 2000, Berezin 2002). In particular, the emotional regime associated with bureaucracies, not least those concerned with policy-making, which has been described as rationalist and sceptical of overt emotions (cf. Hoggett 2000). It follows then that social resistance movements that harbour strong emotions may encounter difficulties if and when they try to gain influence on policy and governance.

There are a number of studies that demonstrate a shift in emotional tactics when a social movement seeks legitimacy within established institutions. For example, the Communist Party of Italy arranged rituals so as to de-emphasise and stigmatise overt expressions of emotions after the Second World War, when it increased its membership drastically and achieved unprecedented influence on the Italian State (Cossu 2010). Feminist movements have struggled with how to approach the State and governance, and part of this struggle concerns the appropriateness of certain emotions, such as anger (Hercus 1999, Polletta and Jasper 2001).

At the same time as bureaucracy has been described as rationalist and emotionless, others have argued that the boundaries between rationality and emotions need to be redrawn in social theory. Jack Barbalet, for example, argues that rationality presupposes emotions, 'which include commitment to the purposes at hand, loyalty to the employing organization, joy in success to encourage more success, and dissatisfaction at failure to encourage success' (Barbalet 2001, p. 59). Barbalet admits, however, that the emotions associated with rationality are often 'under-conceptualised' in comparison to, for example, anger or happiness. What could be called the emotional regime of rational organisations does not, in other words, merely consist of the suppression of emotions. It may also include complex encouragements of certain emotions that are difficult to articulate.

Recent years have also seen a re-evaluation in social science of the emotional regimes of public institutions and private companies. Where before sociologists emphasised the absence of overt emotions in these organisations, contemporary research investigates the more complex ways in which emotions are regulated, used and exploited (Hochschild 2003a, Illouz 2007). Parallel to this social scientific re-evaluation of the emotional regimes in bureaucracies, some writers have discussed how the increasingly complex demands on emotional displays in contemporary work, set high demands for emotional competence among employees (Illouz 2007). To be able to display the right emotions and shift between them when context demands, requires certain skill sets that may be associated with certain forms of family backgrounds and educations.

## 3. Antinormativity in queer theory and beyond

Queer resistance has broadly been associated with the norm concept, and norms have been identified with what the queer movement is resisting. For example, in an official report for the Swedish Government on norm critique and the labour market, Lena Martinsson argues that the norm concept as a tool of critique 'had a significant upswing, particularly in gender studies, when Judith Butler used and theorised it in several of her books' (Martinsson 2014, p. 249). Butler was central to the formulation of queer theory in the early to mid-1990s.

However, this association between queer and critique of norms has recently been interrogated. In a recent issue of the journal *Differences*, a number of writers explore queer theory 'without an allegiance to antinormativity' (Wiegman and Wilson 2015), questioning the fact that:

> [t]hese days it almost goes without saying that queer is conventionally understood to mean 'antinormative,' as can be seen in thumbnail definitions that manage to insist, despite being whittled down to epistemological minimalism, on the primacy of queer's opposition to normativity. (Jagose 2015, p. 26)

One reason to question queer theory's allegiance to antinormativity, is that it may lead to the problematic assumption that old and unproductive norms can be rationally dismissed, or more generally that it might be possible to create a society without exclusionary norms. Given however that norms are defined as basic common assumptions necessary to undertake collective action (Garfinkel 1967, Ahmed 2014), any form of collective resistance, including antinormative varieties, will rest on often implicit norms. Therefore, it is redundant to ask whether norm-critical resistance will be based on norms; rather, a better question is what those norms are and how they are formed.

A further dilemma with an antinormative stance is that it may tie in with contemporary forms of power. In an historical perspective, Michel Foucault argues that norms circulated between what he calls discipline, a specific form of power that operates on the individual body, and biopolitics or regulatory power, which is concerned with masses of people and national populations:

> We can say that there is one element that will circulate between the disciplinary and the regulatory, which will also be applied to body and population alike, which will make it possible to control both the disciplinary order of the body and the aleatory events that occur in the biological multiplicity. The element that circulates between the two is the norm (Foucault 2004, p. 252f).

Given that the forms of power described by Foucault are historical, it is reasonable to ask if contemporary forms of power operate along different axes and whether this impacts how norms circulate. Gilles Deleuze has argued that while the historical forms of power described by Foucault indeed operated within the tension between individual and mass (or population), that is no longer true of emerging forms of dominance, where instead the flow is central (Deleuze 1995). Here, Deleuze is referring to a society where sites and populations are significant only to the extent that they allow for the directing, limiting or increasing of the flow, the mobility, of people. In the work of sociologists Luc Boltanski and Eve Chiapello, bureaucracies are shown to have increasingly come to embrace openness to innovation, change and mobility and presumably emotional regimes conducive to those (Boltanski and Chiapello 2005). Similarly, if we agree with these analyses that the constellation of dominance is currently shifting, it would follow that norms may operate differently. Indeed, if flows, movement and potentialities are more important than, for example, closed institutions, other forms of emotional regimes and norms that govern them are presumably at play.

## 4. Method

Below, I will present an analysis of what Foucault called the enunciative modalities: those positions, sites and relation to the object of discourse that are presupposed by different utterances and which give us a picture of the manifold subject that is allowed to 'speak the discourse', and which the discourse in turn is thus involved in producing (Foucault 1972, p. 50ff). Let me describe the three dimensions of enunciative modalities using Foucault's example of modern medical discourse. The subject's *position* is a formal and informal social one, often associated with requirements like certain competences. The medical discourse, for example, is spoken by medical doctors, that people become after a closely regulated education and so on. The *site* of a discourse is the place where it is spoken – for example the hospital or the ward. Lastly, the subject's *relation to the object* of discourse is the way, for example, that medical doctors approach, investigate and analyse the physical body of their patients.

It is important to stress that I limit myself to an analysis of enunciative modalities; I do not claim on have done a full Foucauldian analysis in any sense of the word. The material I have analysed is small, and can only give indications about the subject that norm critique presumes. Besides, my material is limited to documents only; as Gavin Kendall and Gary Wickham have argued, Foucault does not understand the subject as constructed merely by discourse, but as a nexus that connects discourse and non-discursive elements (Kendall and Wickham 1999, p. 54). Foremost, I can speak of the discursive construction of the norm-critical subject, and only to a much lesser extent of its non-discursive functioning.

# RESISTANCE AND EMOTIONS

In his text on enunciative modalities, Foucault does not mention emotions. Nevertheless, I would argue that to discuss the emotional prerequisites for certain mental operations prescribed for making norm-critical utterances is not far-removed from Foucault's mode of analysis, whereby he seeks various prerequisites on the subject of enunciations. Importantly, the concept of emotions does not assume a unitary subject, which Foucault is critical of. Rather, it can help to further deconstruct that subject and articulate its varying modes of experience (cf. Barbalet 2001, p. 116f).

I have analysed two documents on norm critique than come from two different semi-public or public institutions; the institutions are Tema Likabehandling and Ungdomsstyrelsen (RFSL Ungdom and Birgerson Nordling 2011, Nygren *et al.* 2012). I have translated the documents' titles as *Constructive norm critique. A report on norm critique in the European Social Fund's projects,* and *Open the activity up! Methods about norms and inclusion in open youth activities.* The Tema Likabehandling is a cooperative group jointly directed by public institutions like Linköpings universitet and the Equality Ombudsman, private firms like Swedbank, and civil-society actors like RFSL (the national organisation for LGBT people and issues) and LO (the national umbrella organisation for trade unions). Tema Likabehandling assembles and communicates knowledge to help promote an equal rights agenda in the working life of people and organisations. Meanwhile, Ungdomsstyrelsen, or the Swedish Agency for Youth and Civil Society, works directly under the Swedish parliament and government to evaluate youth policies, distribute funds to various projects and organisations, as well as produce and spread knowledge pertinent to its areas of responsibility.

The social movements that have co-written the documents are RFSL and RFSL Ungdom; the largest Swedish LGBTQ organisation and its sister organisation for young people, respectively. RFSL has organised Swedish LGBTQ people from the 1950s and onwards. Unlike in Anglo-Saxon countries, where different LGBTQ organisations have succeeded each other, Sweden's RFSL has absorbed trends in the LGBTQ community, but remained the same organisation throughout the gay liberation period, the era of AIDS and the queer movement (although it has had LGBTQ critiques throughout these periods). RFSL has nevertheless been central to LGBTQ and queer resistance in Sweden. Its branch for young people, RFSL Ungdom, was formed as late as 1999.

I have chosen to analyse the two mentioned documents, because they are unique in three respects: they (1) treat norm critique not only in schools (see above on norm-critical pedagogy), but in a broader set of institutions; (2) are co-written by people from civil-society and public institutions; and (3) are fairly extensive (66 pages and 73 pages, respectively). No other publically available documents can be found that fulfil these criteria. As the documents are written by organisations that either are, or represent central Swedish institutions (such as RFSL, the parliament, LO and the Equality Ombudsman), they can be read as representing and promoting current developments within those institutions. All quotations from the documents have been translated into English from Swedish by me.

For all intents and purposes, I treat the analysed passages as displaying how one discourse, norm critique, is strategically set up to work within powerful institutions. I will not focus on differences between documents or between different utterances in the same document. My approach may appear to represent the documents as overly homogeneous. However, it is also the case that the two analysed documents display a rather high degree of homogeneity, insofar as they use the same central concepts, use those similarly, take on a similar tone and suggest similar methods for norm critique. Most importantly, the norm-critical subject that they presuppose has similar characteristics.

That said, the two documents display differences; *Constructive norm critique* is an evaluation of a number of norm-critical projects within both the private and public sector that are funded by the European social fund, while *Open the activity up!* gives suggestions and advice for norm-critical work at youth recreation centres. The latter document is more focused on including LGBT youth (although it recognises the need for critique of a wider array of norms), while the former is explicitly broader in its scope. However, despite these differences, both documents spend considerable time explicating the basic concepts and methods of the norm-critical discourse, and my analysis focuses on these parts (albeit not exclusively).

My treatment of the documents as somewhat homogeneous is also a matter of emphasis. This article presents a broad and general analysis of the ways in which the norm-critical discourse has been articulated along the interface between RFSL and other institutions that are constituted by the co-authorship of the analysed documents. While it is an analysis that future articles need to refine and it needs to be extended to other documents, it is also one that may help such future endeavours by pointing out central characteristics and potential points of tension.

## 5. The norm-critical subject

In this section, I will analyse what the documents say and presume about the norm-critical subject; i.e. who can speak the norm-critical discourse. I will follow Foucault's scheme for analysing enunciative modalities; i.e. look at the position, sites and relations to objects that the norm-critical subject discursively occupies (Foucault 1972, p. 50ff). In each of these points of analysis, I will also interrogate the emotionality that the documents presuppose. Overall, I argue that the documents represent an emotional regime that queer resistance needs to adopt when it wins influence in powerful institutions.

### 5.1. Position: the self-surveying, resourceful subject

Who can do norm-critical work? The competence for, or at least interest in, criticising norms, has often been ascribed to people who are directly affected by the norms. However, norm critique takes a different approach and argues that norm-critical work should involve everyone in an organisation: 'Everyone working in the activity/organisation [Sw. Verksamheten] must be involved and be willing to examine themselves' (Nygren *et al.* 2012, p. 52). However, as we will see, although the documents mobilise 'everyone', they also require certain competencies, particularly emotional ones, of its subject. As I will show, this subject needs to be able to overcome emotional crises and feel okay about normative changes. It must be committed to a panoptical form of surveillance in its organisation and it cannot be overly invested in certain values or ends.

The documents encourage norm-critical projects to work particularly closely with resourceful people in the organisation, as these can better effect change:

> It is important that the work towards change is put in a context where people think long-term, and where there are resources for evaluation and development. It is also important to cooperate with activities that can have an impact and that the efforts being made are anchored to the core

activity [of the organisation]' Within the projects [that have been described and evaluated in this document], it is very obvious which co-actors have been missing for the project to have more impact. Employers should therefore be included to a larger extent for change to be possible. (Nygren *et al.* 2012, p. 58)

The logic at play here is that norm critique should avoid what the documents refer to as the 'tolerance perspective', where 'you focus on those who deviate from the norm, instead of focusing on the norm that excludes [them]' (RFSL Ungdom and Birgerson Nordling 2011, p. 33). Or in other words: The point about norm critique is to 'shift focus from "the Others" or the norm breakers, to norms and power' (Nygren *et al.* 2012, p. 13). Norm critique is thus levelled at the norms, not the excluded. As the discourse potentially empowers all people from an organisation to speak, and as those people are presumably part of sustaining norms, it also invites them to look at themselves. 'Norm-critical methods often entail creating situations where those involved must reflect on their own and others expectations, notions and distribution of power' (Nygren *et al.* 2012, p. 14).

Both documents refer to work or project groups that are particularly active in norm-critical work. These include resourceful individuals in an organisation that are, again, invited to reflect on themselves. The first document states that:

> Self-reflection is central to norm-critical work, but to have an impact in the organisation [Sw. verksamhet], the whole work team must be involved. [...] To look at norms and make changes that challenge familiar patterns, can easily yield resistance and then you need each other's support. It can for example be simpler to see things that others say and do, rather than to see what oneself is saying and doing. (RFSL Ungdom and Birgerson Nordling 2011, p. 35)

A similar formulation can be found in the second document:

> To make norms and structures visible within an organisation (Sw. en verksamhet) and to give [the norm critical work] some impact, everyone must be involved in the work. It is therefore important that a project group or a steering committee is actively at work scrutinising itself. (Nygren *et al.* 2012, p. 53)

In other words, the subject of the norm-critical discourse is potentially everyone, but particularly a working committee that ideally includes the resourceful members of an organisation. The task they are given is a self-surveying one.

To Foucault, self-surveillance is central to contemporary forms of power; one of his most famous examples of this is the panoptical arrangement, where the constant risk of surveillance leads people to survey themselves (Foucault 1977). To some extent, an organisation working with norm critique can be likened to a Panopticon; as everyone is potentially involved the norm-critical gaze can come from any direction, thus inciting a need for self-surveillance among members. The norm-critical subject is therefore one that is partly formed within the strictures of disciplinary power, or power focused on the body through (self-) surveillance.

However, as I will elaborate below, it would be wrong to assume that the norm-critical subject has its *self* as object. As Foucault argues, power is never directed at something like the self, but rather at actions (Foucault 1982). Norm critique is indeed directed at actions, particularly those of exclusion or normative presumptions, both of self and others. Through self- and other-surveillance then, a panoptical type of power is put in the service of an anti-normative agenda.

It is significant to recognise the emotional capacities that these quotations require of the norm-critical subject. Norm critique is a discourse of resistance placed in the hands of

RESISTANCE AND EMOTIONS

resourceful members, and directed towards their own actions. As such, they are asked to understand themselves and their organisations in new terms, which may feel emotionally overwhelming, as the documents acknowledge. However, whereas discourses of resistance are elsewhere often framed in terms of strong emotions winning the day, norm critique is about rationality overcoming emotional resistance.

> You may start to see your own life, your relationships and your interests in a new light. Limiting norms can become so evident and so ubiquitous that you can find yourself in a crisis. (RFSL Ungdom and Birgerson Nordling 2011, p. 33)

> It is common to have mental barriers and hidden resistance against scrutinising oneself. One reason may for example be that it is painful to realise that you have advantages and power only because of your skin colour, gender or functionality. (RFSL Ungdom and Birgerson Nordling 2011, p. 48f)

The norm-critical subject is here understood as emotionally competent, as it is able to see itself differently and question its own privileges. While this can initially cause problematic emotions or even a crisis, the norm-critical process is one through which these emotions are overcome. As such, the emotions of the subject are seen as untrustworthy and described only when they signal resistance; with time they are supposed to subside.

The flipside of describing norm critique as an overcoming of negative emotions, is that people involved in the process need to feel okay about taking on a certain norm-critical method: 'If it feels okay in the team, you can check each other by carefully "correcting" one another or add to what is being said [if someone e.g. attributes gender to a non-binary person]' (RFSL Ungdom and Birgerson Nordling 2011, p. 35). Rather than engaging with negative emotions then, the norm-critical process presupposes that people have the emotional competence to feel okay in the face of change. The subject is thus required to handle its emotional crisis, and eventually cross boundaries without significant emotional disturbances. The crossing of boundaries is thus emotionally associated with being okay, rather than with crises. One could say that breaching norms is emotionally de-emphasised.

Both documents present norm critique as a method or a series of methods. Methods, like tools, are usually kept separate from people's aims and ends, and likewise, these methods are described as lending themselves to different ends that people may have.

> It is important to have a common platform, where all participants fight for the same thing, even if not for the same reasons – some focus on the rights to equal rights and opportunities, while others focus on the profits [Sw. affärsnyttan] made from broadening recruitment. (Nygren *et al.* 2012, p. 57)

In this quotation, participants are told to work with the same methods, but not to presume that they all share the same goal or aim. Subjects are therefore allowed to further their own and varying agendas. It is significant that profits are mentioned in the quotation. Indeed, private companies have been important sites for norm critical projects (Vinnova 2016). The argument presented in these contexts is that norm critique can raise profits in companies and enhance the quality of services and products. Thus, norm critique is increasingly presented as a method for the private sector and its often profit-generating aims.

This openness to varying ends and values helps to make norm critique more palatable for various institutions and private firms. In the same instant, it also opens the norm-critical subject position up to a variety of individuals. In short, one does not need to subscribe to any one particular set of values to take on the mantle of the norm-critical subject. Indeed,

I would argue that the norm-critical subject is one that does not adhere to any values or goals with such fervour that it cannot compromise with others in a norm-critical group. This requires a certain emotional detachment to values and goals, without being entirely without them.

Norm critique is thus presented as a means to varying ends. However, at one point it is also described as possible to have as an end in itself:

> Norm critique can therefore be an aim in itself, where the perspective creates an activity or a society that questions, investigates and creates norms through conscious actions and conscious analysis. (Nygren *et al.* 2012, p. 34)

The first thing to note about this quote, is that it presents the reader with a choice between (1) norm critique as a means to unspecified ends; and (2) norm critique as an end to itself. The missing alternative here is norm critique as a means to specified and stable ends. It is difficult to find a line of reasoning in the documents that consistently defends a set purpose for the criticism of norms (such as equal rights). Again, I would argue that this is a way to keep the norm-critical subject position open for a wide array of people.

The second thing to note about the quote is that it presents the norm-critical subject as engaging with norms through consciously acting and analysing. This is a rational subject that has little place for disrupting emotions. Norms are presented as potentially irrational, as long as they are not thought through and changed accordingly. The norm-critical subject is therefore one that can overcome emotions and submit its actions to a rational surveillance. Norm-critical scrutiny could, as it were, be said to liberate these actions from the emotional and irrational reign of norms and put them at the service of a conscious subject. It could be analysed as panoptical-type power in the name of emancipation from norms.

At this point, let me address a possible objection. Some analysts may claim that norm critique is a discourse strategically construed to afford the subject position to resourceful people only to have them deconstruct the basis of their own resourcefulness, and that this explains its slightly vague subject positions. Simply put: could not norm critique be a ruse set within a broader discourse of queer resistance, which has the resourceful and dominant as its object and for which it has devised the discursive snare of norm critique? I would argue not; it is not possible for any discourse to remain faithful to initial intentions, whether these be intentions of resistance or not (cf. Foucault 2004). A discourse can, in a sense, never be a ruse; its subjects are never objects. The subject is indeed a nexus of discursive and non-discursive, and consequently cannot be entirely controlled through discourse. Given the power to speak norm critically, the subject may use the norm-critical discourse for purposes other than those its queer theorist creators may initially have intended.

I have introduced the norm-critical subject in this section; it is kept in a panoptical-like arrangement, where it is supposed to feel okay with normative change. It prioritises rationality and suspects norms of irrational emotions. It cannot be overly invested in specific goals or values. As such, it takes part in the surveillance of self and other, not least, as we will see, through imagining how the site of its operations might be different.

### *5.2. Sites: the (un)settled subject*

The documents describe how norm-critical methods can help to align norms with certain values or goals. Thus, norm critique is not about aborting all norms, but rather realigning norm systems according to extrinsic values or goals. 'There are always norms in an organisation, but [norm critique] is about actively working out which values should be the basis for these systems of norms' (Nygren *et al.* 2012, p. 36). That means that a norm-critical project always entails a discussion about which norms are good and which are bad. Indeed, one source argues, 'it is also however about constructing and creating "new" norms' (Nygren *et al.* 2012, p. 31). This sets up the norm-critical subject as a very peculiar entity. On the one hand, this subject speaks as part of the local organisation and presumably lives within and among its norms. On the other hand, it has goals or values that stretch beyond those norms and the local organisation, goals and values that allow it to judge and change the norms as though they were means. If it manages to create new norms, it will presumably be able to inhabit them as though they were given, rather than set up for ulterior motives. Thus, the subject is able to shift between inhabiting the local and measuring it if not from the outside, then from an imagined alternative version of the local. I will call this subject (un)settled; it simultaneously finds its base in its organisation and seeks to question and change it.

This speaks to the sites that the norm-critical subject inhabits, or rather is unsure how to inhabit. On a methodological note, it also speaks to the problems inherent in Foucault's method for investigating the subject of discourse. Unlike, for example, the medical doctor or the lawyers that Foucault investigates and whose sites are easily identified as the hospital or court (i.e. central institutions in a disciplining society) (cf. Foucault 1977), the norm-critical subject inhabits a rather vague and shifting site. In the documents analysed, it is varyingly called 'an organisation' or 'the activity [Sw. verksamheten]'. But even when this site is identified, it is the norm-critical subject's task to imagine it differently or to seek answers beyond its borders. 'To only ask those that already come to your activities can mean that you get caught in old structures', as one of the documents advises (RFSL Ungdom and Birgerson Nordling 2011, p. 7).

Apart from asking potential inhabitants of their sites, the norm-critical subject is also repeatedly asked to imagine their activities or organisations differently, particularly how they would react or change if excluded groups were involved in one way or another. One document cites a method developed and used at a Swedish hospital, called 'the gender hand':

> The point is to think the opposite of what is the case [Sw. tänka tvärtom]. Each finger on the hand represents an activity in the organisation and you are supposed to ask questions such as; if the patient had had another gender, would you have thought differently? This results in something to remember for each new situation or encounter. (Nygren *et al.* 2012, p. 65)

This method is typical for the norm critique; it involves people who are situated in an organisation or activity, but then asks them to imagine 'the opposite of what is the case'. The point is to have people pay attention to whether their treatment of clients is unduly impacted by the way these clients are categorised. But it also assumes that the norm-critical subject is both enmeshed in the local organisation and can look beyond those boundaries to change its behaviour and engage differently with clients.

The (un)settled character of the norm-critical subject is also illustrated in the following discussion, where readers are introduced to the method of cultural agents: an organisation elects a person to represent the norm-critical project within the organisation itself.

> They learn methods for inclusion and analysis of the companies. The task for cultural agents is to 'spy' on their own working culture, for example during staff meetings or planning meetings, and consider how the culture can be developed. (Nygren *et al.* 2012, p. 45)

The metaphor of the spy displays the kind of emotional competence that is required by the norm-critical subject. To be a spy is to feign belonging, but then serve ulterior purposes in an organisation. However, in this case, the cultural agent does not serve the aims of another organisation, but the purposes of imagined alternatives and norm-critical change. It is thus not that the subject actually belongs elsewhere, but that it attempts to regard the familiar as unfamiliar, to question the given and set its very sense of belonging askew.

Unlike Foucault's doctors and lawyers who look to their organisations and sites as the frames that contain their practices and rationalities, this norm-critical subject seeks to imagine those boundaries differently. The norm-critical methods try to de-emphasise boundaries, for example, by ascertaining that everyone feels okay when pressing for change, or by stressing the importance of self-scrutiny and of imagining alternatives.

As said, I call this mind-set (un)settled; while having and not abandoning a 'base', an organisation or activity, the norm-critical subject nevertheless seeks to transform that base to encompass more of the world. This subject is settled and unsettled at the same time, feeling included and enculturated, and still nervously asking if the current state of affairs is not too familiar or too homely. To imagine one's current organisation differently could be described as a quintessentially (un)settling experience: it allows one to be within an organisation and yet to think it differently in such a way that change becomes logical. As such, this subject is not a Deleuzian nomad who continuously wanders, nor something like the blasé city-dweller who remains unmoved by what s/he sees, as described by Georg Simmel. The (un)settled subject returns to the base after every escapade, finds that it cannot allow itself to call it home and feels committed to change.

Much like other emotions associated with rationality, the (un)settling experience is difficult to describe accurately as an emotion. Sara Ahmed argues that following and breaking norms are associated with feelings of comfort and discomfort (Ahmed 2014). The (un)settled subject, however, fits none of those feelings. It does not seek to imagine itself in the shoes of the uncomfortable. Yet, it is not comfortable with its comfortableness; it somehow manages to inhabit a site that allows it to identify its own actions as disconcerting. To some extent, this fits with the panoptical scheme described by Foucault (1977); to paraphrase him, the spirit surveys the body's actions and finds them wanting. Yet, the norm-critical subject does not inhabit the closed system of the Panopticon. Rather, it is at the porous, flexible boundaries of its loosely defined sites, that this subject operates and where it finds the source of its (un)settledness.

### 5.3. Relations to objects: imagining the target groups

The documents talk about 'target groups'; those whom the norm-critical work will help to include. These can be LGBT people, minority ethnic groups, disabled and so on. A project group leading norm-critical work need not include someone from the target groups. There is in fact no guarantee that a person from the target groups has a better idea about how to change norms than others:

> Even if people from the participant target group have experiences of breaching e.g. linguistic norms and are perhaps negatively impacted by limiting structures, it does not mean that they are automatically conscious of their own notions, values and attitudes. (Nygren *et al.* 2012, p. 30)

As this quotation shows, norm critique is not seen as coming from outside an organisation. Excluded groups are not the subject of this discourse. As I have already explored, the subject is people inside, those who are already included and who may change an organisation from within. The words 'target group' shows that excluded or disadvantaged groups are not engaged as subjects, but seen as the object or target for norm-critical work.

The way that norm-critical subjects are asked to relate to the target group is rather peculiar. Again, we are not in the realm of Foucault's medical doctors or lawyers, who operate directly on the bodies or the actions of their objects. The norm-critical subject needs to relate rather circuitously to the target group. Instead of asking or observing these people directly, norm-critique is more about imagining them. However, this is no empathic exercise – rather, it is a way to explore how 'I' (the subject) relates in thought and action to these groups. In other words, the target is best understood as a means to self-surveillance, not as a way to pretend to be another.

> Another way to create good conditions for your discussions, is if you assume that those engaged in the discussions have different sexual orientations, different gender identities or expressions, different ethnicities or religions and so on. If you assume that different backgrounds, traits and lifestyles are present, it helps you focus on how normative language can be and help you consider what you say. (RFSL Ungdom and Birgerson Nordling 2011, p. 36)

The quotation again displays the importance ascribed to imagining the target group in norm-critical work. But what is not said is also significant; the quotation does not ask the reader to imagine herself as someone from the disadvantaged group, but only imagine others as such. This then is not a method for training empathy, or for feeling and experiencing as another, but a method for reflecting on and training one's responses to these others.

Although never spelled out explicitly, this imagining includes an emotive competence: the subject needs to be able to imagine her/his own potential emotional responses and be able to correct them, or at least be able to emotionally accept changes to her/his actions. I would argue that this is in part accomplished by associating actions with norms as an extrinsic explanation of their problematic character. When the subject critically studies its own responses to an imagined situation, these responses can thus be ascribed to something beyond the self. Indeed, while the documents mention self-reflection as a central method of norm critique, they are never ascribing blame, nor discuss shame or guilt. Rather, the ways that the self responds to the target group is objectified as 'norms', but also as 'normative language'. The relation to the target groups, the problematic ways of talking and so on, can be identified as external to the self and treated as such. In the final analysis then, the norm-critical subject is investigating – by imagining the target group and through self-surveillance – its own actions governed by something that is understood as external to itself, namely norms. It can be said to discipline itself in the name of emancipation; by taking control of its actions, it supposedly liberates them from implicit norms and submits them to its own more thought-through values and goals.

In a recent article, Elisabeth Langmann and Niclas Månsson have sought to problematise norm critique in pedagogy. As I have done here, they assess the subject that emerges in the literature (albeit they use other, more pedagogically focused documents). Unlike me, they conclude that the norm-critical subject is self-reflective and corresponds closely to the modernist essentialised understanding of the self:

> The point of departure for change and emancipation within a norm-critical equality project, is an identifying action that presupposes a stable subject rather than one that is dissolved and full of contradictions. (Langmann and Månsson 2016, p. 91; my translation)

Langmann and Månsson thus criticise norm critique for taking the self as object, and constructing that self as stable and coherent. I am not fully convinced by this analysis, since the norm-critical documents analysed here prescribe self-surveillance rather as a way to imaginatively scrutinise one's actions towards others and consider them governed by external norms. This is a relational, fragmented and situated self that is emotionally flexible and able to change, not a modernist, self-reflective and unchanging self.

Compared with queer theory, norm critique abandons the disadvantaged or excluded as (often explicitly emotional) subject, and instead ascribes the role of discursive (rational) subject to those with resources. The disadvantaged or excluded are accorded the role of target groups, whose voices can only be approached circuitously. The subject is one that can observe and control its own emotions through imagination, and the discourse consequently takes on rationalist overtones.

I would argue that Foucault's method of identifying the subjects and objects of discourses becomes slightly skewed when used to analyse norm critique. Norm critique is a discourse birthed from the insights about discourse that Foucault, among others, were part of uncovering. We should not therefore be surprised when the norm-critical subject reflects on its own actions without taking the self as direct object, or when it critically reflects on its own object-taking when imagining the 'target groups'. However, we should also not hail these quirks of (what could metonymically be called) post-Foucauldian discourses as somehow taking us beyond issues of norms, power and dominance. As I have shown, the norm-critical discourse is as much assigning subject and object positions as other discourses, and presuming emotional competences concurrently with far-reaching rationality of its subject (cf. Barbalet 2001). An important point is therefore that norm critique, while undermining certain norms in the institutions where it is implemented, also inscribes or reinforces other norms, particularly those relating to emotionality and rationality. As we have seen, these norms bolster the porousness of the sites, the temporariness of its members, as well as thinking in terms of potentialities.

## 6. Conclusions

Norm critique can be presented as a way for queer resistance to gain influence in established institutions. As I have shown in this article, however, this influence comes at a cost – namely, the concomitant normative embrace of the rational, emotionally flexible and competent subject. Indeed, in the documents analysed, the queer subject that, for example, feels angry, happy or proud, has been replaced by the resourceful insider with a thoroughly rational mindset. Strong and explicit emotions are replaced by reduced attachment to people, sites and values.

Emotionally, the norm-critical subject feels fine and has the capacity to manage negative emotions and crises. Provocations are not part of the norm-critical project. Its subject does not need to empathise, but simply to retrain its treatment of others. Subjects who engage in norm critique should keep a certain emotional distance from their local organisation and its members, as the latter's perspectives and interests may need to be questioned. I have described this subject as (un)settled; it is simultaneously embedded locally and observes its organisation from the perspective of imagined alternatives. Thus, the norm-critical subject's relations to other inhabitants of its space is ambiguous – e.g. described as that of a 'spy' to the people she/he spies on – as it cannot allow them to claim it for themselves. The norm-critical subject needs to have a certain emotional distance from itself and its normative notions. Norm critique thus seeks to transcend the local and actual, to imagine what could and should happen. This includes transcending one's own currently held values and beliefs, and this makes norm critique deeply reflective and/or associated with self-surveillance.

Finally, Foucault showed how norms are a means of power that historically found its place between discipline and biopolitics. If power in contemporary society predominantly operates along different axes, could it be that norm critique inadvertently assists in repurposing old institutions for any emerging model of power? Indeed, I have shown that norm critique, while operating locally, reimagines local boundaries in relation to flows of people, where current members are merely one of many possible constellations that inhabit a site. In this sense, it repurposes local institutions for a social imagery that is interested in constant change, and has little interest in stable values or ultimate ends (Deleuze 1995, Boltanski and Chiapello 2005). The question that needs to be asked is whether these emerging forms of power are in fact holding norm critique up as a means to dissolve the local and actual, and refocus organisations on flows and potentials. To a certain extent, norm critique would be blind to this kind of power, as it has few concepts or methods by which to understand it. I would therefore contend that the subject constructed by the norm-critical discourse is not one of modernist essentialism as some have recently argued (Langmann and Månsson 2016), but one that is emotionally and empathically detached, operating in relation to imagined and reimagined others, potential actions, groups and people who are only temporarily inhabiting a site.

There are aspects of norm critique that come close to the panoptical scheme famously described by Foucault. The importance of self-surveillance of one's own actions is emphasised. It is ironic, but also in keeping with Foucault's understanding of power, that this self-surveillance is promoted in the name of emancipation from implicit norms. However, the norm-critical subject does not inhabit a closed system, as does Foucault's panoptical prisoners. Rather, the site of a norm-critical gaze is porous and vague, and it often surveys imagined scenes rather than actual actions. Perhaps a new name – Transopticon? – could be devised for this machine of power and surveillance.

The study presented in this article may also be read as indicating the emotional regime that conditions the speaking subject in contemporary Swedish institutions more generally. Of course, given the small sample of texts analysed, I would caution against taking such a reading too far. However, it does point to the fruitfulness of further questioning the classical notion of rational bureaucracies as emotionally sterile organisations, and to combine imagination and precision to describe the various emotions that different types of institutional rationality necessitate.

In view of the norm-critical inscription of norms described here, the queer movement may need to reconsider how its resistance relates to established institutions and its use of the norm concept. Perhaps it would do well to revisit the notion of power (rather than norms) and investigate how current critique of norms may easily be co-opted by emerging forms of power. Perhaps queer theory without antinormativity, although still underdeveloped, may prove more able than norm critique to challenge power in contemporary society (cf. Wiegman and Wilson 2015).

That said, it could be argued that through norm critique, queer resistance has cleverly furthered its agenda by aligning with certain contemporary modes of power. This article is not disputing the critical and transformative potential of norm critique in certain organisations.

## RESISTANCE AND EMOTIONS

Still, the resistance strategy that norm critique entails should be accompanied by an analysis of what its alignment may cost in the long run, and what its pitfalls may be. I hope that this article may contribute towards such an analysis.

## Notes

1. I want to thank the anonymous reviewers of this article for their thorough readings and excellent suggestions. The editors of this special issue on emotions, power and resistance, have also been very helpful with suggestions both early and late in the process of writing this article. All remaining errors are mine, of course.
2. There has not been any inventory of norm-critical initiatives done in Sweden, which makes it difficult to describe the extent to which this practice has entered institutions in the country. One indicator is the list of actors that have received funding for norm-critical projects from the public research foundation Vinnova. From 2014 to 2016, an equivalent of 7 million American dollars has been spent on 72 projects. Among the receivers, about 40% have universities or college universities, while another 20% were private companies and 20% non-profit organisations.
3. I want to thank Åsa Wettergren for help with finding these examples, where social movements have downplayed emotions for the sake of influence.

## Disclosure statement

No potential conflict of interest was reported by the author.

## References

ACT UP, 1990. *The queer nation manifesto*. New York. Available from: http://www.historyisaweapon. com/defcon1/queernation.html.

Ahmed, S., 2014. *The cultural politics of emotion*. Edinburgh: Edinburgh University Press.

Barbalet, J., 2000. Beruf, rationality and emotion in Max Weber's sociology. *European Journal of Sociology*, 41 (2), 329–351.

Barbalet, J., 2001. *Emotion, social theory, and social structure: a macrosociological approach*. Cambridge: Cambridge University Press.

Berezin, M., 2002. Secure states: towards a political sociology of emotion. *The Sociological Review*, 50 (S2), 33–52.

Boltanski, L. and Chiapello, E., 2005. *The new spirit of capitalism*. London: Verso.

Bromseth, J. and Darj, F., 2010. *Normkritisk pedagogik. Makt, lärande och strategier för förändring* [Norm-critical pedagogy. Power, learning and strategies for change]. Uppsala: Centrum för genusvetenskap, Uppsala Universitet.

Cossu, A., 2010. Talking (and silencing) emotions: the culture of mobilization in the Italian Communist Party during the 1940s. *In*: B. Sieben and Å. Wettergren, eds. *Emotionalizing organizations and organizing emotions*. Basingstoke: Palgrave Macmillan, 189–208.

Deleuze, G., 1995. Postscript on control societies. *In*: G. Deleuze, ed. *Negotiations 1972–1990*. New York: Columbia University Press, 175–182.

# RESISTANCE AND EMOTIONS

Foucault, M., 1972. *The archaeology of knowledge and the discourse on language*. New York: Pantheon Books.

Foucault, M., 1977. *Discipline and punish: birth of the prison*. London: Vintage Books.

Foucault, M., 1982. Afterword. The subject and power. *In*: H.L. Dreyfus and P. Rabinow, eds. *Michel Foucault: Beyond Structuralism and Hermeneutics*. New York: Harvester Wheatsheaf, 208.

Foucault, M., 2004. *Society must be defended: Lectures at the Collège de France, 1975–76*. London: Penguin.

Garfinkel, H., 1967. *Studies in ethnomethodology*. Cambridge: Polity.

Hercus, C., 1999. Identity, emotion, and feminist collective action. *Gender & Society*, 13 (1), 34–55.

Hochschild, A., 2003a. *The commercialization of intimate life: notes from home and work*. Berkeley: University of California Press.

Hochschild, A., 2003b. *The managed heart: commercialization of human feeling*. Berkeley: University of California Press.

Hoggett, P., 2000. Social policy and the emotions. *In*: G. Lewis, S. Gerwitz and J. Clarke, eds. *Rethinking social policy*. London: Sage, 141–155.

Illouz, E., 2007. *Cold intimacies: the making of emotional capitalism*. Cambridge: Polity.

Jagose, A., 2015. The trouble with antinormativity. *Differences*, 26 (1), 26–47.

Kalonaityté, V., 2014. *Normkritisk pedagogik – för den högre utbildningen [Norm-critical pedagogy – for higher education]*. Lund: Studentlitteratur.

Kendall, G. and Wickham, G., 1999. *Using Foucault's Methods*. London: Sage.

Langmann, E. and Månsson, N., 2016. Att vända blicken mot sig själv: En problematisering av den normkritiska pedagogiken [To turn the gaze at oneself: problematizing norm-critical pedagogy]. *Pedagogisk forskning i Sverige*, 21 (1–2), 79–100.

Martinsson, L., 2014. Intersektionell normkritik – om jämställdhet, arbetsliv och omvandlingar av makt [Intersectional norm critique - on gender equality, working life and transformation of power]. *In: Delegation for equality in working life: Inte bara jämställdhet. Intersektionella perspektiv på hinder och möjligheter i arbetslivet. Swedish Government Official Reports 2014:34*, 247–272. Available from: http://www.regeringen.se/rattsdokument/statens-offentliga-utredningar/2014/10/sou-201434/.

Nygren, K. *et al.*, 2012. *Konstruktiv normkritik. En rapport om normkritik i Europeiska socialfondens projekt* [Constructive norm critique. A report on norm critique in the European Social Fund's projects]. Available from: http://www.jamstall.nu/wp-content/uploads/2014/02/Konstruktiv-normkritik.pdf.

Polletta, F. and Jasper, J.M., 2001. Collective identity and social movements. *Annual Review of Sociology*, 27 (1), 283–305.

RFSL Ungdom and Birgerson Nordling, C., 2011. *Öppna verksamheten! Ett metodmaterial om normer och inkludering i öppen ungdomsverksamhet* [Open the activity up! Methods about norms and inclusion in open youth activities]. Available from: https://www.mucf.se/sites/default/files/publikationer_uploads/oppna-verksamheten.pdf.

Rosenberg, T., 2002. *Queerfeministisk agenda* [A queer feminist agenda]. Stockholm: Atlas.

Vinnova, 2016. Normkritisk Innovation 2016 [Norm Critical Innovation 2016]. *Utlysning*, p. Vinnova. Available from: http://www.vinnova.se/EffektaXML/ImporteradeUtlysningar/2014-06304/Revider adutlysningtextNormkritiskinnovation2016.pdf(731607).pdf.

Wasshede, C., 2013. Med hat och smuts som vapen. Queeraktivisters självpresentationer på internet [With hate and dirt as weapons. Queer activists' self-presentations on the Internet]. *Lambda Nordica*, 2013 (1), 35–60.

Wiegman, R. and Wilson, E.A., 2015. Introduction: antinormativity's queer conventions. *Differences*, 26 (1), 1–25.

# Resistance against material artefacts: university spaces, administrative online systems and emotions

Anna-Lena Haraldsson and Mona Lilja

**ABSTRACT**

This article traces some of the attempts that have been made to analyse time and emotions in order to gain a broader understanding of how power and resistance entangle in online administrative systems in university spaces. Rising levels of Internet usage in the university sector, and society in general, imply a new era for public administration. Online administrative systems have moved into the university sector, creating different reactions, new practices, temporalities and emotions. The administrative online systems, which govern through, as our respondents understand it, various time-consuming scripts (for example, the travel expenses programmes or programmes regulating working hours or duty periods) or through online communication systems (for example, emailing), give rise to a rich and varied resistance against the different systems, which informs the employees' temporalities and spent time (clock time). Among other things, people reacted emotionally with avoidance, time-travel, manipulations, ignorance and by exact rule following.

## 1. Introduction

This article explores strategies of temporal resistance that are used by university staff members in their encounters with different computer-based administrative systems within university spaces. Rising levels of Internet usage in the university sector, and society in general, imply a new era for public administration. Many universities have entered different pathways to maximise the benefits of the Internet age. Among other things, online administrative systems have moved into the university sector, creating different reactions, new practices, temporalities, emotions as well as resistance.

Technological tools, such as administrative online systems, to some extent, can be seen as 'scripts' that govern our movements and limit which actions we can take. Technological systems comprise common frameworks for expressing and creating different temporalities, i.e. our understandings of time and how we organise it. Among other things, calendars, schedules, travel expenses programmes and communication systems all depart from standardised systems for classifying, allocating or managing time.

Administrative online systems have material-semiotics of their own, which makes it important to acknowledge the analytic stances that grant agency to non-human entities as well as embracing the entanglement between matter and our discursive constructions. When emphasising the agency of matter – such as the framing, staging and fostering aspects of computerised administrative systems – it is important not to lose sight of the subjects 'behind' these products. Administrative systems have been developed, managed and implemented by designers, technicians and public administrators, who are invisible in the moment of interacting with the systems. Administrative online systems are material artefacts that mediate between those who demand and shape these systems and their users.

Computerised systems, in some senses, can be seen as a way of governing self-managing subjects, through technological systems. However, we are not only governed but we also resist different technologies that shape our relationship with time. In this, emotions become an engine that creates motivation as well as reasons to resist. Although emotions have not been the core of resistance studies, they play a silent but fundamental role in many theories of resistance (for example, Scott 1990). In this paper, we will explore *how emotions emerge in the meeting with administrative online systems, thereafter entangling in different practices of temporal resistance.* Thus, the article will display how the promotion of different temporalities prevails as a form of resistance, or as a means to resistance, in order to negotiate current discourses and future prospects. Moreover, we will elaborate on different forms of temporal resistance in the light of power *that are mediated* through different administrative online systems. The analysis is inspired by the 'affective turn' and takes emotions as a starting point in order to examine different strategies of resistance.

To explore the temporal and affective resistance of university staff members in their meeting with different computer-based administrative systems, we have conducted five in-depth interviews in Sweden. The respondents are all university employees who hold different positions such as head of department, lecturer and administrator.[1] All of the interviews were open-ended and semi-structured. Respondents were given the opportunity to address questions of relevance to them. This approach was designed to capture a more in-depth understanding of resistance practices. In this, we followed the works of John Gerring, who states that:

> (…) the case study – of an individual, group, organization or event – rests implicitly on the existence of a micro-macro link in social behaviour. It is a form of cross-level inference. Sometimes, in-depth knowledge of an individual example is more helpful than fleeting knowledge about a larger number of examples. We gain better understanding of the whole by focusing on a key part. (Gerring 2007, p. 1)

In-depth studies, with few subjects, sometimes tell us more than broad but shallow studies. In the forthcoming sections, we will present some themes that we found during the coding process. Before that, however, we will introduce some of the main concepts of the paper: emotions, resistance and time.

## 2. Theoretical approaches, new public management, time and affects

The neoliberal era has brought great changes in society, not least through new reforms and changes in policy in the public sector. A large portion of these changes are influenced by the most current trend in organisation development, called New Public Management (NPM). The NPM has incorporated ideas and models from the business sector into public organisations. The aim has been to increase the effectiveness as well as the quality of work through clearer management that is guided by objectives and performance monitoring (Røvik 2008).

NPM has had an impact on most universities in the European Union even though it differs in how it has been implemented, adopted and the consequences that it has had (Bleiklie *et al.* 2010). Within the university sector, as well as in other public sectors, authorities have been increasingly centralised and managers engage more and more with different formalised controls (Røvik 2008). Digital administrative online systems are becoming increasingly important as tools for the management and control of university employees as well as students.

Technology is often perceived as neutral but can be used for everything, including one-sided information, control of work processes, information gathering and the systematisation and standardisation of procedures. In a sense, new technology is used to replace human intelligence and abilities, and to increase control over the individual employee's work performance. One consequence is that power and hierarchy are becoming increasingly anonymous and invisible (cf. Orlikowski 1991, Anderson 2006, Menzies and Newson 2007). In addition to this, university staff members are expected to govern themselves more and more through the systems. Below, we will present a number of concepts, such as time and emotions, through which we can gain a broader understanding of how power and resistance entangle in online administrative systems in university spaces.

### 2.1. Time, temporality and acceleration

Time is a difficult notion to conceptualise. Time is not just a category or the rhythmicity of the physical environment that we organise ourselves according to, during our lifetime. We are involved daily in a material world with a temporal core (Hörning *et al.* 1999). Adam states: 'Time is about god and the universe, life and death, knowledge practices and the human condition. The relationship to time is at the very root of what makes us human' (Adam 2006, p. 119).

In one way, 'time' refers to everyday biological processes such as birth and the ageing of things and bodies, which proceed moment by moment. On the other hand, we constantly *do* time when we organise, understand and spend time. Time is made in every moment (Dinshaw 2007). The enactment of temporalities is to some extent performative, i.e. bodies act out temporalities which they establish to some extent.

The concept of temporality is useful when addressing our social constructions of time. 'Temporality' refers to our understandings of time, the social patterning of experiences and how we organise our time (cf. Amin 2014). There are often multiple temporalities operating in the same moment (Dinshaw 2007, p. 110). Moreover, not only do subjects embrace different temporalities but different functions, institutions and spaces (the school, media, artists, the political arena) are organised according to different understandings of time, thereby producing different notions of time. In addition, there are places such as museums that function as sites of memory and history.

The social organisation of time can also be seen as a biopolitical temporal strategy: different temporal patterns or political interventions – patterns of acceleration, deaccelerating, establishment programmes for migrants, parental leave – structure and organise our time. New forms of temporality prevail within neoliberalism, increased transnational contacts, worldwide migration patterns, etc. In addition, new technological systems also generate new forms of time. Computerised administrative systems work to control, coordinate or regulate a wide variety of time concepts (clock time, travel time, working time, etc.). Administrative online systems have also spawned a whole range of new metaphors for time, such as timeless, virtual and instantaneous time.

Time concepts and temporalities, then, interact with technological changes in governing subjects as well as whole populations. Moreover, research shows that contemporary understandings of time must embrace the 'time-space' compression that we live under. Rosa (2013), for example, identifies an acceleration in the pace of life and how the present is marked by the 'shrinking of the present'. Time seems to flow ever faster, making our relationships to each other and the world fluid and hard to understand. Rosa's way of displaying time has previously been neglected in sociological theory. There is a particular lack of more nuanced analysis of what areas are accelerating, which ones are not and which ones cannot do so. Culture cannot always, for example, be consumed at a faster rate and we cannot always think faster.

Rosa distinguishes different processes in the acceleration. One is the technical, often goal-oriented and focused on rationality and efficiency; for example, through faster transport, faster communication and more efficient production processes. Technological acceleration affects social relationships and the temporality of personal life.

Technology is expected to result in time savings, but also means, paradoxically, that the number of actions and experiences per unit of time are objectively increased. A simple example of this is that there is more and more mail to be answered in an increasingly shorter timespan. The increased pace of life is experienced as a subjective sense of time pressure, lack of time, fear of not keeping up and so on.

Rosa believes that the pace will reach, or has already reached, the critical threshold where the perception of reality changes. This applies in particular when the experience and knowledge can no longer be used to plan or manage expectations and new systems. The pace of change is faster than the ability to integrate the new, which can create experiences of chaotic uncertainty and the extension of time itself becomes temporalised – everything depends on the situation – time itself.

### 2.2. Universities, time and technology

Within the academy, teaching, research and administration are various temporalities, or what Scott and Wagner (2003) call different temporal zones. Submitting applications, lecturing or coding data all follow different temporal logics, rhythms and cycles that are different from administrative tasks. Currently, less and less time is spent on research and teaching, and instead, more and more time is spent on administration (Ylijoki and Mantyla 2003). Temporal changes are challenging for many university employees as it is difficult for them to emotionally tune in and manage duties that demand time for concentration, creativity and reflection, when one is lagging behind and there is a 'speed problem'.

Online administrative systems try to time-determine and systematise work. However, when different temporalities meet, difficulties and tensions emerge in the intersections between slow and fast institutions and tasks. Political institutions and processes or research follow a different logic than temporalities that are at work in markets or various business fields.

The concept of 'scripts' can illuminate some of the ways in which university staff are managed and governed through online administrative systems. Scripts can be compared 'like a film script, technical objects define a framework of action together with the actors and the space in which they supposed to act' (Akrich 1992, p. 208 in Oudshoorn and Pinch 2005, p. 9). Here, the 'script' is the outcome or 'the end product' of the designers' activities, planning and visions. Thereafter, however, the artefact in itself comes to define a 'framework of action'. The script could then be seen as the trace left by human agency once the artefact was made. The notion of a 'script' can be used to capture how technical objects limit the relationships between people as well as between people and things. When using scripts in the analysis, the designers, implementers and users all become visible in the technical development (Oudshoorn and Pinch 2005)

It follows from the above that online administrative systems are governing university employees into computerised self-management in their present-day working life. Longer and longer chains of anonymous interactions, via online systems, mark the university space. Time standards in the forms of deadlines, process planning, speed premiums, time-management, time-planning, etc. come to structure the employees' time (Rosa 2013). The more complex computerised systems are, the more difficult it is for employees to change and influence their working environment.

New technologies and compression of time–space not only affect performance of work but also our emotions (Thrift 1996 in Urry 2000) and, thus, individual employees' subjective experiences. Studies of organisations, technologies and time often lack subjective perspective (see for example Scott and Wagner 2003).

Virtual technologies can be emotionally demanding, but also create new ways to work and express emotions, such as giving people who are shy, socially insecure or belong to a discriminated group greater opportunity to express themselves. But using only virtual communication and personal computers can create feelings of isolation and one's experiences of the outside world become limited. Sometimes, feelings of worthlessness, helplessness and boredom occur. Virtual work affects both our social and emotional lives (Fineman *et al.* 2010).

### 2.3. Emotions and resistance

As stated above, affects and emotions have not been the core of resistance studies. Still, James Scott, for example, brings in *fear* of reprisals and repressive actions as an important aspect when discussing everyday resistance, without emphasising 'emotions' as an important aspect (Scott 1990).

Due to the intermingling of emotions and resistance, this paper is inspired by the sociology of emotion, more generally, and affect theory, in particular (Goodwin *et al.* 2001, Ahmed 2004). Emotions affect people and we need to consider how they work; how they, for instance, mediate the relationship between the individual and the collective (Hochschild 2003). Recent research has specified the role of emotions in social movements and related forms of political actions (Goodwin *et al.* 2001). What political subjectivities are emotions generating? Hochschild (2003, p. 114) shows, in her study on emotions, how resistance can be incorporated into a situation that appears to be nice and pleasant on the surface. Moreover, Jansson and Wettergren (2013) display how communities draw upon collective

# RESISTANCE AND EMOTIONS

emotional resources when they feel threatened by the social and political advancement of marginalised groups.

According to Sara Ahmed, emotions are not private matters; she describes emotions as economic – they circulate between signifiers (Ahmed 2004, p. 119). She concludes:

> How do emotions move between bodies? (…) I argue that emotions play a crucial role in the 'surfacing' of individual and collective bodies through the way in which emotions circulate between bodies and signs. Such an argument clearly challenges any assumption that emotions are a private matter, that they simply belong to individuals, or even that they come from within and then move outward toward others. It suggests that emotions are not simply 'within' or 'without' but that they create the very effect of the surfaces or boundaries of bodies and worlds. (Ahmed 2004, p. 117)

Emotions move and circulate between bodies and bodies, and bodies and signs. However, the subjects' reflections upon the emotions must be added to this. Techniques of the self, here, involve practices through which individuals inhabit subject positions while reflecting upon signs and, we argue, entangled emotions (cf. Foucault 1988, Foucault in Nixon 1997, p. 322).

Thus, to hate, desire or love are relational reactions, embedded in social contexts that create the possibility for us to communicate, share, negotiate and circulate emotions (entangled in discourses), while still having an individual attachment to them. Overall, scholars who promote the 'affective turn' argue that emotions and interpretations are inseparable (Hemmings 2005, 2014). Subjects embrace and experience emotions while interpreting various signs.

As we will see below, the double dimensions of emotions, as circulating while simultaneously creating various subjectivities, are interesting for the forthcoming analytical sections. In the interaction with administrative online systems, and the governing dimensions of these, different emotions, such as frustration and fear, emerge. These emotions are coloured by, and/or emerge from circulating signs and discursive 'truths' that are produced in the meaning-making around the systems.

Moreover, when administering oneself, the classical figuration of the research scientist is broadened and merges with other related subject positions, such as the administrator. This negotiation of oneself, through administrative online systems, also seems to create emotional reactions. In addition to this, the systems demand time and might sometimes be difficult to fill in, leaving the employee with a sense of failure. In the material-semiotic situation of filling the administrative online systems with the data that these systems demand, material artefacts, non-present authorities, complex forms, circulation of discourses, negotiated selves, feelings of failure or a sense of losing of one's identity altogether, entangle in, and shape, different emotions. Thus, in the moment of interaction with online systems, emotions are created from an assemblage of material signs, expectations and different (hidden) power relations.

Emotions, in turn, become an engine that creates subjective reactions, motivations and various resisting practices. Resistance is a complex and broad umbrella concept that needs to be elaborated in specific contexts with specific aims and ways of acting. 'Resistance' might be played out by organised large groups and movements as well as individuals and subcultures, based on everyday relations. Resistance is an act or patterns of actions, which might undermine or negotiate different power relations, but sometimes end up reproducing and strengthening relations of dominance (Lilja 2016).

Regardless of type, resistance exists in relation to power (and violence) and the type of power often affects the type of resistance employed as well as the effectiveness of various resistance practices: violent or non-violent, open or hidden, organised or individual, conscious or unconscious, etc. Power is not only about the ability to influence a decision in a particular direction but also about agenda setting, determining what can be discussed and about dominant discourses (Lilja 2016, cf. Hollander and Einwohner 2004).

By taking the above into consideration, we understand resistance as a subaltern practice that might challenge, negotiate or undermine power. Such a subaltern practice arises from below and might be performed by someone from a subordinate position or on behalf of and/or in solidarity with someone in a subaltern position (proxy resistance). This means that resistance studies is primarily about studying how various practices from below relate to power (or its varied manifestations, such as discipline, hierarchy, coercive force, violence, etc.), and as such it is focused on studying resistance strategies and practices. However, resisters and dominators should not be dichotomised. There are multiple systems of hierarchy, and individuals can be simultaneously powerful and powerless within different systems (Hollander and Einwohner 2004).

## 3. Constructing then, now and the future: practices of resistance

In the text below, we will explore strategies of resistance used by university staff members in their encounters with different computer-based, online administrative systems within university spaces. In particular, we will add to the discussion of resistance and technology by departing from the concepts of time, temporalities as well as emotions.

### 3.1. Resistance in the face of fear of a threatening future

Technology in itself is often connected to time, pace and flexibility but also with pressure, waste and scarcity. We save more and more time while we have less and less time in the workplace. Technology in workplaces is also associated with standardisation, discipline, control, prediction, destruction, divestment, irritation and provocation. People affect, interpret and translate the technology to their own needs and everyday contexts. Technological systems are thus part of how reality is constructed: however, not in a simple way but in line with current discourses, the users' specific needs, complex contexts, materialities and in-the-moment decisions. Even though there are 'scripts' for how to use the systems, users consume, modify, control, change, as well as resist technological systems.

Various administrative, material systems gave our respondents different possibilities to shape the future. The systems also, in themselves, affected people's futures. One concern in this regard is how computer-stored information about students might affect their grades. One respondent said:

> All examiners have the possibility to go into the grading system and look up the result and past performances of individual students. How damn good is that? Can all teachers do that too? I mean, knowing the past performances of individual students, colours how we view him or her now! One fundamental principle for our work is that it must have legal certainty and be humane and efficient. I do not think that these systems correspond to that. Because we judge a person from his past. If a person been troublesome in the past we expect him/her to be that in the future too. (IP CD)

# RESISTANCE AND EMOTIONS

This quotation can be understood through the concept of 'linear time'. The idea that time is linear – the past is separate from the present and comes before it – has been taken for granted in European cultures. Edkins argues: 'time appears as a succession of 'nows', a sequence of presents, and the existence of something is confirmed by its continuing presence through a series of such moments'. (Edkins 2003, p. 34). This notion of time affects how we understand the future and the past in relation to now. Or as Maria Stern expresses it: 'memory (and thus remembering stories) are as much a part of the present as they are a part of the past. They are also shaped by expectations for the future'. (Stern 2005, p. 62). One common logic drawn from this is that what was true then is true now, and will probably be true in the future (Lilja 2008). This logic is also what coloured the above quotation. The above citation stretches between the past and the present as the respondent argues that there is a risk that we tend to shape our expectations for today and for the future from the notions of the past. The reasoning goes that if a student got bad results then, she/he will also get that in the future. This way of thinking might lead to poor grades for individual students in the present day due to past mistakes.

A similar pattern was displayed in regard to university employees. Private information about employees was displayed within administrative systems. One respondent told us that the administrative online systems give staff members insight into different personal details of their colleague's lives, such as various health problems. According to our respondents, the system threatens the integrity of faculty employees and thereby their well-being. In our interviews, personal 'sensitive' information leaking out was linked to anxiety and, overall, seemed to work as a narrative of fear. The future was imagined as an unpleasant place, where their precarious situation could become known by others. These imagined scenarios of the future created concerns for the respondent in the present. Therefore, the transparency of administrative systems was considered erroneous from the beginning and it was also resisted by the respondent, who manipulated the systems in order to not display too much 'uncomfortable' information. One respondent stated:

Interviewer: I talked to one of the university teachers about the administrative systems. We also talked about this with Retendo. He said that Retendo makes it possible for him to control what others do.

Respondent: Yes.

Interviewer: And that he thought was creepy.

Respondent: Yes, it's – very uncomfortable. We have also been talking about, because you know (…), you sometimes give people some room of manoeuvre, some space, for health reasons or because they have had a tough time. But you do not want to display that to everyone at the department. Instead, I have to invent, new, pretended boxes in the system or come up with other creative solutions. (IP CD)

The respondent was afraid that personal information would leak out and put employees in a difficult position. Fear is an emotion experienced in the face of something that is threatening to our potential well-being. It involves the future, which is understood as indefinite, threatening and awaiting. Fear, then, as stated by Ahmed (2004, p. 65), includes a temporal dimension; it arises in response to something that can hurt one in the future. Fear moves between the present and the future; between the immediate experience and potential future hurt (Ahmed 2004, p. 65). Or, departing from Heidegger, fear relates to that 'as something that threatens us, is not yet within striking distance, but it is coming close' (Heidegger 1962, p. 180). In the above case, the respondent expressed fear for other's future well-being.

The time-travelling between then, now and the future creates emotions, which also shape our practices and how we act in order to change the future. How one acts 'now' is expected to change 'then'. This, in some senses, involves agency and resistance against what otherwise would be an inevitable future. In the above quotation, the respondent reveals how she/he manipulates the administrative system in order to avoid an undesirable situation in the future, in which the integrity of employees is put at risk:

> I have to invent, new (pretended) boxes in the system or come up with other creative solutions ... One must lie to the system, we have talked a lot about that. Almost every semester we have a case like that, someone who is in a precarious situation and you do not want others to know. (IP CD)

This form of resistance can be interpreted as proxy resistance, which is played out by someone in solidarity with an employee in a precarious situation. In addition to this, the respondent might be driven by a fear of what will happen if it is revealed that she/he has manipulated the system.

### 3.2. Resistance through time-theft and escape

In the above, the quotations show how administrative online systems sometimes entangle in constructions of future scenarios, emotions (fear) and different resisting practices. Other respondents argued that the administrative online systems allow them to remember and recall the past. One respondent, for example, suggested a time-travel that was made possible by administrative systems themselves, as a kind of 'resistance by escape'. While travels, fieldtrips and conferences in the past are saved in the computerised systems, the past has gained a new materiality on the screen. Through the system, dates, places and other travel details are saved, and are possible to view each time one enters the system. Thus, while entering the system to fill in new travel expenses, past travels becomes displayed and the past becomes part of the present. The respondent argued that this gave him/her the possibility to 'resist by escape', spending his/her working hours going through past trips instead of preceding with his tasks within the travel expenses system. The respondent said:

> It [to see the accounts of past fieldtrips/conference] creates memories of course. It contributes to create memories, it is pretty fun actually. (…) In case one is bored, it is just to enter the system and look at one's travel history and all trips one have done and so I do the trips once again. Actually, I will do that the next time I am expected to fill out an expense report, instead of filling in the travel-expenses, I will relive my past travels. (IP GH)

This can be understood as resistance by time-theft. The respondent argues that she/he will not do what she/he is expected to do with his/her time, i.e. filling in the administrative systems. Instead, she/he will spend his/her time reconstructing memories of the past. The 'resistance by escape' – escaping the present by reconstructing travels in the past – implies that the past is reconstructed in 'now' as a form of resistance. In this, the respondent *does* time as she/he organises, understands and spends time differently from what is expected. The enactment of temporalities is to some extent performative, i.e. bodies enact temporalities, which they, to some extent, establish (Dinshaw 2007).

This resistance is made possible by the administrative systems that the respondent experienced as being forced upon them. Thus, the very power relation between the respondent and the administration made the resistance possible. The resistance is parasitic upon power and the materiality of computers, chairs and desks. Power mediated through material artefacts clearly shows 'how matter comes to matter' (Barad 2008, p. 120).

The above quotation could also be interpreted as resistance by bringing in a new temporality. While the respondent is expected to be in the present 'now', by filling in his/her travel expenses in the system, she/he chooses to bring in another temporality, a longer time perspective, in which the 'past' is reconstructed in the 'now'. She/he states: '(...) it is just to enter the system and look at one's travel history and all trips one have done and so I do the trips again'. By playing out multiple temporalities that are operating in the same moment – being both in the present and in the past – resistance is played out. Resistance then, builds on, as Dinshaw put it, 'temporal heterogeneity – of the multiplicity of temporal systems, or time frames, or time consciousness in any present moment' (Dinshaw 2013, p. 4).

The engine of resisting was the frustration that the respondent experienced as she/he was expected, and to some degree forced, to engage with the administrative online systems. She/he stated: 'To experience that you are frustrated is not very nice. The frustration becomes an engine or a drive to resist. Because you do not want to experience that frustration again' (IP GH). As stated above, affects and emotions have not been the core of resistance studies. Still, they have played a silent but fundamental role in many theories of resistance (Scott 1990). Emotions create motivations and various resisting practices.

## 3.3. Emailing, stress and resistance by deceleration

As stated above, Rosa (2013) identifies acceleration in the pace of life and how time seems to flow faster and faster. In this, Rosa distinguishes sped-up communication as one aspect of the acceleration. In our interviews, emailing prevails as a phenomenon that informs the respondents their understanding of their presence, past and future as well as their resistance strategies. Emailing is faster than other ways of communicating and easier to use. Therefore, it is often employed indiscriminately, without much careful consideration. Few reflect on the emotional consequences of the overload of emails, and the impact on workers, who are exhausted by the accelerated communication (cf. Fineman 2003). One described, for example, how students send emails without too much hesitation and expect immediate responses:

> They want answers faster too. (They had not asked these things) if they had no e-mail, because you may not dare to go here (to the university) and write a note, either. It is that easy ways to communicate that opens up all sorts of feelings and practices. (IP AB)

Each email also adds to the working load. One respondent stated:

> It could be, to take an example, as economy, how many percent (...) and it's really a rush. (...). Then I have to talk to the director of studies and perhaps with NN directly. So, it takes some time to get the answer to that simple question: (...) (It) can take me half a day to get the information. It is not effectively used time, but before I get hold of people and before I succeed and find out ... So a seemingly simple question can take a very long time for me to answer. (IP CD)

The call to constantly respond to the fast-flowing stream of emailed requests seems to impact our respondents' relation to time. The demand to instantaneously respond can, according to Urry (2000), lead to time being turned into an extended present, i.e. people must stay and live in 'real time'. In our case, the extended present is occupied by others' demands. As one respondent put it:

# RESISTANCE AND EMOTIONS

> People expect that you read the e-mail as soon as they send them 'you haven't read my e-mail', 'No I have not read your mail' and then it just arrived 10 min ago. Thus people have no patience, I think … When they send the e-mails, they want answers right away. (IP IJ)

Constant emailing thereby requests immediate reactions from the senders, which fragments the day for many employees and the time–space paths of individuals are often desynchronised. The requirement to constantly engage in multiple, often disparate activities, preferably simultaneously, and being constantly interrupted by new requirements create, according to Bloch (2001), the basic conditions for stressful experiences. Stressful experiences in turn create feelings of irritability, difficulty in concentrating, but also emotions such as shame when one fails to live up to the accelerated tempo. Bloch also argues that the increased volume of experience in every 'now' can lead to a breakdown between the past, present and future. The heavy workload sometimes becomes an obstacle to rest in the 'now', something which, in prolongation, can induce stress and resistance. The opposite of stress is, according to Bloch, having the opportunity to pay proper attention to activities that require it (Bloch 2001, see also Csikszentmihalyi 1998).

For the researchers who were interviewed, it seems crucial to have time, without interruption, to perform one's research and teaching-related duties – a so-called timeless time (Ylijoki and Mantyla 2003). There is some space for our respondents to postpone their responses (to various e-mails), but, as argued by Urry (2000), the accelerated tempo has increased the demand for fast or instantaneous action. This seems to awaken various resisting responses in our respondents. One university employee said:

> Respondent: And speaking of that, there is the advantage of e-mails, you can pretend that you haven't seen them.
>
> Interviewer: Yes, okay. Do you?
>
> Respondent: It has happened. Not that I do that ... but sometimes I have thought that they do not know if I have read this. I may have been busy all day, so they have to calm down a little. I could have been in a meeting, and so you have the possibility to say 'I take it in the afternoon'. It's also a way to cope. Phones are the worse, then you have got the information. (IP CD)

As stated above, power and resistance are often reactions to one another. Resistance mostly exists in relation to power, and what type of power prevails affects the type of resistance that emerges as well as the effectiveness of various resistance practices. Thus, if emailing and other related communicative, technological systems govern people's lives through acceleration in the pace of life, one resistance strategy is to deaccelerate the pace created by technological acceleration. This pattern was displayed in our interviews, and not just through the ignoring of emails. One respondent turned off his email when he had to work. He stated:

> It's so that the phone does not ring anymore because people are e-mailing. And in case people do not turn off their e-mail programs – as I do –then it adversely affected the work. As soon as I have to work to do I turn off e-mails. Previously, I turned off the phone, but I do not need to do that now, people do not call anymore. (IP GH)

To turn one's email off – to deaccelerate time – can be seen as resistance against being governed by technological systems, which then impacts how time is spent. Feelings of stress and lack of control seem to be strongly correlated with various resistance practices (Menzies and Newson 2007).

### 3.4. Quick implementations, slow systems and resistance through avoidance and approaching

A current trend is that administrative online systems are implemented and changed at an accelerated speed (Fineman 2003). This can also create stress. One respondent described the pace of technological change in relation to the teaching and the use of, for example, PowerPoint. She/he said:

> (…) but it is a stress factor before you get there and before it works, but we have a very good support system, I think. You can call and so you get assistance but it's always a concern and so they changed the cables and so they changed their technology and so they changed the equipment. And then when it comes to a new equipment, it doesn't fit with the computer you have, then you have to call again. (IP IJ)

To learn a new system takes time and one of our respondents stated: 'as soon as I have learnt this system, they implement a new administrative online system and I must start all over again' (IP GH). The respondent also stated that the new systems are neither properly completed nor lead to any improvements. She/he said: 'Those who develop technology equate change with improvement and therein lies a big, big mistake. And there is also a rush to let go of the new systems long before they are ready, which makes the already bad system worse' (IP GH).

With new systems, older administrative online systems are outdated. In an accelerating era where technology is an engine, knowledge and skills are considered passé much faster (Rosa 2013). It is impossible to learn everything that is new and the previously learnt skills are becoming unusable at a faster rate. This means that, as a respondent said: 'The incentive to learn a new system is so small that I do not do it' (IP GH).

Each change requires time for adjustment, both emotionally and cognitively, not least to manage and interpret the employees' own role in relation to the change (Jacobsen 2013). It takes time to sort, organise and manage any new information. If time (clock time) runs short, this sometimes contributes to experiences of anxiety and uncertainty (cf. Berger and Luckman 1967).

One reason for implementing digitised systems is efficiency. Paradoxically, our respondents seem to experience the systems as time-consuming (IP GH), creating anxiety and more work (IP IJ). Several functions previously performed by institution administrators today are expected to be self-managed by the employees themselves. A frequently occurring example is the management of travel expenses and other expenses. These administrative online systems were considered slow and complicated. One of our respondents described how the reporting of travel expenses before took 15 min, but now 'after two weeks of juggling with the system the travel bill is still not approved' (IP GH).

There are, according to Pratt and Doucet (2000), two ways of responding to role conflicts, societal changes and increased complexity within organisations. One way is to approach; another is to avoid the changes/conflicts. Both are to be regarded as forms of resistance. Negative approach reactions can be emotions of anger, frustration and rage. The milder forms of negative approach reactions involve moving towards the target through voicing criticism, derogatory comments or using humour.

The other way of handling organisational change, such as the implementation of time-consuming online systems, is avoidance (cf. Pratt and Doucet 2000). This can be exemplified by one of the respondents, who avoided incurring expenses in order to keep away from the online travel expense system. The respondent said:

> It's almost as if I avoid to take on expenses because I can't be bothered... I understand that it would be so much work to get the money back and so. (IP AB)

The quotation can be interpreted as a mild form of avoidance, and a more extreme form was to exit the organisation. One of our respondents explained why she/he left for another position: 'I thought it was too little student contact (…) and too much administrative work in online systems and so …' (IP AB). In this latter case, avoidance could be seen as a light version of the resistance of the withdrawal that James Scott outlines in his 'the art of not being governed'. (2010)

As stated above, Pratt and Doucet (2000) argue that not only avoidance, but also 'approaching the system' is a strategy for handling different administrative online systems. This can be exemplified by the cynical or distanced attitudes the employees displayed when talking about the different systems. One respondent said: 'the use of several systems is minimal'. (IP CD). Another respondent argued: 'There is a lot of bullshit data that are fed into the system' (IP CD). The negative attitudes, in these quotations, can be regarded in relation to the system itself or to the pointless actions they experience that they are forced to undertake. But since emotions and resistance arise in relation to objects, and in situations when our respondents are alone with the digital system, the employee cannot object, for example, through humour to superiors in the organisation. One of our respondents instead expressed resentment through using the system according to the manual which she/he knew would create negative consequences:

> There is an expectation that you should fill in the systems in a certain way, but if you take the system to its ultimate rationality and do exactly what the system wants, then it will almost always go wrong, and it creates extra work for those who have a high system confidence and their high faith will start to crack. '(…)' because then the system breaks down. (IP GH)

This resistance was played out by an individual in her/his office without any audience. It is also hard to distinguish this kind of resistance and few will notice it unless the system breaks down. To only follow the system, without the flexibly of adapting to the faults of the system, does not appear as resistance on the surface. It is an everyday, hidden form of resistance, which uses, and is parasitic on, the constructions of power, i.e. the scripts that the administrative online systems compose. But resistance, in this case, does not affect those who constructed, implemented or decided that the system should be used. Instead, the administrative staff members, who must rescue the situation, become an interface between the decision-makers, technicians and the resisting staff members. Thus, the resistance seems highly ineffective in terms of impact – at least in the short term.

### 3.5. Shadow systems as resistance

When technical systems are perceived as pointless and time-consuming, as well as not adapted to reality, our respondents tended to create 'shadow systems' in order to be able to perform their duties in a meaningful way. The shadow system is based on more complex and context-sensitive information than the public system can offer (cf. Moser and Law 2006). There are shadow systems for evaluation, work allocation models, budget and other planning systems. For example, one respondent preferred his/her own course evaluation 'model' over the online system. Information was collected by posing questions directly to the students in order to, as she/he put it: 'find out what you really need to know' (IP AB). She/he stated:

> I try to listen to the students after the lectures and at the end of the course. By chatting I get a sense of their situation and the general mood. As a professional teacher, I think I have developed a sense for what works and what does not work. You are sensitive to whether or not they grasp all the topics at the course. That kind of information is also accessible through reading the students e-mails, homework and so. As professionals, we must make use of that information. (IP AB)

Another respondent described how one of the staff members used both Excel and the university's standardised work allocation system to manage her work:

> so s/he did it first in Excel (the own system), then s/he transferred the numbers to the system that was decided, and I wonder what that kind of (double) work costs? (IP CD)

The administrative online systems are part of the new governance of public organisations but also a result of technology development. They seem to be designed without flexible user's demands, with the consequence being that staff members spend time on creating their own systems (cf. Scott and Wagner 2003). The creation of the shadow system can be understood as a struggle to maintain pride and a positive identity as an intellectual and professional academic (cf. Clegg 2011, cf. Fineman 2003, Anderson 2006). These shadow systems can also, in this context, be understood as resistance, i.e. as practices that might challenge, negotiate or undermine power, in the form of different obligatory administrative online systems.

Time-consuming technical systems are, thus, often experienced as meaningless and lead to innovative forms of resistance, such as the creation of shadow systems. This is somewhat different from Scott's assumption that the resisting subject is being exploited and dominated. The issue here is qualitatively different, in that the resisting subject is resisting being coerced into tasks that prevent them from doing their job in, what they experience as, a meaningful or effective way. This makes it relevant to reflect upon domination and 'modern' bureaucracy, acting directly upon individuals through 'a management of individuals' self-management'. According to Weber, bureaucracy is conceived as instrumentally rational – as an efficient means to an end. However, at a certain point, the bureaucracy becomes an end in itself. At that point, responsibility/agency is taken away from employees in order to make the perfect system, which, in some senses, becomes inefficient at achieving outcomes, such as educating students and research, but highly effective at reproducing itself. In a study of Portuguese bureaucracy, for example, (Clegg *et al.* 2016), it was found that the system was specifically set up *not* to generate outcomes for its clients. Similar to Hannah Arendt, the study describes a 'government by nobody' as the ultimate tyranny (1970, p. 38). This is an interesting conclusion and, overall, the theoretical entrances of Weber, Arendt and Clegg become highly relevant reflecting upon the results of this study.

## 4.  Concluding discussion

Today, information in organisations is sent out with the help of technology, either directly from various devices or gathered through mass dissemination of emails from the immediate supervisor. More and more tasks are handled through various technological systems, which reduce the possibility of encountering colleagues or supervisors at joint meetings, etc. Increased time pressure also makes people opt out from interacting with others when it does not occur naturally. In all, one has more freedom to determine the time for information while losing the opportunity to deliberate with others, including those in leadership positions (see Urry 2000)

The introduction of technical systems enables the division and planning of employees' time to be done in different systems. By extension, this also means that contact between leadership and employees becomes restricted to email communication. The organisation may not consciously aim to discipline employees through one-way communication via administrative online systems, but the consequence is that employees are increasingly isolated from each other and have few opportunities to confront the leadership.

Administrative online systems, which govern through, as the respondents understood it, various time-consuming scripts (for example, the travel expenses programmes or programmes regulating working hours or duty periods) or through online communication systems (for example, emailing), create individual resistance as well as people absorbing and adapting to the systems. In this article, we have focused on a few university employees and their strategies and relationships with different administrative online systems. In particular, we have outlined various ways in which these staff members resist the systems, which they are expected (and to some degree demanded) to feed or react to. Interestingly enough, although we conducted only five interviews, we found a rich and varied resistance against the different systems, which informs the employees' temporalities and spent time (clock time). Among other things, people reacted with avoidance, time-travel, manipulations, ignorance and by exact rule following. Most strategies appeared very subtle and made us think of James Scott's concept of 'everyday resistance'.

The manifoldness of strategies might be the result of different kinds of governing that the systems imply. Different online systems seemingly present different scripts, i.e. they function as technical objects, which define a framework of action together with the actors and the space that they interact within. The artefacts, through which the online systems work, limit the relationships between people as well as between people and things. They decide how to act, and what practices are possible, in the interaction between human and the machine. This must be regarded as a form of governing. In addition, filling in the administrative online systems is also a result of direct decision-making power. Someone has decided that you (as an employee) *must* feed the systems (it is part of your duty plan) or react to emails. Systems also create different time-related issues; they create temporalities, inform different constructions of the present and past, steal time units, etc. The different kinds of power, described above, entangle with each other, but also with different emotions that they create (fear, frustration and anger), which become engines of resistance. As a reaction to the temporal aspects, mentioned above, much of the resistance is time related. Resistance is played out by time-travel, stealing time (the administrators), deceleration, etc.

The acts of resistance, which are mapped in the analytical sections, seem to have little or no significant impact on the power relations that are at stake. The long distance between authority and employees in today's organisations, and the fact that power is often mediated through technical systems, moderates the impact of resistance. Resistance seems to lose significance when it takes place against the system: no one experiences/notices the resistance and the administrators become 'airbags' between the superiors and the staff members. Materiality becomes an important unit of analysis in this regard. Current governing happens through the different materialities of the administrative online systems – a materiality that lessens the impact of resistance. The leadership seldom meets their employees face to face,

# RESISTANCE AND EMOTIONS

which lessens the opportunity to play out resistance against bodies (not machines). Still, while resistance might be ineffective from a more instrumentalist perspective, it could have important effects on shaping resistance subjectivities and/or giving the employees a sense of agency. Thereby, the resistance, and its outcomes in terms of agency, could be a platform on which later public resistance is built.

We do not know how widespread the resistance described is, as we conducted a very limited number of interviews. But if more (all?) university employees employ these kinds of resistance strategies, the effectiveness of online administrative systems needs to be further explored.

Digital systems seem to have increased significantly as tools for the NPM and the governing of universities. Not least in order to control and monitor employees' actions and productivity. More and more people gain access to the systems and through the transparency of these systems, more and more people get the opportunity to monitor other people's actions, although this was not the intention when implementing the system. Do we see a new panopticon evolving?

Through accelerating time, time pressure and technological development, and through digital systems and their scripts, the logic of the clock, productivity and instrumentality penetrates deeper into academic practice. How deep, and with what consequences, is an empirical question. Digitalised systems have an impact on people's actions and thinking, where some employees carry out resistance in order to maintain the quality in their work, while others adapt to the system. The latter customises the resistance practice to the system, with other consequences.

There is a risk that accelerating time in institutions has an impact on the perception of work, the professional role and the university as an organisation. Here, emotions seem to matter. Different emotions can be understood as forces, which in some senses undermine the governing of the university employees. Emotions seem to create resistance, non-governable subjects, chaotic administration processes and undermine the very core of various self-disciplinary systems. But emotional rule can also stop the employees from expressing themselves.

## Note

1. The respondents will remain anonymous in the article.

## Disclosure statement

No potential conflict of interest was reported by the authors.

## References

Adam, B., 2006. Time. *Theory, culture and society*, 23 (2–3), 119–138.

Ahmed, S., 2004. *Cultural politics of emotions*. New York: Routledge.

Amin, K., 2014. Temporality. The complete keywords section of TSQ. *Transgender studies quarterly*, 1 (1–2), 219–222.

Anderson, G., 2006. Carving out time and space in the managerial university. *Journal of Organizational Change Management*, 19 (5), 578–592.

Arendt, H., 1970. *On violence*. London: Penguin.

Barad, K., 2008. Posthumanist performativity: toward an understanding of how matter comes to matter. *In*: A. Stacy and S. Hekman, eds. Material feminisms. Bloomington, IN: Indiana University Press, 73–98.

Berger, P. and Luckman, T., 1967. *The social construction of reality*. New York: Anchor.

Bleiklie, I., Enders, J., Lepori, B. and Musselin, C., 2010. New public management, network governance and the university as a changing professional organization. *In:* T. Christensen and P. Laegreid, eds. *The ashgate reasearch companion to new public management*. Farnham: Ashgate, 161–176.

Bloch, C., 2001. *Flow og stress – stemninger og fölelsekultur I hverdagslivet*. Köbenhavn: Samfundslitteratur.

Clegg, S., 2011. Academic identities re-formed? Contesting technological determinism in accounts of the digital age. *Contemporary Social Science*, 6 (2), 175–189.

Clegg, S., *et al.*, 2016. Kafkaesque power and bureaucracy. *Journal of Political Power*, 9 (2), 157–181.

Csikszentmihalyi, M., 1998. *Flow. Den opitmala upplevelsens psykologi*. Stockholm: Natur och Kultur.

Dinshaw, C., 2007. Temporalities. *In:* P. Strohm, ed. *Middle English, Oxford twenty-first century approaches to literature*. Oxford: Oxford University Press, 107–123.

Dinshaw, C., 2013. All kinds of time. *Studies in the age of chaucer*, 35, 3–25. Available from: http://english.as.nyu.edu/docs/IO/3693/Dinshaw_Presidential_address.pdf/ [Accessed 23 February 2017].

Edkins, J., 2003. *Trauma and the memory of politics*. Cambridge: Cambridge University Press.

Fineman, S., 2003. *Understanding emotion at work*. Los Angeles, CA: Sage.

Fineman, S., Yannis, G., and Sims, D., 2010. *Organizing & organizations*. Los Angeles, CA: Sage.

Foucault, M., 1988. Technologies of the self. *In*: L.H. Martin, H. Gutman, and P.H. Hutton, eds. *Technologies of the self: a seminar with Michel Foucault*. Amherst: University of Massachusetts Press, 16–49.

Gerring, J., 2007. *Case study research: principles and practices*. Cambridge: Cambridge University Press.

Goodwin, J., Jasper, James M. and Polletta, F., 2001. *Passionate politics: emotions and social movements*. Chicago, IL: The University of Chicago Press.

Heidegger, M., 1962. *Being and time*, translated by J. Macquarrie and E. Robinson. London: SCM Press.

Hemmings, C., 2005. Invoking affect: cultural theory and the ontological turn. *Cultural Studies*, 19 (5), 548–567.

Hemmings, C., 2014. The materials of reparation. *Feminist Theory*, 15 (1), 27–30.

Hochschild, A.R., 2003. *The managed heart: commercialization of human feeling*. Berkeley, CA: University of California Press.

Hollander, J.A. and Einwohner, R.L., 2004. Conceptualizing resistance. *Sociological Forum*, 19 (4), 533–554.

Hörning, K.H., Ahrens, D. and Gerhard, A., 1999. Do technologies have time?: New practices of time and the transformation of communication technologies. *Time & Society*, 8 (2), 293–308.

Jacobsen, D.I., 2013. *Organisationsförändringar och förändringsledarskap*. Lund: Studentlitteratur.

Jansson, A. and Wettergren, Å., 2013. Emotions, power and space in the discourse of 'People of the Real World'. *Journal of Political Power*, 6 (3), 419–440.

# RESISTANCE AND EMOTIONS

Lilja, M., 2008. Gendering legitimacy through the reproduction of memories violent discourses in Cambodia. *Asian Perspectives*, 32 (1), 71–97.

Lilja, M., 2016. *Resisting gendered norms civil society, the juridical and political space in Cambodia*. New York, NY: Routledge.

Menzies, H. and Newson, J., 2007. No time to think. Academics' life in the globally wired university. *Time & Society*, 16 (1), 83–98.

Moser, I. and Law, J., 2006. Fluids or flows? Information and qualculation in medical practice. *Information Technology & People*, 19 (1), 55–73.

Nixon, S., 1997. Exhibiting masculinity. *In:* S. Hall, ed. *Representation: cultural representation and signifying practices*. London: Sage.

Orlikowski, W.J., 1991. Integrated information environment or matrix of control? The contradictory implications of information technology. *Accounting, Management and Information Technologies*, 1 (1), 9–42.

Oudshoorn, N. and Pinch, T., 2005. How users matter. The co-construction of users and technology. Cambridge, MA: The MIT Press.

Pratt, M.G. and Doucet, L., 2000. Ambivalent feeling in organizational relationship. *In:* S. Fineman, ed. *Emotions in organizations*. London: Sage, 204–226.

Rosa, H., 2013. *Acceleration, Modernitet och identitet. Tre essäer*. Daidalos: Göteborg.

Røvik, K.A., 2008. *Managementssamhället. Trender och idéer på 2000-talet*. Malmö: Liber.

Scott, J.C., 1990. *Domination and the arts of resistance: hidden transcripts*. New Haven, CT: Yale University Press.

Scott, J.C., 2010. *The art of not being governed: an anarchist history of upland southeast Asia (Yale Agrarian Studies Series)*. New Haven, CT: Yale University.

Scott, S.V. and Wagner, E.L., 2003. Networks, negotiations, and new times: the implementation of enterprise resource planning into an academic administration. *Information and Organization*, 13, 285–313.

Stern, M., 2005. *Naming security – constructing identity: 'mayan-women' in Guatemala on the eve of 'peace'*. Manchester, NH: Manchester University Press.

Urry, J., 2000. *Sociology beyond societies: mobilities for the twenty-first century*. London: Routledge.

Ylijoki, O.-H. and Mantyla, H., 2003. Conflicting time perspectives in academic work. *Time & Society*, 12 (1), 55–78.

# Martyrdom and emotional resistance in the case of Northern Kurdistan: hidden and public emotional resistance

Minoo Koefoed ⓘ

**ABSTRACT**
Violence, deaths, fear and sorrow characterise the everyday lives of those in Turkey's Kurdish region, also known as Northern Kurdistan. Through ethnographic field research, this article explores connections between resistance and emotions by scrutinising empirical observations and activists' narratives during and after participation in a ceremony for a 16-year-old Kurdish boy who had been killed by Turkish forces – a 'martyr' in the eyes of the activists. By fusing empirical ethnographic data with James Scott's theoretical works on hidden resistance and Arlie Russell Hochschild's theorisations of emotional management, two distinct forms of what will be termed *emotional resistance* will be pointed out. Emotional resistance refers to conscious attempts to manipulate or manoeuvre around one's own emotional expressions or reactions in order to undermine the power of psychological or direct violence in political contexts.

## 1. Introduction

The violent conflict between the Partîya Karkerên Kurdistanê [Kurdistan's Workers' Party] (PKK) and the Turkish government dramatically escalated in intensity after a pro-Kurdish activist delegation at the border city of Suruç was bombed in July 2015. The attack led to the end of peace negotiations between the PKK and the Turkish State that had been in place since 2013. The result was the emergence of a massive wave of political detentions, arrests, executions, street fighting, bomb blasts, shelling from helicopters, prolonged curfews and increased political crackdowns on Kurdish political parties, organisations, institutions and media outlets (HRW 2016a). Between August 2015 and July 2016, as many as 355,000 people in the region were temporarily displaced due to the escalation of the armed conflict (HRW 2016b). In the same period, 338 civilians were killed either by gunshots or by mortar explosions (HRW 2016b). Furthermore, 22 Kurdish towns and neighbourhoods have also been subjected to prolonged, round-the-clock military curfews, which disable people in this region from maintaining a normal life, going to school or work, or buying groceries, due to the risk of being shot or detained by Turkish armed forces (HRW 2016b). After a failed coup attempt in July 2016, which is understood to have been propagated by the exiled Islamic leader Fethullah Gülen and his supporters, repression of politically dissenting individuals, organisations, institutions and non-governmental organisations radically increased all over Turkey. Subsequently, violent crackdowns on the Kurdish movement also increased.

Within the field of psychology, it is well-documented how prolonged conflicts, low- and high-intensity warfare, refugee-hood and high levels of political repressiveness have devastating effects on the emotional and psychological well-being of affected individuals (Berceli 2008). Post-Traumatic Stress Disorder, depression, anxiety, sleeping disorders and aggressive behaviour are psychological reactions associated with traumatic experiences from conflict settings. Berceli (2008) shows how living under prolonged violent conflicts often implies living with constant fear, which increases the risk for depression, the feeling of apathy and a sense of disempowerment (Berceli 2008).

Subsequently, since the 1990s, social science scholars have been increasingly interested in the implications of emotions in the study of social movements (see e.g. Goodwin *et al.* 2000, 2001, Flam and King 2005, Goodwin and Jasper 2006, Gould 2009, Jasper 2011, Hogett and Thompson 2012). Goodwin and Jasper suggest that 'feelings such as apathy and fear' could be seen as destructive for movement activism, political resistance and social movement organization (Goodwin and Jasper 2006, p. 626). This is because such feelings often have a 'demobilising' effect that reduces activists' beliefs in the prospects of the desired social change, which then leads to them losing hope and their sense of agency (Goodwin and Jasper 2006, p. 626). As a result,

> (f)or a movement to succeed (…) activists must devote enormous efforts to giving participants a sense of their own agency. They need confidence in their own ability to act, something that requires the suppression of demobilizing emotions such as apathy and fear. (Goodwin and Jasper 2006, p. 626)

This view seems to resonate with ideas circulating among activists in Northern Kurdistan, as illustrated by, for instance, the following quote of 'Gülçin', a Kurdish political activist in her mid-40s, after she had participated in yet another funeral for a Kurdish martyr:

> If we don't have faith in the struggle, in the movement, in the ideology, how will things ever improve? In Nusaybin, in Cizre, in Farqîn, in Silvan, they have come much further than us because there the people have faith! There, the organization and resistance is strong! If you say that things will never change, you complain that there are 15 days of curfews, that people are martyred every day, that our work doesn't mean much, then things will not change. The truth is that many things have already changed! When I first joined the party, I was the only woman. The only woman! Now, how do the party and the Municipality look like? Now we are many women in the party. ('Gülçin', 20 November 2014)

If we are to believe the suggestions mentioned above by Goodwin and Jaspers, it is reasonable to assume that the political violence of the Turkish State could also influence Kurdish activists in a way that halts their resistance and demobilises their movement. Therefore, it becomes particularly interesting that, despite the high level of violence that characterises the situation in Northern Kurdistan, it continues to be a region where extensive, large- and small-scale forms of grass-roots political organising, self-organised institution-building and massive political mobilisation efforts are taking place on a day-to-day basis (see TATORT, 2011). This raises crucial questions as to how, or rather, whether, activists in Northern Kurdistan also apply strategies to handle the psychological terror that is imposed on them by the State to avoid such demobilising feelings that Goodwin and Jaspers mention. More precisely: What would a particularly *emotional resistance* – a form of resistance with the explicit aim of undermining the psychological power of violent state activities – potentially entail? – By drawing on empirical observations and interviews during ethnographic fieldwork in Northern Kurdistan, this article seeks to address this question through exploring some of the intersections between emotions and resistance in the particular context of martyrdom among participants in the Kurdish movement in Northern Kurdistan.

The complex, multifaceted and diverse ways in which martyred members of the Kurdish guerrillas are given symbolic and political importance in the discourses, political rituals and cultural expressions among Kurdish movement participants, could undoubtedly have been a useful starting point for exploring the role and meanings given to violent resistance within the Kurdish communities in Turkey. However, such an exploration goes beyond the scope and aim of this article. Martyrdom has traditionally been associated with self-sacrifice in religious contexts and for religious purposes (see Cormack 2001 for further details). However, the use of martyrdom and self-sacrifice as political tools is far from unique to Northern Kurdistan (see e.g. Fierke 2013). For instance, Tibetans self-immolate as a means of protest against violations of human rights and lack of freedom, in the context of the Tibetan–Chinese conflict (see Fischer 2012, Woeser 2015). Other examples are the political use of hunger-strikes (see Sweeney 1993) and suicide bombings (see Brym and Araj 2006). Self-immolations, hunger-strikes and suicide bombings have also been used as political tools to achieve political goals in the history of the Kurdish movement in Turkey.

As death is a deeply existential matter, it naturally becomes an emotional and highly charged issue. This makes the context of martyrdom particularly useful for exploring some of the potential connections between emotions and resistance in the case of Northern Kurdistan.

By analysing ethnographic empirical material along with theoretical works by Erving Goffman (1956), Hochschild (2003) and Scott (1985, 1990), this article brings a phenomenon that I will term *emotional resistance* to the surface. Here, *emotional resistance* will be understood as a distinct sub-type of what Scott terms *hidden resistance* by virtue of being low-key, unorganised, individually performed activities conducted on an everyday basis. Based on Kurdish activists' narratives and experiences, two conceptually distinct forms of *emotional resistance* will be pointed out. These will be analysed according to Hochschild's conceptualisations of *deep acting* and *surface acting* in the context of her work on *emotional management* (Hochschild 2003). The two forms of emotional resistance will be termed *hidden emotional resistance*, and *public emotional resistance*, respectively.

This article concludes that emotional resistance is particularly important for movement persistence and long-term engagement in high-risk political contexts such as Northern Kurdistan. In the particular context of martyrdom, this article shows how emotional spaces represent spheres within which political resistance is nurtured and serve the purpose of regaining agency over subjects' own emotional landscapes amid political violence.

I will start this article with a short note on methods and methodology, followed by a discussion on the relevance of emotions for the study of resistance. This will be followed by a discussion mapping out the conceptual and theoretical ideas that will later be applied in order to investigate the empirical material that will be used in this article. After that, I will present a contextual background where I describe some of the roles and meanings given to martyrdom in the context of the Kurdish movement in Turkey. I will then turn to the empirical case of emotional resistance in Kurdistan, discussing two different aspects of emotional resistance in the context of a martyr's funeral in the city of Wan.

## 2. A note on methods and methodology

As a component of a larger research project on constructive forms of resistance in Northern Kurdistan, this research is rooted in ethnographic research methodologies with emphasis on participant observation, informal conversations and informal semi-structured interviews during a fieldwork exercise over seven months that was conducted in 2015 and 2016 in the predominantly Kurdish towns of Amed (Diyarbakir), Wan (Van), and Gewer (Yüksekova) in Turkey's Kurdish region. Movement access, security and language were some of the challenges that I faced during this fieldwork.

The informal, semi-structured interviews were conducted mainly during the first four months of my fieldwork with representatives and staff at Kurdish self-organised institutions, parties, municipalities, organisations, council delegates, and members of cultural and educational centres in different cities and towns, and conducted with informal translation. Most communication and informal interviews during the last three months of the fieldwork were conducted in Kurdish, with some assistance from a couple of English-speaking movement participants whom I befriended.

The participant observation consisted of regular and frequent participation in demonstrations, protests, martyr's funeral and ceremonies, and other cultural and political events organised by different Kurdish movement sub-groups. I also participated in the everyday work of one particular neighbourhood council in Wan over a period of three months, and attended Kurdish language training for six months in total at the Kurdish movement's own language school, the Kurdî-Der. The Kurdî-Der is an institution that is designed to preserve and promote the Kurdish languages to Kurds who have lost, or partly lost, their Kurdish language skills due to assimilation. I also participated in meetings of the coordination committee of the Mesopotamia Ecology Council in Wan, and volunteered for some time as an English teacher at the Kurdish self-organised educational organisation MAPER. During the two presidential elections in June and November 2015, I also participated as an electoral observer for the Kurdish party the HDP. I frequently wrote field notes that included quotes, personal experiences and observations. However, due to security considerations, I did not use a voice recorder. All names and identities of the individuals that are quoted in this article have been changed due to security and anonymity concerns.

The aim of the next section is to map out the theoretical foundations on which the later empirical and theoretical analysis will be grounded.

## 3. The emotional turn and the turn to affect: their relevance for resistance studies

In their work on emotions and social movements, in a large edited volume that maps out the field of *Sociology of Emotions*, Jeff Goodwin and James Jasper present three different historical *waves* of how emotions have been dealt with in Social Movement Research (Goodwin and Jasper 2006). Until the 1960s, social movement scholars often focused on what could be seen as one-dimensional, spontaneous 'reflex emotions' like fear, anger, joy, surprise, disgust and shock 'to dismiss protestors as irrational or immature' (Jasper 2011, p. 287).

# RESISTANCE AND EMOTIONS

In contrast, from the 1960s until the 1990s emotions were a largely ignored issue in social movement research in 'an effort to demonstrate that protestors are rational' (Jasper 2011, p. 287). With the emergence of the *Sociology of Emotions*, in the 1990s scholars began to again set their sights on the role of emotions where cultural studies were fused with research on emotions. However, these studies were rarely directly connected to politically oriented research. Researchers now discuss what is known as the *emotional turn* (Flam and King 2005, Gould 2009, pp. 1–49, Hogett and Thompson 2012) and *the affective turn* (Clough and Halley 2007, Ahmed 2012, Hogett and Thompson 2012, Wetherell 2012), respectively. As there are also overlapping definitions of emotions within these two different strands of literature, an attempt to comprehensively discuss and describe the differences and similarities between them lies beyond the scope of this article. In recent years, renewed interest in emotions and affect has entered the sphere of social movement studies, protests and related political issues (e.g. Goodwin *et al.* 2001, Flam and King 2005, Goodwin and Jasper 2006, Gould 2009, Jasper 2011, Hogett and Thompson 2012).

However, Jasper and Goodwin argue that '(t)he study of emotions in politics and protests has emerged (or re-emerged) in the past decade through a messy inductive process of recognising the obvious: Emotions of many sorts permeate political action' (2006, p. 611). This emphasis on the importance of emotions in politics seems to also resonate with the views of Arlie Russell Hochschild, who, in her ground-breaking book *The Managed Heart: Commercialization of Human Feelings*, argued that '(s)ince feeling is a form of pre-action, a script of a moral stance toward it is one of culture's most powerful tools for directing action' (Hochschild 2003, p. 56). Yet, the definitions and approaches to terms like *emotions*, *affect* and *sensations* remain contested, diverse, blurred and complex.

In this article, I have chosen to stick with the understanding of Deborah B. Gould, who defines affect in pre-discursive terms as, 'nonconscious and un-named, but nevertheless registered, experiences of bodily energy and intensity that arise in response to stimuli impinging on the body' (Gould 2009, pp. 19–20).Thus, an example of this is blushing and changes in the rhythm of the heartbeat, where I understand affect as being registered and experienced, but at the same time '*nonconscious* in that this sensing is outside of the individual's conscious awareness and is of intensities that are inchoate and yet inarticulable' (2009, pp. 19–20). I understand the term *emotion,* on the other hand, in line with Hochschild's definition as discursive and conscious '(…) like the sense of hearing or sight. In a general way, we experience it when bodily sensations are joined with what we see or imagine' (Hochschild 2003, p. 17). By referring to Freud, she also holds that emotions have what she calls a 'signal function' (Hochschild 2003, p. 17). As a result, she argues, it is from 'feeling we discover our own viewpoint on the world' (Hochschild 2003, p. 17).

Despite what thus appears to be a growing acknowledgement of the importance of emotions in politics, emotions have for some reason not been met with an equal level of interest in the emerging field of resistance studies (see e.g. Scott 1985, 1990, Colburn 1989, Abu-Lughod 1990, Ortner 1995, Brown 1996, Hollander and Einwohner 2004, Seymour 2006, Kastrinou-Theodoropoulou, 2009, Lilja *et al.* 2013, 2015, Lilja and Vinthagen 2014, Vinthagen 2015, Juris and Sitrin 2016, Johansson and Vinthagen 2016). However, a few recent examples do exist, such as the work of Lilja *et al.* (2015) who theorise the interconnections between affect, temporality and resistance in the case of environmental activists in Japan. It is also necessary to point out how the feeling of fear of repression is the backbone of the emergence of James Scott's theorisation of *hidden resistance*, *everyday resistance* and *infrapolitics*, which I will return to below (Scott 1990, 1985).

If we are to accept the propositions by Hochschild, as well as those of Goodwin and Jasper – that emotions of different kinds are preconditions for political actions – I argue that emotions could be understood as crucial building blocks for resistance practices and movements. Furthermore, the proposition that emotions have a 'signal function' that helps us to articulate and become aware of 'our own viewpoint on the world', seems to be crucial for developing and articulating awareness about dissent (Hochschild 2003, p. 17). These propositions strengthen the argument for the relevance of emotions in relation to resistance.

In the section below, I will map out the main theoretical concepts that I use to analyse the empirical context of martyrdom in Northern Kurdistan.

## 4. Front stage/back stage, emotional management and hidden resistance

In his work from 1956, *The presentation of self in everyday life*, Erving Goffman used the metaphor of theatre and dramaturgy to make sense of human interaction and presentation of the self. Seeing the individual as *an actor* and society as *a stage*, Goffman argued that human beings could be understood as playing several different *roles* in their everyday lives. The roles that individuals take depend on the *audience* who observes them, as well as social factors like class, social hierarchies and social norms. By making a distinction between what he sees as *the front stage* and *the back stage* of human self-presentation, he convincingly shows how humans may present one image of self in public (front stage), and a different one in the private sphere (back stage).

In my opinion, Goffman's work becomes interesting when put in the context of the work on resistance by Scott (1985, 1990). In his work *Everyday Peasant Resistance: Hidden Transcripts*, Scott shows how *hidden resistance* or *everyday resistance* could be found in what he terms the *hidden transcripts* of subordinates. Similar to Goffman, Scott also points out the discrepancy behind '(…) what is said in the face of power and what is said behind its back' (Scott 1990, pp. 2–5). The aspects of open, visible social communication between the subordinates and the dominant conducted on the front stage are referred to by Scott as 'the public transcripts' (Scott 1990, pp. 2–5). The public transcripts are defined as '(…) a shorthand way of describing the open interaction between subordinates and those who dominate' (Scott 1990, pp. 2–5). The so-called *hidden transcripts*, on the other hand, are viewed as the 'discourse that takes place "offstage", beyond direct observation by power holders' (Scott 1990, pp. 2–4).

By assessing the discrepancy between what is being expressed and done on the back and the front stage, Scott shows how resistance does not necessarily need to be conducted publicly, outspokenly, or even loudly. Neither does it need to be organised or experienced by the actor herself/himself as an act of resistance. On the contrary, he argues, resistance might just as well be '(…) disguised, low-profile, [as well as] undeclared (…)' (Scott 1990, p. 198). To put it simply, this is what Scott terms *hidden resistance*. This brings us to the work of Hochschild, which is useful for making sense of how emotions could potentially relate to Scott's understanding of *hidden resistance*.

By studying flight attendants at Delta Airlines in America, in her book *The Managed Heart: Commercialization of Human Feelings*, Hochschild introduces the terms *emotional management*, *emotional labour* or *emotional work* (Hochschild 2003). Hochschild also investigates the discrepancies between what she terms '(t)he private and the public faces', but uniquely focuses on emotions (Hochschild 2003, p. 7). She explores the discrepancies between how people actually feel and how they try to portray themselves to be feeling, noting that people, particularly in service-oriented professions, sometimes pretend or act out as if they were in emotional states other than what they are actually feeling (such as smiling, being pleasant and 'caring' for the clients). In the case of flight attendants at Delta Airlines, such *emotional labour* was an explicitly defined part of their job description. Hochschild shows how flight attendants thus did an additional type of 'labour', which was not acknowledged or compensated for as work. She defines *emotional labour* as: '(…) the management of feeling to create a publicly observable facial and bodily display' (Hochschild 2003, p. 7). *Emotion work* or *emotion management* is used synonymously '(…) to refer to these same acts done in a private context where they have *use value*' (Hochschild 2003, 7). She furthermore elaborates that:

> This labor requires one to induce or suppress feeling in order to sustain the outward countenance that produces the proper state of mind in others – in this case, the sense of being cared for in a convivial and safe place. This kind of labor calls for a coordination of mind and feeling, and it sometimes draws on a source of self that we honor as deep and integral to our individuality. (Hochschild 2003, p. 7)

Interestingly, just as Scott refers to hidden resistance as having *theatrical* elements, so does Hochschild in her theorisation of *emotional management*. She does this to the extent of talking about emotional labour as *acting*. When referring to Constantin Stanislavski, the founding father of a particular theatrical approach known as *method acting*, she distinguishes between what she terms 'surface acting' and 'deep acting' (Hochschild 2003, p. 35).

*Surface acting* can be understood as representing an extroverted aspect of what could be seen as emotional self-presentation, referring to attempts to 'change how we outwardly appear' (Hochschild 2003, p. 35). Examples of surface acting in the context of emotional labour could, for instance, be the act of pretending to be happy by smiling while the person might be, in reality, in a bad mood, sad or exhausted.

*Deep acting*, on the other hand, in my understanding, represents a more introverted aspect of emotional self-presentation that is understood as acting where emotional '(…) display is a natural result of working on feeling; the actor does not try to seem happy or sad but rather expresses spontaneously, as the Russian director Constantin Stanislavski urged, a real feeling that has been self-induced' (Hochschild 2003, p. 35). In other words, individuals not only manage their own visible emotional expressions (*surface acting*). Through *deep acting*, subjects manage how they actually feel, and could thereby even contribute to changing their actual emotions. She suggests that '(i)n managing feeling, we contribute to the creation of it' (Hochschild 2003, p. 18).

I will now turn to the empirical context where these theoretical concepts will be discussed and analysed later. But before presenting the particular narratives and observations from the ceremony that will be used in the analytical discussion, in the following section I will present a very brief contextual description of some of the various roles martyrdom and martyrs play in the Kurdish movement in Northern Kurdistan.

## 5. Contextualising martyrdom in Northern Kurdistan: a brief background

Kurdish guerrillas or political movement participants who are killed as a consequence of their political struggle in the Turkish–Kurdish conflict are considered martyrs. I was surprised by the visibility and frequent commemoration of martyrs in Northern Kurdistan during the initial phase of my fieldwork. Martyrs are visually present in Kurdish society, both in institutional as well as private spheres. Portrait photos of martyrs are often placed on walls of Mala Gels (People's House), People's Councils, Kurdish self-organised organisations, offices of Kurdish political parties or Kurdish municipalities and in the homes of families. Such portraits are also often printed on banners and on posters that are used in political demonstrations. Furthermore, numerous Kurdish self-organised institutions are named after famous Kurdish martyrs, such as the case with the *Navenda Çand û Hunerê ya Nûda* (the Nûda centre of culture and arts), the *Navenda Çand û Hunera Bêrivan* (the Bêrivan centre of culture and arts) as well as the *Akademi şehît Nûdaye* (the Martyr Nûda Academy) in Wan/Van.

In the wake of the autonomy declarations – after the break in peace negotiations between the Turkish State and the Kurdish movement during the summer and autumn of 2015 – there were also cases where districts and neighbourhoods that were declared autonomous by the Kurdish movement were re-named after Kurdish martyrs. This was the case with the Esiltepe neighbourhood of Gewer, which for a period was re-named 'Martyr Bêrîtan Neighbourhood' after its autonomy declaration in late July 2015 (Rojhelat 2015). A Kurdish friend of mine from Amed chose to name his newly born baby daughter after a famous Kurdish martyr. Additionally, when visiting autonomous institutions such as the Mala Gel in the autonomous Ormanê neighbourhood in Gewer, activists often used the names of martyrs as code-names when they were organising political and social activities. In such situations, I too was frequently given a martyr's name by the youth, which was a gesture of inclusion. I also came to meet guerrillas and former guerrillas who used the names of martyrs as *nom-de-guerre*, which one might argue is a paradox given that these are individuals who themselves perhaps run a greater risk of being subjected to martyrdom due to their involvement in armed resistance.

Every time someone dies a martyr, which is unfortunately a frequently recurring event in Northern Kurdistan, a ceremony called *tazîye* is organised. The *tazîye* are open to the public, and during certain periods, especially towards the end of my fieldwork, there were several *tazîye* every week – an indication of the degree to which the conflict had escalated. Some would take time off work to attend these ceremonies, which were normally carried out during work hours. Large and small, more or less public funerals are also sometimes held, as was the case in late-July 2015 after the bombing of Suruç, where multiple bodies were transported to Amed and thousands of people showed up to witness the burial. The coffins were covered in fine cloths and ribbons in the Kurdish colours, and participants shouted political slogans while marching, which partly muffled the sounds of the Turkish military helicopters that were circling in the sky above as a symbolic exposition of control and surveillance.

In his ethnographic research from the region, Orhan (2016) shows how there is extensive communication between the PKK guerrillas and the social base in Northern Kurdistan, which is an important aspect of what he sees as processes of *political socialisation*, and is crucial for strengthening what he terms a *militant habitus* among people in the movement. During his fieldwork, he experienced villagers having meetings with PKK militants where stories of the two female martyrs Bêrivan and Zakiye Alkan were raised as examples to illustrate the importance of women in the Kurdish movement and the significance of female liberation. In these dialogues, Bêrivan was portrayed as a young Yezidi woman who joined the PKK in Europe, and who, through her participation, contributed to changing the way the PKK was perceived in Europe. Zakiye was discussed at the meetings because of her self-immolation in Diyarbakir prison back in the 1990s, and the guerrillas explained that she 'burned the fire of *newroz* in her own body' (Orhan 2016, p. 134). According to Orhan, such *militant biographies* fascinated, impressed and inspired the villagers and made them consider how women could play a part in the Kurdish resistance movement (Orhan 2016).

I argue that martyrs in the region could be seen to (re)produce a collective sense of unity. In the ceremonies, funerals, *tazîye* and demonstrations, activists are united in an emotional connectivity centred on martyrdom – a powerful symbol of both injustice and resistance. The martyrs embody both victimhood and agency, and reaffirm a dual Kurdish identity or self-image of being both victims as well as resisters. In this way, they presently play an important role in the Kurdish resistance struggle despite being physically absent. The political symbolism of the martyrs is therefore paradoxical, partly contradictory, and, loaded with meaning. Perhaps as a result of these poetic paradoxes, stories of Kurdish martyrs are often themes in popular Kurdish songs, films, literature and theatre. In reading that I have undertaken, the martyrs thus become a political intermediary between injustice and victimhood on the one hand – and resistance and hope on the other.

I will now describe my observations and experiences at a martyr's ceremony during my fieldwork in Wan, and the subsequent conversations that I had with Kurdish movement activists during and in the aftermath of the ceremony.

## 6. A case of emotional resistance: a martyr's ceremony in Edremit, Wan

The *tazîye* are announced through the Kurdish local party, the DBP's SMS-list, of which most of the Kurdish activists in the region are members. They normally happen at a local mosque where food is served, and are normally partly organised by the local Peoples Democratic Council in the neighbourhood where the ceremony is taking place. The *tazîye* are normally also partly organised by the Kurdish, self-organised organisation, MEYA-DER, which is funded by the DBP-run Kurdish municipalities. The section below reflects my own field observations during my participation at one of these *tazîye*:

> One day in Wan, everybody received an SMS from the DBP, announcing that there would be a ceremony – tazîye – the next day. A 16-year old boy from the Edremit district in Wan had been killed in battle in Rojava, a former guerrilla soldier with the YPG. Together with some friends from the Council we drove to the event the next morning. *A couple of hundred people showed up, including some well-known faces from the movement, but mostly just ordinary people, friends, family of the martyr, and general movement participants. As is the common practice, photos and posters of the martyred boy were hanging on the walls of the mosque, together with the KCK flag, and a poster of Abdullah Öcalan. While I was served food where I was sitting, listening to the Imam giving his speech, I was surprised to notice that I could not see a single person crying. Most people looked moved and saddened by the situation – but nobody cried. Obviously, the etiquette and norms for the public display of feelings could vary much from culture to culture. But while I was sitting and observing, I remembered my Kurmanji teacher 'Gülistan', who many times had burst out in tears even before we knew each other well, over, amongst other things, listening to songs about the Kurdish motherland or repression during the 1990s. Other friends too, had many times mentioned how they viewed sensitivity and emotional openness as something positive and admirable, rather than something one should hide or suppress. Therefore, the fact that nobody cried in a situation like this appeared to me peculiar and unexpected. There was some kind of friction or ambiguity at stake that I could not

really comprehend. I tried to recall other *tazîye* that I had participated in before, and I quickly came to the conclusion that at most of them, perhaps six or seven in total, I could only recall very few incidences where I had seen people crying. I asked my friends from the council if the mother and the other family members of the martyr was there, and they pointed towards a table in the middle of the room, informing me that it was the table where the family of the martyr was sitting. However, his mother was not here, they said, she was inside her house, mourning. One of the friends from the council, 'Gülçin', said that we might get the opportunity to visit the mother of the martyr in her house after the ceremony had ended to offer our prayers and condolences.

After the ceremony, we did visit her home. It was packed with people; piles of shoes were lying in front of the doorstep at the entrance door, and it was difficult to walk through the entrance hall because of all the jackets that were hanging on the walls, as well as due to the crowdedness of people. For a while, I and the other women from the council (only women were allowed in) were standing in a line to enter the little living room to greet the mother of the martyr. However, when it was our turn, I was shocked to see that not even his mother cried. Her face was pale and thin, but she greeted everyone politely without showing any evident sign of emotional breakdown or grief. We left her home after about fifteen minutes, after a short prayer and after we had expressed our condolences.

After the ceremony we all returned to the council together to drink tea. I think it was my friend and fellow fieldwork partner Axel Rudi who then introduced the conversation by asking why nobody had been crying at the *tazîye*. After all, it was difficult, even for us, coming from the outside, not to become emotionally affected by the situation. Furthermore, whenever information on a new martyr reached us through the DBP SMS list, our friends from the council were always talking about it with much emotional presence. This developed into a heated discussion where a handful of different people from the council shared their thoughts, experiences, reflections and views. 'Heval', for instance, explained that people in the movement 'generally do not to cry' when someone is martyred. However, he also emphasized how the non-crying was about being respectful to the martyr in question, adding as an explanation that, after all, 'they are contributing to the struggle after their death' ('Heval', November 2015).

According to this logic, if we had cried at this 16-year-old boy's *tazîye*, it might be interpreted as a lack of acknowledgement of his continued political contribution, thus reducing the importance of his suffering, political activities, and person, or reducing the political value of martyrdom all together. 'Gülçin', a woman aged in her mid-40s, who was generally active in the council, also contributed eagerly to this discussion. She began talking about her own experiences when her brother was martyred as a guerrilla fighter several years before in order to shed some light on why nobody had been crying at the *tazîye*.

It had been a psychologically terrible experience, she explained. His death had come as a shock to the entire family. She emphasised the psychological aspects of the war waged by the Turkish State, arguing that of course the police and government wanted to see them, Kurds, emotionally destroyed. Therefore, she argued that she did not want the Turkish authorities to find out that their violence actually had the effect on her that she assumed it was meant to have. She did not want to give that victory to the State, she said, and added that it was particularly important that the police and other representatives from the Turkish State would not see her, or any other Kurdish person, crying, especially in a political context such as when people were martyred. Several other people participating in the discussion nodded in confirmation as she spoke. 'Gülçin' explained that she had actively been struggling to avoid crying in public in the wake of the killing of her brother. However, because she had been completely emotionally devastated, she mainly stayed inside, for weeks, where she could cry. However, when she was outside, she never cried, she said.

The experiences of 'Gülçin' appeared to resonate with others at the council, some of whom confirmed how they viewed the killings, war and violence by the State as a conscious attempt to make them feel bad, and that the attempt not to cry where the public could see was a way of portraying themselves as strong and unaffected – as if they were under observation by the State itself.

In relation to Hochschild's theorisation of *emotion work*, combined with Scott's idea of *hidden resistance* as well as Goffman's distinction of the *front stage* and *back stage* of human self-presentation, I think we could use the experiences of 'Gülçin' to broaden our understanding of the connections between emotions and resistance.

## 7. Public emotional resistance: front stage surface acting

When observed by others, the act of crying could be seen as a non-verbal sign of affect that communicates something about the emotional state of mind of the person who cries. Inspired by James Scott's work, the act of crying in public could therefore be seen as an example of a *public transcript* – a concept used to describe the overt communication between the subaltern and those in power. In the case of 'Gülçin' it would have been a *public transcript* of sadness and sorrow.

However, by circumventing that transcript, what 'Gülçin' did in the aftermath of the killing of her brother, was to engage in what Hochschild termed *emotional work*. This was done through (what she presented as) a conscious attempt to avoid crying in public after the State had killed her brother. But unlike the case of Hochschild's flight attendants who were engaged in *emotion work* and *emotional management*, because it was professionally expected from them by Delta Airlines, 'Gülcin' engaged in emotional management based upon an underlying political rationale.

As demonstrated above, 'Gülçin' thought that the Turkish State consciously aimed to see the Kurds emotionally destroyed through what she framed as the *psychological warfare* of the State. The Turkish State was experienced as responsible for a very explicit type of domination, which in my view could be seen as a type of *power over*, perhaps in its most extreme and explicit form; that is, the act of killing in a political context of overt ethnic conflict. However, as 'Heval' said later, 'out of respect for the martyrs', or, in the words of 'Gülçin' 'not to let the enemy win', these Kurdish movement participants were negotiating with the power of the State by playing a *theatrical game* through consciously avoiding displaying their own sorrow. On the *front stage*, 'Gülçin' would put on *a mask* and pretend to be emotionally unaffected by forcing herself not to cry in front of people, whereas on the *back stage*, in her own home, the situation would be different, she would be *mask-less* and crying. The motivation to do this was to create an image to those in power that she was stronger than the emotional violence caused by the political injustices wrought upon her by the authorities: that they did not have the ultimate power to control or influence her emotional state of being.

As mentioned, when 'Gülçin' was at home, she allowed herself to cry, but outside she refused to do so. To use Goffman's terminology, it is clear that in this case, there was a clear discrepancy between the way 'Gülçin' presented herself to the public on the public *front stage*, and how she presented herself on the private and hidden *back stage*. In the words of Hochschild, thus, she was engaged in *surface acting*. Furthermore, there was clearly a discrepancy between her public and hidden transcripts.

As stated in the theoretical framework earlier, and following the understanding of James Scott, assessing the discrepancies between what is expressed in the face of power (public transcripts) with what is expressed behind the scene (hidden transcripts), could be a useful tool to shed light upon manifestations of what he sees as *hidden resistance*.

When taken in connection with the discussion of the case of emotional management and emotional labour of 'Gülçin' above, I argue that we could also use this to illuminate the existence of what I propose should be understood as a sub-version of *hidden resistance*. I term this sub-version *emotional resistance*.

If we understand acts of direct and psychological violence as materialised manifestations of power, 'Gülçin' could be seen as being subjected to both, given that she is a close relative of a man who was killed by the State for his political engagement as a member of the Kurdish guerrillas. If resistance is a reaction to power, which at the same time attempts to undermine that power (see Vinthagen 2015, p. 7), I argue that this conscious act of not crying should be seen as an act of *emotional resistance*. By refusing to comply with what perhaps otherwise would have been their emotional expressions, and explaining this refusal with the political rationale of portraying the power of the State as less effective or weaker than it actually was, I argue that they are undermining this power itself.

When taken in context with the emphasis on how destructive feelings such as apathy and fear, as proposed by Goodwin and Jaspers, could have devastating effects on social movement activities, it becomes particularly relevant to resist or circumvent such feelings and thereby undermine the power of direct and psychological violence.

I call this form of emotional resistance *public emotional resistance*. It is public because it relates to an expression that would have been visible to outsiders (surface acting, public transcript). It is emotional because the act of crying reflects an emotional state of mind (sadness, grief), and because crying can be seen as a sign of affect. And it is non-compliant, because the act of not crying refuses that expression. It also refuses to accept or react according to the direct and psychological violence imposed by the Turkish State.

But whereas the narrative of 'Gülçin' above illustrates how emotional landscapes could represent a form of emotional resistance with the aim of portraying oneself in a certain way to those in power, there is another aspect of her experiences and reflections about herself that could shed additional light on the understanding of emotional resistance, addressed in the section below.

## 8. Hidden emotional resistance: back stage deep acting

Another interesting point that came up during this conversation with 'Gülçin' and the others at the council after the funeral was that 'Gülçin' also explained how she, when her brother was killed, not only had been consciously attempting to avoid crying in public. She explained that she additionally had been working with herself to suppress the feeling of sadness that she felt inside, based on a similar political reasoning as the one discussed above. Given that she experienced the political violence from the State as so illegitimate and unjust, she expressed how she refused to accept its personal emotional implications in herself as best as she could. As a result, she had consciously attempted to manipulate her own feeling of sadness and sorrow in the aftermath of the killing of her brother. Of course it had not been possible to completely force these feelings away, but she said that she nevertheless had tried to suppress them – she did not want to allow the effects of the State's emotional warfare to crush her.

'Gülçin' thus expressed how she was actively trying to manipulate or change her own feeling of grief in the wake of the political killing of her brother because she saw that sorrow as a result, and therefore also as an extension, of the power of the Turkish State. To her, the Turkish State's domination and warfare in Northern Kurdistan had a clearly psychological aspect, which in her narrative was intentional: with their violence and terror the attempt of the State is 'to crush us'. As a result, in order to resist that power, she consciously attempted to suppress her own feeling of grief. Regardless of the extent to which such an attempt would be successful, I argue that the attempt itself should be understood as an act of resistance.

In Hochschild's terms, 'Gülçin', according to her own statements, could thereby also be seen as to having been involved in *emotional work* in another way as the earlier example with the refusal to cry in public. By consciously trying to manage her own feeling of sorrow by consciously trying to suppress it, she could also be seen as, to use Hochschild's terminology, engaging in *deep acting*. On the *back stage*, she was engaged in an introverted form of emotional resistance far away from the sight of the Turkish State, but nevertheless silently undermining its power over her. This example, I argue, illustrates how emotional landscapes, in light of Hochschild's conceptualisations, also represent a sphere within which *hidden transcripts* of resistance could be found. Emotional landscapes thus represent a *back stage* sphere where hidden resistance could be articulated.

I term this manifestation of emotional resistance *hidden emotional resistance*. The power in question here would be the same; the 'power over' reflected in the political violence of the State. The emotional reaction to that power would be sadness and grief. However, in this hidden aspect of emotional resistance, the emotional resistance directly addresses the subjective emotional experience rather than the visual expression of such experiences. Thus, the emotional resistance here would be the conscious attempt to suppress or manage one's emotional reaction of grief and sadness. It is hidden, because the act of trying to manage one's own feelings reflects the inner lives of that individual and is absolutely invisible to the outside world. It is emotional for obvious reasons: managing sadness means managing emotion. It is non-compliant because the core of the action is a rejection of the emotional reaction that it is in response to. Similar to the example of public emotional resistance discussed above, this also resists complying with the emotional effect of the political violence by the Turkish State.

The discussion above demonstrates how observations from a martyr's funeral in Wan, combined with narratives and reflections by participants in the Kurdish movement, could be used to highlight two distinct aspects of what I have chosen to term *emotional resistance*.

## 9. Conclusion: prefiguring a sensation of freedom

Despite the renewed interest in emotions in various social science disciplines reflected in what have been termed *the turn to affect* and *the emotional turn*, resistance studies has not substantially emphasised the role that emotions can and do play in the articulation and emergence of resistance practices. By drawing on personal narratives from Kurdish activists and their experiences from a *tazîye* ceremony for a 16-year-old Kurdish martyr in the city of Wan, this article has, among other things, highlighted how emotional spaces represent spheres within which political resistance is articulated and nurtured, and serve the purpose of regaining agency over subjects' own emotional landscapes amid political violence. In doing this, three distinct terms related to some of the ways in which emotions could be understood as related to resistance have been introduced.

By drawing on works by James Scott, I have demonstrated what I have chosen to generally term *emotional resistance*. In the nature of being un-organised, covert, performed by individuals rather than collectives, and circumventing the power of the dominant without being noticed by those in power, this could be seen as a specific sub-type of what Scott terms *hidden resistance*.

Inspired by Arlie Russell Hochschild's work on *emotional management*, I have utilised the empirical case of activist narratives in Kurdistan to point out two different forms of emotional resistance. The term *public emotional resistance* has been utilised to describe a form of emotional resistance that corresponds to what Hochschild terms *surface acting*. This refers to situations where individuals consciously try to manipulate or change their own emotional expressions in order to give an image to those in power that their emotional state differs from the experienced reality. In the case from Wan, this aspect was evident in the way activists managed their own public display of grief. Participants at the martyr's *taziye* argued that they consciously tried not to cry in public when a martyr had been killed to give an image to the Turkish State that they were strong and could not be crushed.

The second distinct type of emotional resistance has been termed *hidden emotional resistance*. This refers to a form of emotional resistance corresponding to Hochschild's subsequent term *deep acting*. Observations and participation from Wan showed how 'Gülçin' consciously attempted to suppress her internal emotion of grief after her brother was killed by Turkish forces. In her logic, this was an attempt to reject what she framed as *the intended effect* of the psychological warfare perpetrated by the State. Thus, she had a highly political approach to her own inner emotional landscape with the aim of undermining the psychological effects of the political violence conducted by the State, which is understood here as a form of cohesive or direct power.

There has been some focus in academic research on the risk of burnout among movement activists (see e.g. Weixia Chen and Gorski 2015). Public and hidden emotional resistance resist feelings like apathy, fear, sorrow, as well as the extroverted reactions to those feelings such as inactivity, avoidance and visible grief. Emotional resistance should be understood as important weapons in the struggle to capture human agency, to sustain resistance and make activists emotionally more resilient: to prefigure a sensation of freedom.

Further research is needed to advance understanding of the implications, meanings and impacts of hidden and public forms of emotional resistance for broader resistance strategies undertaken by social movements and resistance communities in Kurdistan and elsewhere.

## Acknowledgement

I would like to thank all my Kurdish interview partners and friends who made it possible to do the research for this article. I would also like to thank Annika Vestel, Mona Lilja, Maria Eriksson Baaz, Camilla Orjuela, Stellan Vinthagen, Majken Jul Sörensen, Jörgen Johansen, Daniel Ritter, Jens Sörensen, Viggo Vestel, Ben and Laura for useful comments and feedback on this article.

## Disclosure statement

No potential conflict of interest was reported by the author.

## ORCID

*Minoo Koefoed* ⓘD http://orcid.org/0000-0001-8485-4051

## References

Abu-Lughod, L., 1990. The romance of resistance: tracing transformations of power through Bedouin women. *American Ethnologist*, 17 (1), 41–55.

Ahmed, S., 2012. *The cultural politics of emotion*. New York: Routledge Taylor and Francis Group.

Berceli, D., 2008. *The revolutionary trauma release process: transcend your thoughts*. Vancouver: Namaste Publishing.

Brown, M.F., 1996. On resisting resistance. *American Anthropologist*, 98 (4), 729–735.

Brym, R.J. and Araj, B., 2006. Suicide bombings as strategy and interaction: the case of the second intifada. *Social Forces*, 84 (4), 1969–1986.

Clough, P.T. and Halley, J., eds., 2007. *The affective turn: theorizing the social*. Durham: Duke University Press.

Colburn, F.D., 1989. *Everyday forms of peasant resistance*. New York: Routledge Taylor and Francis.

Cormack, M., 2001. *Sacrificing the self: perspectives on martyrdom and religion*. New York: Oxford University Press.

Fierke, K.M., 2013. *Political self-sacrifice: agency, body and emotion in international relations*. New York: Cambridge University Press.

Fischer, A., 2012. The geopolitics of politico-religious protest in Eastern Tibet. *Cultural Anthropology Online – Hot Spots* 4, 1–6.

Flam, H. and King, D., 2005. *Emotions and social movements*. New York: Routledge Taylor and Francis.

Goffman, E., 1956. *The presentation of self in everyday life*. New York: Anchor Books.

Goodwin, J. and Jasper, J.M., 2006. Emotions and social movements. *In:* J.E. Stats and J.H. Turner, eds. *Handbook of the sociology of emotions*, 612–631. New York: Springer.

Goodwin, J., Jasper, J.M. and Polletta, F., 2000. The return of the repressed: the fall and rise of emotions in social movement theory. *Mobilization: An International Quarterly*, 5 (1), 65–83.

Goodwin, J., Jasper, J.M. and Polletta, F., 2001. *Passionate politics: emotions and social movements*. Chicago, IL: University of Chicago Press.

Gould, D.B., 2009. *Moving politics: emotion and act up's fight against aids*. Chicago, IL: University of Chicago Press.

Hochschild, A.R., 2003. *The managed heart: commercialization of human feeling*. Berkley, CA: University of California Press.

Hogett, P. and Thompson, S., 2012. *Politics and the emotions: the affective turn in contemporary political studies*. New York: Bloomsbury Publishing.

Hollander, J.A. and Einwohner, R.L., 2004. Conceptualizing resistance. *Sociological Forum*, 19 (4), 533–554.

HRW, 2016a. *Human rights watch world report 2016: Turkey, events of 2015*. New York: Human Rights Watch.

HRW, 2016b. *Turkey: state blocks probes of southeast killings: allow UN to investigate cizre abuses; repeal new law to block prosecutions*. New York: Human Rights Watch. Available from: https://www.hrw.org/news/2016/07/11/turkey-state-blocks-probes-southeast-killings

Jasper, J.M., 2011. Emotions and social movements: twenty years of theory and research. *Annual Review of Sociology*, 37, 285–303.

Johansson, A. and Vinthagen, S., 2016. Dimensions of everyday resistance: an analytical framework. *Critical Sociology*, 42 (3), 417–435.

Juris, J. and Sitrin, M., 2016. Globalization, resistance and social transformation. *In:* David Courpasson and S. Vallas, eds. *The Sage handbook of resistance*. London: Sage Publications, 31–51.

Kastrinou-Theodoropoulou, M., 2009. Editorial note: political anthropology and the fabrics of resistance. *Durham Anthropology Journal*, 16 (2), 3–7.

Lilja, M. and Vinthagen, S., 2014. Sovereign power, disciplinary power and biopower: resisting what power with what resistance? *Journal of Political Power*, 7 (1), 107–126.

Lilja, M., Baaz, M. and Vinthagen, S., 2013. Exploring 'irrational resistance'. *Journal of Political Power*, 6 (2), 201–217.

Lilja, M., Baaz, M., and Vinthagen, S., 2015. Fighting with and against the time: the Japanese environmental movement's queering of time as resistance *Journal of Civil Society*, 11 (4), 408–423. London and New York: Taylor and Francis.

Orhan, M., 2016. *Political violence and kurds in Turkey: fragmentations, mobilizations, participations and repertoires*. New York: Routledge Taylor and Francis Group.

Ortner, S.B., 1995. Resistance and the problem of ethnographic refusal on JSTOR. *Comparative Studies in Society and History*, 37 (1), 173–193.

Rojhelat, 2015. Kurdish youth declared autonomy. *Rojhelat*, 31 July 2015. Available from: http://rojhelat.info/en/?p=1575

Scott, J.C., 1985. *Weapons of the weak: everyday forms of peasant resistance*. London: Yale University Press.

Scott, J.C., 1990. *Domination and the arts of resistance: hidden transcripts*. London: Yale University Press.

Seymour, S., 2006. Resistance. *Anthropological Theory*, 6 (3), 303–321.

Sweeney, G., 1993. Irish hunger strikes and the cult of self-sacrifice. *Journal of Contemporary History*, 28 (3), 421–437, Sage Publications.

TATORT, 2011. *Democratic autonomy in Northern Kurdistan: the council movement, gender liberation, and ecology – in practice*. Porsgrunn: New Compass.

Vinthagen, S., 2015. Editorial: an invitation to develop 'resistance studies'. *Journal of Resistance Studies*, 1 (1), 5–11.

Weixia Chen, C. and Gorski, P.C., 2015. Burnout in social justice and human rights activists: symptoms, causes and implications. *Journal of Human Rights Practice*, 7 (3), 366–390, Oxford University Press.

Wetherell, M., 2012. *Affect and emotion*. London: Sage Publications.

Woeser, T., 2015. *Tibet on fire: self-immolations against Chinese rule*. London and New York: Verso.

# Everyday resistance in psychiatry through harbouring strategies

Mona Lindqvist and Eva Olsson

**ABSTRACT**
The purpose of this article is to study emotion management by focusing on emotion labour in relation to organisational resistance in psychiatry. Drawing on focus group interviews and individual interviews with 11 therapists in psychiatry, and on theories of emotion management and *harbouring work* (i.e. managing emotion work and renewing energy in a team), we argue that individual workers in psychiatry have to create strategies on their own. The main findings show that emotions are harboured alone and resistance strategies created in solitude can be characterised as everyday resistance and organisational misbehaviour, performed in deep backstage spaces such as the bathroom.

## 1. Introduction

Significant research has been done in the field of emotion work that is performed by healthcare workers (Smith 1992, 2011, Bolton 2000, 2003, Bolton and Boyd 2003, Mann and Cowburn 2005, Olsson 2008, Theodosius 2008). Smith (1992) and Theodosius (2008) describe, for example, how nurses distance themselves from patients and from their own feelings to protect themselves from emotional strain and drain. In order to withdraw emotionally, they objectify and depersonalise patients by choosing to perform technical duties (such as taking blood pressure) rather than engaging with patients' emotions. These technical duties are not an option for employees of psychiatric care (Mann and Cowburn 2005). Mann and Cowburn (2005) have studied emotional labour in mental healthcare and psychiatry and found that as long as emotion work appears to be invisible, it easily becomes the sole concern of the individual. They also found that intensity of emotion seems to influence how much the employees are drained of energy at work. If employees do not have opportunities to reflect on their own emotions, on the emotions of patients and colleagues as well as on norm-bound emotions during the working day, they may become ill themselves (Hochschild 1983, Olsson 2008). This is due to what Olsson (2008) refers to as harbouring work, which is a strategy to contain emotions of their own as well as emotions from the patients and the emotional demands from the organisation (see also Smith 1992, Larson and Yao 2005). This is also described as an act of organisational resistance when performed in a team (Olsson 2008). Hochschild (1983) emphasised resistance in her description of how flight attendants could express their frustration and anger towards passengers to their colleagues in the cabin. Bolton and Boyd (2003) also acknowledge that employees will find opportunities and venues to cultivate their emotional work by practising organisational resistance or misbehaviour.

However, much is still to be done – especially on how to organise emotion work; i.e. how to handle difficult emotions arising at work that require some kind of retention of another person's (the patient's) feelings. There is also a gap in research when it comes to acknowledging how healthcare workers, i.e. therapists, create space for themselves in order to be able to manage and resist the increasing demands of emotion work at the workplace. We will focus on this gap below.

The purpose of this article is to further the study of emotion management by focusing on emotion labour in relation to organisational resistance in psychiatry. In order to explore this matter, we have chosen to examine how a specific category of employees in psychiatry, namely therapists, work with emotions and how they carry out containing or 'harbouring work' (Olsson 2008), depending on the context. We use qualitative methods, such as interviews, and take an abductive approach to our analysis (Alvesson and Sköldberg 2009). We analyse this harbouring work by concentrating on the strategies in transitions between different duties used by individual therapists to manage and harbour the emotions that arise in them. This, we argue, becomes an act of resistance against a greedy organisation that is characterised by the pursuit of profit (Lindgren 1999, Rasmussen 2004). While harbouring work is emotion work and a strategy to deal with emotions, it could also be understood as a form of resistance. Nevertheless, this resistance partly takes a covert expression and might therefore remain unnoticed by management (Scott 1989, 1990, Huzell 2005, Mann and Cowburn 2005). The resistance arises partly as an opposition to greedy demands but also as a need for a space for reflection in order to be able to give 'a gift' to the patient as will be explained later in this text.

In what follows, we present previous research and theory on emotional labour and strategies to manage emotions by employees in healthcare organisations (here psychiatry). Thereafter we present previous research and theory that focuses on everyday resistance, organisational misbehaviour and emotions, as well as the theoretical concepts used in our analysis. This is followed by a methods section and then an analysis of how care employees in psychiatry manage emotions in their work. In the analysis, we emphasise the therapist's strategies and how the organisation is forcing them to seek recovery by withdrawing themselves in different ways.

Finally, we present and discuss our results and argue that those who provide care individually also resist the organisation and its pressures individually, and thus are perhaps at a greater risk of becoming ill themselves. Thereby, it is important that this is seen as emotion work that needs to be made visible.

## 2. Emotion work and emotional labour in healthcare

There are different opinions on what makes emotion work in healthcare taxing, and also how emotional labour, managing emotions for a wage in relation to customers or patients, differs from other emotional work such as emotion work in relation to colleagues in an organisation (James 1992, Wharton 1999, Hochschild 2003). Both emotion work and emotional labour are, according to Hochschild (1983), guided by emotion rules and display rules[1] that are rooted in social norms (derived from society as well as from the profession in question), or within the individual herself. This demands not only mental work but also working with emotions in order to perform emotion work/labour at work. Thus, emotion work and emotional labour demand emotional management of employees and ultimately emotional management strategies (Hochschild 1983, Fineman 2000). It would therefore seem that all emotion work that an employee performs is emotional labour (Olsson 2008). The emotion work should, however, have very different effects depending on the demands from both the prevailing organisational culture and the prevailing organisational and professional emotion rules. This includes the prominence of managing emotions in the specific profession (Zammuner *et al.* 2003, Wharton 2009).

Managing emotions is a major feature of psychotherapeutic work (Greenberg and Paivio 2003). However, therapeutic work mostly concerns helping patients to manage their emotions. The therapist's feelings and emotions are generally seen as instruments to achieve results for the patient (cf. Greenberg 2002, Aldao *et al.* 2010). The duration and intensity of the interaction and the variety of emotions expressed by employees performing emotional labour in different types of jobs have also been discussed (Morris and Feldman 1996). Mann and Cowburn (2005) conducted a study in which psychiatric nurses answered questions in relation to a number of patient interactions. Their survey results indicated that the more intense an interaction is and the more varied emotions are perceived to be, the more emotion work (emotional labour) was reported. Here it is conceivable that if employees harbour strong emotions from patients, such as violent grief or anger, the employees' emotion work increases. Mann and Cowburn (2005, p. 160) also found that surface-acting emotion work is a more important predictor of interaction stress than deep-acting emotion work,[2] and could result in a high degree of emotional dissonance (cf. Hsieh and Guy 2008). Emotional dissonance refers to discrepancy between felt emotions and emotional display required by and appropriate for the working context (Hochschild 1983, Zapf *et al.* 1999, Zapf 2002). Emotional dissonance thus describes the discrepancy between felt emotions on the one hand and displayed emotions as part of the job on the other. Previous research supports the notion that suppression of true feelings has harmful effects on health and wellbeing (Smith 1992, Bone 2002, Mann and Cowburn 2005, Mark and Mann 2005).

Moreover, this work also requires management of harbouring work,[3] where an employee must be able to hold and manage emotions (Olsson 2008). While harbouring work is important in somatic healthcare, it is considered a prerequisite for employees in psychiatry, since there are organisational as well as professional demands to harbour the emotions of the patient (Lindqvist 2016).

Emotional harbouring work is regulated by professional ethics and professional emotional rules, as well as by expression rules that apply to the organisation in question. However, it is the emotional culture of the workplace that ultimately decides what is permissible to feel and to express (Olsson 2008, Smith 2011). There is also an understanding that healthcare workers in somatic and psychiatric care relate differently to the emotional content of their work depending on how (emotion) work is organised at the workplace. Emotion work may be performed either as teamwork or individually (Olsson 2008, Lindqvist 2016). However, when individual emotion work becomes too prominent and there are fewer opportunities to manage emotions as a team, this may prove a breaking point where emotion work might become too damaging to the employee. One of the most pressing issues for healthcare professionals is therefore how to create emotionally supportive cultures in their workplaces in order for them to give each other emotional support and to prevent the development of negative coping strategies and burnout (Smith 1992, p. 139).

Research on strategies for dealing with the effects of emotional labour has, however, mostly concentrated on the kind of emotion work that has the most harmful effects (Diefendorff *et al.* 2005). It has been questioned whether it is more harmful to pretend to feel the emotions that are required at work by surface-acting, or to really feel the emotions inside oneself by deep-acting (Mann and Cowburn 2005). And what about the display of natural feelings, which are distinct from both surface and deep-acting (Wharton 1999, 2009, Bolton 2003)? It has also been discussed whether Hochchild's dichotomy, emotion work and emotional labour, is sufficient in order to be able to analyse the emotion work performed in a professional situation (Bone 2002, Bolton 2003).

These different perspectives imply that there is an interesting divide in the previous research and theorisation, and a need to adopt a balanced approach that takes into account the complexity of the emotion work involved. We therefore proceed by outlining Bolton's (2003) emotion management perspective, which takes into account more aspects rather than just the emotional labour/emotion work and deep-acting/surface-acting dichotomies.

## 2.1. Strategies to manage emotions at work

Bolton (2003) argues that there are many variables that affect how emotions are managed within an organisation, and this in turn affects how management strategies are used by employees. Strategies result from many intersecting influences, including variables such as the nature of work, types of patients, professionals' status, their seniority in the organisation and their personal life stories. According to Bolton (2003, 2005), the type of strategy used depends on all these variables. Bolton's typology has, however, been criticised for not taking into account that employees' emotion work is always commercialised in relation to the employer, which means that employees also engage in organisational resistance when they can (Brook 2009). Even her critics, however, are open to the use of Bolton's typology as providing a more nuanced analysis of emotion work (Brook 2009). In what follows, the point of departure is the emotion management perspective formulated by Bolton (2000, 2003, 2005), as well as Olsson's (2008) further development of this perspective. Our main point is that both Bolton and Olsson indicate that individual workers are capable of using different emotional management strategies including organisational resistance, depending on contextual circumstances. Olsson develops Bolton's perspective by adding the specifics of care work, namely patient confidentiality. This certainly complicates emotion work when it is performed without support from a collegial group (Olsson 2008).

Bolton (2003) argues that the need for emotional management can be attributed to the emotional rules of the organisation, profession and society (Bolton 2003, p. 7). We focus on both organisational and professional codes of emotional control along with social and cultural rules that prevail and regulate performance. Sometimes, commercial, professional and social rules collide with each other, but Bolton (2003, p. 12) argues that employees constantly search for – and find – ways to circumvent the process and the dilemmas that arise in the organisations where they work. This can be illustrated by Bolton's typology of four different emotional coping strategies (Bolton 2003, p. 7, 13f.). She describes them as pecuniary, prescribed, performance-oriented and philanthropic approaches. Bolton's pecuniary management corresponds to Hochschild's emotional labour, and it is governed by commercially and organisationally decided emotion rules. Presentation management corresponds to emotion work, and is thus governed by social and cultural emotion rules. Prescriptive management is a variation of pecuniary work, but it is not commercial. Emotions can be closely prescribed by, for instance, professional codes of ethics and professional rules. Philanthropic management, on the contrary, is a variation of all the previous categories. Philanthropic performance of emotion work means giving away emotions because you want to, without expecting any reward. Bolton (2005) refers to this emotion work as 'a gift'. The distinction Hochschild (1983) makes between emotional labour (paid work) and emotion work, is thereby resolved and replaced by distinctions based on classification of the emotional rules that govern the emotion work strategy. There are different motivations for using these different kinds of emotion management, and they in turn lead to different performances, identities and consequences.

Bolton (2003) argues that employees should not be seen as victims of demanding employers, since employees also have opportunity to use their learned social and emotional skills at work. Employees are as much social agents and emotion workers when earning wages as in their private lives. They can thus make use of their different emotions and their social skills depending on situational requirements. The argumentation here is based on the notion that employees will find arenas of resistance during their working day, and that they have possibility to take advantage of these venues to perform 'presentation' or 'philanthropic' emotion work, as appropriate to well-socialised and knowledgeable individuals. Bolton's typology offers a conceptual tool for understanding workplace emotion in a way that recognises both structural constraints and social actors as knowledgeable agents.

In order to counteract organisational demands, replenish energy and make some space for managing emotions, employees create strategies of resistance. In the next section, we describe our perception of organisational resistance and how we use the theories and concepts in our analysis. Based on our empirical data, we decided to focus on the concepts of everyday resistance and organisational misbehaviour. The resistance of the interviewees often takes a hidden form; it is not revolutionary, organised or loud. Such resistance is often completely overlooked by management, but can nevertheless serve to hearten employees.

## 3. Everyday resistance and organisational misbehaviour

Employees need to experience both dignity and autonomy in their work. If they are denied this, employees tend to respond through various forms of organisational resistance (Karlsson 2011). According to Hodson (2001), a sense of dignity is essential if employees are to experience work as meaningful and satisfying, and this, in turn, is important if work is to be perceived as enjoyable (Sandelands and Boudens 2000). Organisational resistance does not only occur due to discomfort or the fact that employees do not experience their work as dignified or autonomous. It also occurs in response to intensified workloads and bad management. In some cases, resistance is also a reaction to lousy leadership that impairs employees' ability to do justice with their patients (Olsson 2008, Karlsson 2011). Resistance is created due to various forms of circumstances and configurations in organisations (Ackroyd and Thompson 1999).

In existing research, resistance may be characterised as either formal, organised resistance or informal, unorganised resistance (Huzell 2005). Resistance is a very broad concept, and we therefore narrow it down here to what Scott (2008) calls everyday resistance and what Karlsson (2011) describes as organisational misbehaviour. These two concepts are not exactly synonymous, but could be used in the context of this study to describe everyday coping as well as opposition against an unreasonable (emotional) workload. Furthermore, there is a growing interest in the informal, personal and hidden forms of resistance within organisations (see e.g. Ackroyd and Thompson 1999, Prasad and Prasad 2000, Fleming and Sewell 2002). Resistance need not necessarily always be expressed through large, visible public performances such as strikes and demonstrations, but may instead be expressed through hidden and invisible power acts beyond a management's (organisational) control (Scott 2008, Lilja and Vinthagen 2009). According to Paulsen (2010), 'everyday resistance' involves resisting without directly confronting the establishment. Resistance may be disguised as cooperation in order to get benefits, to defend interests in the organisation passively, or to reduce the effects of oppression.

Organisational misbehaviour (Karlsson 2011), i.e. breaching management rules, involves anything one consciously is, does, or thinks at work that one is not supposed to be, do or think. Organisational misbehaviour is thus included in everyday resistance and gives a sense of control and power to the worker beyond control of the organisation/management (Karlsson 2011).

Paulsen (2015) presents non-work as one form of everyday resistance. Non-work is, according to Paulsen, wasting of paid time or employing empty labour as a resistance strategy. We interpret this waste of time in psychiatry as a form of resistance and as a harbouring strategy. Resistance includes taking a break in an exceedingly (emotionally) pressured working day as well as reacting against a greedy organisation and inconvenient working conditions. Since most therapy work is performed in the absence of colleagues, resistance strategies tend to be individual.

Resistance, as it appears in everyday work, can be divided into open/overt and hidden/covert resistance, and can be performed individually or collectively (cf. Collinson and Ackroyd 2005). However, as mentioned above, individual work will mostly result in individual forms of resistance.

Inspired by previous research (see e.g. Fleming and Sewell 2002, Huzell 2005 and Paulsen 2015) and the growing focus on informal and hidden forms of resistance within organisations (cf. Huzell 2005), we explore the strategies employees use not only for endurance but also for finding relief from a greedy organisation. As the focus is on the individual's performance and interpretations of the work situation, we avail ourselves of the notions of 'everyday resistance' and 'organisational misbehaviour'.

Relevant previous research on resistance in work situations therefore includes research on the performance of informal rather than formal acts of resistance (Karlsson 2011). Huzell (2005) discusses the difference between resistance (open and systematic opposition), misbehaviour (acts of unruliness) and dissent (hidden and informal resistance taking the form of linguistic/normative ideological disagreements). In our case, resistance includes misbehaviour and acts of dissent. The resistance that emerges from our data does not take the form of a large-scale political strategy in the sense of a serious drive to change the organisation. In our analysis, resistance is further expressed as advanced emotion work that takes the form of emotional harbouring work in solitude. Therefore, we conclude by describing how we relate emotion work, harbouring work and resistance to each other, and

## RESISTANCE AND EMOTIONS

focus on the difference between individual emotional work and emotional work carried out with support of a collegial buffer group.

### *3.1. Emotion work, harbouring work, and resistance*

It is important to distinguish between effects of individual resistance and resistance that occurs in groups, and the emotion work that is done, respectively. Astvik *et al.* (2014) conclude that when a group jointly resists an employer, individuals enjoy psychological protection since they do not have to stand alone in their opposition. This can be compared with the buffer group – a group of colleges who work together and know each other well (Olsson 2008), and its importance for individual survival. Emotion work is done collectively in the buffer group (roughly synonymous with the team) and the group protects the individual from a greedy organisation (Olsson 2008).

The development of a buffer group requires not only time to socialise, but also some form of similarity, closeness and common problem definition (Lysgaard 1967, Lindgren 1999). That is, people need to be able to identify with each other, and there have to be opportunities for interaction and some kind of common understanding of different situations. The harbouring work described below is best done in a buffer group (Olsson 2008).

Harbouring work is a generic description of how healthcare professionals relate emotionally to patients, colleagues, themselves and the organisation. A prerequisite for performing harbouring work is, however, that there is adequate time (Olsson 2008, Lindqvist 2016). If enough time is not available, a gap may occur between expressed and perceived feelings. Hochschild (1983) names this gap emotive dissonance. Emotive dissonance can cause emotional numbness and lead to an experience of estrangement; i.e. alienation from oneself. As work requirements become more complicated, the tempo increases and monitoring of the work is reinforced. The resulting emotive dissonance can then cause an employee to resign or become ill (Hochschild 1983). This has important implications for healthcare professionals due to specific professional ethics as well as emotion rules.

Olsson (2008) suggests that healthcare workers carry out a particular type of emotional labour as part of their harbouring work. Individuals working in human services vocations who are subject to the constraints of patient confidentiality will need to work through their experiences with the help of colleagues. This further implies that colleagues and a buffer group are very significant in terms of how individual employees will, in the long term, endure the emotional labour that healthcare work entails. As a strategy, employees can also create various forms of resistance to ensure emotional survival at work and to maintain their dignity (Huzell 2005).

How individual employees use strategies to manage and keep/contain/harbour the emotions that arise during their work duties is important. These strategies, we argue, may become acts of resistance against greedy employers. While harbouring work is emotion work and a strategy to deal with emotions, it also constitutes a form of resistance, although this form of resistance is expressed covertly and might therefore remain unnoticed. An act that is considered resistance would possibly benefit an employee more if she/he were consciously aware of it as opposition. It could thereby be an act that strengthens the employee.

Building on prior research, we use a theoretical framework that consists of emotion theory and theory of resistance in work organisations. The emotion–theoretical framework includes theories of emotional labour (Hochschild 1983), and strategies for managing both one's own and others' emotional states, as well as strategies for recovery during the working day (Bolton 2003, Astvik *et al.* 2014). We also use the concepts of a buffer group and resistance to analyse the narratives of our participants (Huzell 2005, Olsson 2008).

We mainly draw upon Bolton's (2003, 2005) concepts and typology of emotion management, and on Olsson's (2008) concept of harbouring work. We show how emotional attunement works in different work situations, as well as emotional strategies that arise from this. We further use the notion deep backstage by Meyrowitz (1986) that builds on Goffman's (1959) use of the theatre as a metaphor for society. Roughly speaking, frontstage is what happens in public and backstage refers to actions that take place behind the scenes with your colleagues. Meyrowitz (1986) describes an even more private space than the backstage as the deep backstage. Again, using the theatre as a metaphor, the open space behind the scene constitutes the backstage, and the dressing rooms to which actors withdraw between performances on stage constitute the deep backstage. This deep backstage is then to be understood as an even more private space than the backstage, where actors can drop their masks and relax for a moment.

## 4. Method

This study analyses interview data to provide insight into workplace resistance. Interviews were conducted with 11 therapists' in psychiatry; six of them were interviewed in a focus group and five were interviewed individually. The method may be described as a qualitative interview study with some auto-ethnographic elements (Ellis 2004, Baarts 2010), since the first author also works as a therapist and is therefore situated within the site. Yet, our main focus falls on the interviews. Although prior experience in the field might benefit understanding, it can also act as a hindrance (Chenail and Maione 1997). Doing research on colleagues thereby placed the participants and the researcher on a more equal footing, yet it may be naïve to assume comprehension – it may rather serve to obstruct the process. Therefore, conducting open-minded, open-ended interviews was important (see e.g. Holloway and Wheeler 2013).

The empirical data were collected through focus group interviews as well as individual interviews. Participants were recruited through network referrals and key persons who knew many therapists working in the field. The focus group interviews took place on three different occasions at the respondents' workplace. The focus group interview method was chosen to obtain different perspectives and experiences on the issue of therapists' emotions (Wibeck 2000).

On all three occasions the same six therapists working at the same clinic were interviewed. The focus group interviews were then supplemented with five individual interviews to obtain the views of a wider range of therapists and to refine the perspectives on the emotion work of therapists. These five individual interviews were conducted with therapists who worked both in outpatient clinics and in closed wards. In all, 11 therapists were interviewed. The purpose of the individual interviews was to get an opportunity to dig deeper (Epstein 2009) into work experiences and to obtain a broader overview of emotion work and the resources employed by therapists in order for them to recover during a working day. The individual interviews were only held on one occasion, mainly due to the interviewees' lack of time. All the interviews were recorded with the participants' permission and were transcribed. All but one of the participants were women aged between 30 and 60. This clearly shows the gender distribution among therapists. The interviewees had been working in mental healthcare between three and 35 years.

The selection of interviewees was limited to therapists with experience in treating migrants (due to the doctoral dissertation that this study is part of). All the respondents were informed of the ethical rules and signed a consent form (Swedish Research Council 2004). (The study and methods were approved by the Regional Ethical Review Board in Uppsala, Sweden and the study was conducted in agreement with the guidelines of the Swedish Research Council.)

The transcribed interviews were then read and thematically categorised, using sensitising concepts (Blumer 1954). We started with a theory developing approach. Going through the empirical data, we found indications of some form of resistance at the workplace. After a more detailed analysis, we found theory that supports a deeper and more nuanced discussion of everyday resistance. On the whole, this study thus followed an abductive approach and the scope of the theory we used thereby developed during the course of the study (see e.g. Dubois and Gadde 2002).

In this article excerpts from interviews have been edited into a more readable form, but without changing the content (Malterud 2003). All names have been changed in order to protect participants' anonymity and further precautions have been taken to preserve the original character and content of the statements without compromising confidentiality.

### *4.1. Further ethical considerations*

Ethical issues arise when the research area is resistance in an organisation. The researcher is responsible for conducting the analysis and publishing results in such a way that participants will not be harmed. In this case, the analyses reveal how employees can use different strategies, such as withdrawing to get a moment of peace and quiet or time for recovery. We believe that what happens is not unique to this particular workplace, but probably occurs more generally where employees have fewer venues at work for recovery. Therefore, it is also important to show how certain work environments compel employees to find their own strategies and spaces to have a break and to cope with the pressures of increasing productivity and doing emotionally exhausting work.

## 5. Results and analysis

There is no doubt that all the therapists interviewed felt the need to recover during the working day. Most of the interviewees in this study said that they needed to have a chat or a conversation with colleagues to replenish their emotional energy. However, since working conditions were mostly designed according to a new public management (NPM) style that did almost not allow any unplanned, spontaneous conversation with colleagues, the therapists thus needed to find strategies to recharge their batteries in their own ways. The NPM model suggests new techniques and practices, drawn from the private sector, to manage and control activities in the public sector, with the aim of enabling more efficient and rational resource utilization (Lane 2000).

In the following discussion we only focus on individual covert forms of managing emotions and resistance. There are opportunities available to engage in open, collective resistance through, for example, trade unions that openly oppose increased work tempos. Nevertheless, the interviewees only seldom made use of this opportunity. Yet, as shall be seen below, individual work seems to generate individual hidden resistance strategies. Employees are driven by increased demands for measurable work performances that leave very little space for reflection and emotional harbouring work between patients. In order to do a good job, and even give a little extra attention to the patient as 'a gift' (see Bolton 2005), therapists have to oppose the rapid tempo in order to recover between therapy sessions.

The analysis shows how the interviewees in this study use non-work and deliberate absence as a way of doing their harbouring work, resisting demands and creating free zones at work to withdraw for a moment to recover from the hectic emotional tempo. Examples of 'deliberate absence', a way of performing organisational misbehaviour, might include performing unimportant actions in order to look busy. It might include finding something to do at the other end of the hallway and actively walking back and forth, organising and re-organising one's desk, printing or copying papers without an immediate purpose, talking to the secretary about something administrative that is not especially urgent, as well as to going to the bathroom (Lindqvist 2016). These are all actions that constitute transitions between duties.

The bathroom deserves to be explored in more detail, since it serves as a significant marker in the empirical data. There are not many places at work where employees can withdraw to be completely on their own. Yet, the bathroom or toilet is an obvious place where one will be left alone without people knocking on the door asking for advice and attention. There are of course designated resting areas at work, such as the lunchroom and other spaces intended to be used by employees on regulated breaks. Yet, the openness of these official spaces is problematic: these spaces are under management control, not only in relation to time but also in relation to the actions of the employees. When it comes to emotion work and impression management, the lunchroom can be seen as a sort of backstage where therapists are supposed to be relaxing, but where they still have to behave accordingly to the organisational norms. The employees therefore have to be cautious with what they say and do and they have to act according to the current emotion rules (cf. Bloch 2008). They cannot relax for even a moment. The bathroom, on the other hand, is a space where one is supposed to get rid of excesses, not only concretely but also metaphorically. Here a therapist can drop her mask (cf. Goffman 1959) and does not need to present a proper professional face; in the bathroom no impression management is needed (Goffman 1959). As one of the interviewees noted, 'in the bathroom you can let go of your face, no professionality [is] needed'.

### 5.1. Deep backstage

When work sometimes gets too hectic and therapists cannot manage more emotional relating to others, they just have to take a break. Since breaks are regulated at work, they have to creatively make their own space in the current context. As Karlsson (2008, p. 21) shows in his vignette of 'the stairs', employees approve of a staircase at work, yet it is not the staircase itself that is useful, but the space behind the stairs that has gone unnoticed by management. In this study, employees are using another existing space at work. This space, the bathroom, is however intended for slightly different activities than what the participants in this study use the bathroom for. Yet, the participants in our study can be sure that no one will ask what they actually do in the bathroom, since that would be a violation of their privacy. The bathroom can therefore be used as space for the employees' intentions where the management cannot exert control over them. To use Meyrowitz's (1986) vocabulary, it thus becomes a deep backstage. A break, even if it only lasts a few minutes, can make a difference to the therapist, giving her the opportunity to pause and deal with emotions between executing different duties, as shall be seen below.

Thus the bathroom serves as a deep backstage where therapists do not need to display a professional face and where they can void themselves mentally and emotionally. Some of the therapists explain that they go into the bathroom to cry, as they are deeply affected by the narratives and emotions of their patients. Therapists are supposed to abide by professional rules and should not let their emotions get out of control in therapeutic relationships or in other encounters in psychiatric care. The organisational rules on emotion of the professional framework prevent therapists from expressing certain emotions openly through crying and anger. These kinds of emotions have to be stored only to be let out in the deep backstage, the bathroom. As Maria says:

> It was really tough. There was a young girl who told me about her sister's death. It was just awful. I just sat there and listened to her story and tried to be calm and show compassion. After the session, I went to the bathroom and cried. I just had to let my feelings out.

This indicates that the harbouring vessel will soon be filled and is liable to run over. This may also be interpreted as feeling inadequate in response to the patient's suffering and thereby creating an urgent need to manage feelings of inadequacy. The bathroom then becomes an obvious space, since it is relatively accessible (Lindqvist 2016).

On the front stage, therapists have to maintain a certain kind of professional face; they need to remain calm and display empathy. Therapists have to show a certain kind of coolness (cf. Stearns 1994), and should not really show some emotions when facing patients. Crying is not the only expression of emotion that cannot be shown frontstage, and it can only be let out in the bathroom. Anger is another emotion that is merely supposed to be expressed behind the scenes, if at all. As Inger explained:

> All these stupid ideas of things we have to do. They (the management) always come up with new things to control and measure everything we do. I get really angry so I sit there [in the bathroom] having an imaginary conversation with the management about who actually knows what the work is all about.

However, since Inger does not dare to confront the management directly, expressing her resentment is her own way of resisting the limits at work. The bathroom is a management-free zone: management exerts no control over what an employee does in the bathroom and cannot restrict bathroom visits in number or length. Therapists somehow have to recover during working hours in a way that does not necessarily fit in with the management's plans. As a result, employees arrange a break by themselves to resist the increasing strain and work tempo, while simultaneously performing a certain kind of harbouring work on their own.

Interviewees gave examples of different activities to do in the bathroom. All these activities are intended to release an emotional load, to constitute 'emotional void'; i.e. doing things that are not supposed to be done in the bathroom or perhaps doing nothing at all, and just trying to pause time for a moment (cf. Rosa 2013). Since almost all workplaces provide internet access, so-called cyberloafing (Lim 2002) has become common, which can also be seen as an act of resistance. As seen below, the internet is frequently used for different purposes, but it is not even needed when a therapist indulges in self-talking.

## 5.2. Cyberloafing and self-talking

The interviewees often use surfing the internet as a way of loafing or avoiding work. They chat with friends on social media, play online games and check Facebook, and so on. Lim (2002) calls the act of employees using their corporate internet for personal use during working hours, cyberloafing. Cyberloafing has become a common phenomenon in workplaces with access to the internet. Many researchers see cyberloafing as another type of deviant behaviour at work, while others believe that cyberloafing can be productive and make employees more efficient. In both cases, however, cyberloafing is seen as a misuse of internet resources during the working day (Zoghbi-Manrique-de-Lara 2012, Paulsen 2015). Cyberloafing occurs in the office between seeing different patients, but is even more frequent in the bathroom where the organisation cannot exert any control. A therapist cyberloafs on her mobile phone or tablet in order to escape for a moment from the workplace, as explained by Maria, who sees this as a relief:

> I take my phone to the bathroom to check Facebook, I chat with friends and it's such a relief to know that there's a world out there. It is so easy to get sucked into it (the work) when you are just working, working, working.

As Maria noted, cyberloafing provides a momentary respite in a hectic workspace and relieves the pressure. As she later explained, the breaks are not very long but are extremely important for her to recover. Katia explained that she needs to empty her 'system' (i.e. her mind and her emotions) between patients and therefore plays a game on her phone. However, she is not really explicit about the space where this happens. It might in be the bathroom, but it might also be in some other space at work where her playing can go unnoticed:

> Every now and then I play a game on my phone in order to cleanse my mind and my system between each patient.

Here the cyberloafing itself seems more important than the space where it happens, but it still needs to be a covert, hidden act that is not performed openly (cf. Huzell 2005). Being alone in an empty space with an emptied 'system' seems to give her the emotional cleansing needed to face the next patient.

Chatting with friends on Facebook is one option, but if friends are not available or the matter cannot be discussed with friends, self-talk is always a possibility. Pia talks to herself and daydreams in the bathroom, thus displaying yet another way of mindscaping from the premises:

> I talk to myself about a lot of things mostly about holidays I think I am going to have someday in faraway places.

## 5.3. The comfort of emptiness

Astrid sometimes uses the bathroom for no particular reason except to be on her own or to rest:

> I go there, I sit, I do nothing, I just want to be on my own for a while. No one demanding my attention, no phones ringing. It is just me with myself for a while.

Ylva similarly described her need to withdraw for a while when there are no colleagues to talk to:

> I need to be on my own. I am not sure what I do. Probably I just stare into the walls. I don't even think I think, it's just a moment of space out.

As Astrid and Ylva explained, there seems to be an obvious need to not be constantly available, to not anticipate other peoples' (emotional) requests at every moment. This can be seen as an individual harbouring strategy – a way of dealing with oneself when the buffer group is missing (Olsson 2008).

To secure their withdrawal to the bathroom, some of the interviewees appear to give an explanation before entering the space so as to be sure that they will not to be questioned about why they spend a lot of time in the bathroom: 'I am having my period' and 'having a bad stomach' were never questioned. Withdrawing to the bathroom for a moment is thus always a possibility if space is needed to take an unquestioned rest. It also indicates that this is where therapists are able to recover and to manage their emotions in preparation for further encounters with patients. Several interviewees pointed out the need for recovery between patient visits, to cope with and once more provide emotional work as a gift to a patient – they draw strength from these recovery periods to perform 'presentations' or 'philanthropic' emotional work, as suggested by Bolton (2003).

There are probably more things employees in psychiatry do in the bathroom that they are not supposed to do, think or feel during working hours. Presumably all strategies were not revealed in the interviews. But going back to what Karlsson (2008, 2011) denotes as organisational misbehaviour, these can include anything the employees think and do that management would want to prevent. We would like to add that it also includes emotions that management would not want employees to feel during working hours such as sadness, resentment or the anger expressed by Inger in this study.

### 5.4. Emotional recovery and emotional gifts

The psychiatric staff's resistance seems mainly to have resulted from the high emotional workload and the dense harbouring of emotions: the workers' own emotions, the patients' emotions and the emotional rules and norms of the organisation; i.e. the official discourse of psychiatry. Our results indicate an unreasonably high workload comprising: (1) large patient turnover; (2) difficult (emotional) matters; (3) patients' precarious situation (psycho-social problems, unemployment, relative poverty, etc.); (4) lack of opportunities to receive support from colleagues; and (5) lack of support from management and the organisation.

These aspects correspond to the characteristics of greedy organisations: responsibility is decentralised, but disproportionately so in the light of available resources. A greedy organisation combines more attractive aspects such as greater responsibility and greater freedom at work with less favourable aspects such as centralised management and control of resources (Rasmussen 2004). Resources, such as the time allocated to various tasks, are under pressure and employees are forced to increase their work tempo and to cut corners in their work (cf. Astvik *et al.* 2014). At an individual level, this can result in employees being forced to intensify their focus on their work duties as well as their focus on persisting at work (Rasmussen 2004, Håpnes and Rasmussen 2007).

Accordingly, a therapist accumulates emotions during several patient encounters that could be let out. A greedy organisation also tends to reinforce gender norms in relation to care work, meaning that women are supposed to provide care naturally and that this kind of emotional care is not supposed to require a salary and above all it is not actually considered work or labour at all (Rasmussen 2004, Wettergren 2013). The greedy organisation thus generates resistance; in order to endure these conditions, employees have to create space for their recovery and their survival at work. Work has become more rationalised and doing harbouring work is no longer possible. Implementing the conceptual apparatus of NPM in psychiatry then forces staff to respond more instrumentally to their work so that they can perform all their duties. This instrumentalisation can be considered to be counteracting their professional ethics as well as personal convictions about the importance of relations in human encounters in therapy. A space for reflection/harbouring is needed to counteract instrumentalisation in the workplace. Change over time is thus required so as not to accumulate an increasing amount of stored emotions during the working day. Doing 'heavy emotional lifting', as one of the participants called it, requires a moment of balancing between patients, a short break to gather strength to do the next 'emotional lift' (Lindqvist 2016). Anyone who has done something emotionally or mentally taxing, such as feeling compassion or showing empathy with a patient (who may have experienced acts of torture, in this study), needs harbouring after being exposed to social suffering and feelings of extreme vulnerability. As Katia noted:

> Patients often tell horrible stories about their lives and it touches me deeply, I can feel sadness and anger because people have been treated so badly. While I am at the same time impressed that it is possible to continue living after being raped twenty times without collapsing completely, I still feel powerless about not being able to offer more.

Pia, another interviewee, concluded:

> You want to share the feelings then with your colleagues. It feels so undignified to only write all this down in a journal and keep working.

Yet, it is not patients' narratives of extreme experiences per se that result in stress and possible staff burnouts, but rather the turnover of patients during a working day. It becomes harder to recover and if resources are scarce this makes it difficult for a therapist who wants to do a good job. Since there is no space to work through the emotions raised by working with a patient, harbouring work is rationalised and must be carried out in secret in the bathroom. The bathroom therefore becomes the place where therapists will be able to recover and work through their emotions, making it possible to go out and meet a new patient. Several interviewees have pointed out the need for recovery between patient visits so that they can cope with once again providing emotional labour as a gift to the next patient. In this way they draw strength to perform 'presentation' or 'philanthropic' emotional work, as Bolton (2003) suggests, but they can also be seen as acts of organisational resistance.

## 6.  Concluding discussion

The purpose of this article is to further the study of emotion management by focusing on emotion labour in relation to organisational resistance in psychiatry. We have shown the importance of buffer groups and how it becomes a problem that resistance is done individually. Another important argument we want to emphasise is that emotional work needs to be recognised as 'work' of the employer and thus needs to get recognition in the organisations. It becomes difficult to emphasise these kinds of work if they are made invisible. Furthermore, it is essential that individual employees understand their emotional work in the struggle against the 'emotion rules' as a form of resistance against greedy organisations. It is thus important that this is seen as resistance to make this particular emotion work more visible. One significant conclusion from our analysis is that the bathroom offers the most important space for therapists' individual harbouring work and resistance within a time-pressed and greedy organisation. Crying, talking to oneself, chatting with friends, talking on the phone, surfing the internet, stretching, just sitting doing nothing – all these actions have been described by the therapists as happening in the bathroom, besides the obvious.

Psychiatry mostly involves mental and emotion work, since there are no actual physical duties to be performed as in somatic healthcare where employees can excuse themselves by 'having' to perform something such as getting clean sheets. This path does not exist in psychiatry. Since all props are supposed to be in 'the minds' of employees, organisational resistance takes the form of hidden or covert resistance, which probably goes unnoticed by colleagues and management. At the same time, 'self-talk' provides a way of resisting a greedy organisation and also a way of managing one's harbouring work: one needs to work as much on one's harboured feelings, as one needs to resist the greedy organisation.

One explanation for the hidden or covert form that resistance takes (and for harbouring emotions alone) may be professional demands, such as patient confidentiality. Therapists are supposed to absorb a large amount of emotional material that can only be released in a transformed form. Another explanation may be that staff fear reprisals if they protest too loudly. The covert form leads to mental/emotional distancing of oneself from the work at hand, which may be disastrous in relation to patients. Yet, it may entail spatial distancing. We have shown how the use of the toilet as a deep backstage space provides a place where one can let go of emotional material. The toilet is a space where you can be on your own, in a sense it is a 'private space' to which patients, colleagues, management or the organisation has no access. Using the terminology of Goffman (1959) and Meyrowitz (1986), this is a backstage beyond the backstage. This is the only space in the organisation where one can be alone, without anyone asking what one is doing.

Although it is not clearly evident from our analysis, we want to stress that employees certainly have to use their social and relational abilities and knowledge to mitigate the effects of an emotionally taxing job. They deliberately seek to recover between patient visits to be able to contain/harbour patients' emotions and difficult experiences. We have noted and described how particularly difficult experiences in one encounter are transferred to the next patient encounter if they are not taken care of. The interviewees were well aware of this and also acted in a socially (and emotionally) reflective way by finding ways and venues where they can process their emotions (Bolton 2003, 2005). They do so in solitude; however, they do this because they do not have access to their colleagues or a buffer group – the organisation of the work does not allow for that (Lindqvist 2016). Since the duration of each patient visit is limited by the management style, there is pressure to deal with as many patients as possible during a working day (Lindqvist 2016).

Decreasing time for recovery is a problem in many work organisations at present (Moyers 2005), and more sick leave is taken due to mental illness in Sweden. These two facts are deemed to be related. (We also have examples of incipient signs of burnout in our interview material.) An overly tightly structured working day, during which employees are not given opportunities to consult each other in order to talk about matters not related to work, or to sit down for joint recovery, has effects. A consequence of this might be adopting solitary forms of 'loafing' or 'non-working' as an individual approach to harbouring work and of carrying out (organisational) resistance. We have argued that employees will find arenas of resistance during their working day, and that they have the opportunity to take advantage of these venues to perform 'presentations' or 'philanthropic' emotional work, as suggested by Bolton (2003). The therapists interviewed in this study noted that extended bathroom visits give them the space they need for recovery and thereby give them an opportunity to attune to a patient's feelings. In doing so, they get the energy and the strength that they need to be able to offer empathy and compassion to the suffering person. It is thus because of their visits to the bathroom that they are able to offer 'a gift' to the patient – not because they are required to do so. They do this in solitude as they lack a buffer group to share their emotion harbouring work with.

By talking to themselves in the bathroom they might create imaginary colleagues and thus create a team and a buffer zone (Olsson 2008) where they can manage their emotions and do harbouring work in order to keep a sense of dignity for themselves and patients. In other words, they construct a sort of split-personality where they harbour heavy emotional material for themselves by becoming their own colleagues.

## Notes

1. Emotion rules and display rules are norms and rules guiding what we are allowed to feel on specific occasions, and what and how we are allowed to show our feelings (Hochschild 1983).
2. Surface-acting can be defined as pretending to feel the emotions that are required at work, while deep-acting means that one actively tries to really feel the emotions inside themselves.
3. Health care workers get emotions from working with the patients. They accommodate emotions of the patients (and occasionally emotions of colleagues), which results in a containing function for both their own feelings and for the feelings of the patients/colleagues.

## Disclosure statement

No potential conflict of interest was reported by the authors.

# References

Ackroyd, S. and Thompson, P., 1999. *Organizational misbehaviour*. London: Sage.

Aldao, A., Nolen-Hoeksema, S., and Schweizer, S., 2010. Emotion-regulation strategies across psychopathology: a meta-analytic review. *Clinical Psychology Review*, 30 (2), 217–237.

Alvesson, M. and Sköldberg, K., 2009. *Reflexive methodology: new vistas for qualitative research*. London: Sage.

Astvik, W., Melin, M., and Allvin, M., 2014. Survival strategies in social work: a study of how coping strategies affect service quality, professionalism and employee health. *Nordic Social Work Research*, 4 (1), 52–66.

Baarts, C., 2010. Autoetnografi. *In*: S. Brinkmann and L. Tanggaard, eds. *Kvalitative metoder: en grundbog*. Copenhagen: Hans Reitzels forlag, 275–288.

Bloch, C., 2008. Akademins lunchrum – mys eller hierarki? [Lunchrooms of academia – cosiness or hierarchy]. *In*: Å. Wettergren, B. Starrin, and G. Lindgren, eds. *Det sociala livets emotionella grunder* [The emotional foundation of social life]. Malmö: Liber AB, 215–236.

Blumer, H., 1954. What is wrong with social theory? *American Sociological Review*, 19 (1), 3–10.

Bolton, S.C., 2000. Who cares? Offering emotion work as a 'gift' in the nursing labour process. *Journal of Advanced Nursing*, 32 (3), 580–586.

Bolton, S.C., 2003. *Introducing a typology of workplace emotion*. Lancaster: Lancaster University School, Working paper 2003/064.

Bolton, S.C., 2005. 'Making up' managers the case of NHS nurses. *Work, Employment & Society*, 19 (1), 5–23.

Bolton, S.C. and Boyd, C., 2003. Trolley dolly or skilled emotion manager? Moving on from Hochschild's managed heart. *Work, Employment and Society*, 17 (2), 289–308.

Bone, D., 2002. Dilemmas of emotion work in nursing under market-driven health care. *International Journal of Public Sector Management*, 15 (2), 140–150.

Brook, P., 2009. In critical defence of 'emotional labour'. *Work, Employment and Society*, 23 (3), 531–548.

Chenail, R.J. and Maione, P.V., 1997. Sensemaking in clinical qualitative research. *The Qualitative Report*, 3 (1), 1–10.

Collinson, D. and Ackroyd, S., 2005. Resistance, misbehavior, and dissent. *In*: S. Ackroyd, R. Batt, P. Thompson and P. Tolbert, eds. *The Oxford handbook of work and organisation*. Oxford: Oxford University Press, 305–326.

Diefendorff, J.M., Croyle, M.H., and Gosserand, R.H., 2005. The dimensionality and antecedents of emotional labor strategies. *Journal of Vocational Behavior*, 66, 339–357.

Dubois, A. and Gadde, L.E., 2002. Systematic combining: an abductive approach to case research. *Journal of Business Research*, 55 (7), 553–560.

Ellis, C., 2004. *The ethnographic I*. Walnut Creek: Alta Mira Press.

Epstein, I., 2009. *Clinical data-mining*. Oxford: Oxford University Press.

Fineman, S., ed., 2000. *Emotion in organizations*. London: Sage.

Fleming, P. and Sewell, G., 2002. Looking for the good soldier, Švejk. *Sociology*, 36 (4), 857–873.

Goffman, E., 1959. *The presentation of self in everyday life*. Garden City, NY: Doubleday Anchor Books.

Greenberg, L.S., 2002. *Emotion-focused therapy: coaching clients to work through their feelings*. Washington, DC: American Psychological Association.

Greenberg, L.S. and Paivio, S.C., 2003. *Working with emotions in psychotherapy*. New York: Guilford Press.

Håpnes, T. and Rasmussen, B., 2007. Familievennlige kunnskapsbedrifter: Fleksible vs. Byråkratiske organisasjonsformer? [Family-friendly knowledge companies: Flexible vs. Bureaucratic organizational forms?]. *In*: E. Kvande and B. Rasmussen, eds. *Arbeidslivets klemmer. Arbeidets konstruksjon av foreldreskap* [Working life's clamp. The construction of parental work]. Bergen: Fagbokförlaget, 146–167.

Hochschild, A.R., 1983. *The managed heart: communication of human feeling*. Berkeley: University of California Press.

## RESISTANCE AND EMOTIONS

Hochschild, A.R., 2003. *The managed heart: commercialization of human feeling.* Berkeley: University of California Press.

Hodson, R., 2001. *Dignity at work.* Cambridge: Cambridge University Press.

Holloway, I. and Wheeler, S., 2013. *Qualitative research in nursing and healthcare.* New Jersey, NJ: John Wiley & Sons.

Hsieh, C.-W. and Guy, M.E., 2008. Performance outcomes: the relationship between managing the 'heart' and managing client satisfaction. *Review of Public Personnel Administration*, 29 (1), 41–57.

Huzell, H., 2005. *Management och motstånd: offentlig sektor i omvandling- en fallstudie* [Management and resistance: public sector in transformation - a case study]. Doctoral dissertation. Karlstad: Karlstad University Studies.

James, N., 1992. Care = organisation + physical labour + emotional labour. *Sociology of Health & Illness*, 14 (4), 488–509.

Karlsson, J.C., 2008. *Den smidiga mellanchefen* [The smooth floor-walker]. Malmö: Gleerups.

Karlsson, J.C., 2011. *Organizational misbehaviour in the workplace: narratives of dignity and resistance.* Basingstoke: Palgrave Macmillan.

Lane, J.E., 2000. *New public management.* London: Routledge.

Larson, E.B. and Yao, X., 2005. Clinical empathy as emotional labor in the patient-physician relationship. *JAMA*, 293 (9), 1100–1106.

Lilja, M. and Vinthagen, S., 2009. *Motstånd* [Resistance]. Malmö: Liber.

Lim, V.K., 2002. The IT way of loafing on the job: cyberloafing, neutralizing and organizational justice. *Journal of Organizational Behavior*, 23 (5), 675–694.

Lindgren, G., 1999. *Klass, kön och kirurgi: relationer bland vårdpersonal i organisationsförändringarnas spår* [Class, gender and surgery: relationships among health care professionals in organizational change]. Malmö: Liber.

Lindqvist, M., 2016. Organisering av tid och emotioner i psykiatrin [Organization of time and emotions in psychiatry]. *Arbetsmarknad & Arbetsliv*, 22 (1), 27–41.

Lysgaard, S., 1967. *Arbeiderkollektivet* [Labor collective]. Oslo: Universitetsforlaget.

Malterud, K., 2003. *Kvalitative metoder i medisinsk forskning* [Qualitative methods in medical research]. Oslo: Universitetsforlaget.

Mann, S. and Cowburn, J., 2005. Emotional labour and stress within mental health nursing. *Journal of Psychiatric and Mental Health Nursing*, 12 (2), 154–162.

Mark, A. and Mann, S., 2005. A health-care model of emotional labour: an evaluation of the literature and development of a model. *Journal of Health Organization and Management*, 19 (4/5), 304–317.

Meyrowitz, J., 1986. *No sense of place: the impact of electronic media on social behavior.* Oxford: Oxford University Press.

Morris, J.A. and Feldman, D.C., 1996. The dimensions, antecedents, and consequences of emotional labor. *Academy of Management Review*, 21 (4), 986–1010.

Moyers, P., 2005. Introduction to occupation-based practice. *In: Occupational therapy: performance, participation, and wellbeing*, 221–234.

Olsson, E., 2008. *Emotioner i arbete: En studie av vårdarbetares upplevelser av arbetsmiljö och arbetsvillkor* [Emotions in work: a study of healthcare workers' experiences of the working environment and working conditions]. Doctoral Dissertation. Karlstad: Karlstad University Studies.

Paulsen, R., 2010. *Arbetssamhället* [The working society]. Stockholm: Carlssons.

Paulsen, R., 2015. Non-work at work: resistance or what? *Organization*, 22 (3), 351–367.

Prasad, P. and Prasad, A., 2000. Stretching the iron cage: the constitution and implications of routine workplace resistance. *Organization Science*, 11 (4), 387–403.

Rasmussen, B., 2004. Between endless needs and limited resources: the gendered construction of a greedy organization. *Gender, Work & Organization*, 11 (5), 506–525.

Rosa, H., 2013. *Social acceleration.* New York: Columbia University Press.

Sandelands, L.E. and Boudens, C.J., 2000. Feeling at work. *In:* S. Fineman, ed. *Emotion in organizations.* London: Sage, 46–63.

Scott, J.C., 1989. Everyday forms of resistance. *The Copenhagen Papers*, 4, 33–62.

Scott, J.C., 1990. *Domination and the arts of resistance: hidden transcripts.* Yale: Yale University Press.

Scott, J.C., 2008. *Weapons of the weak: everyday forms of peasant resistance.* Yale: Yale University Press.

Smith, P., 1992. *The emotional labour of nursing*. Basingstoke: Palgrave Macmillan.

Smith, P., 2011. *The emotional labour of nursing revisited: can nurses still care?*. Basingstoke: Palgrave Macmillan.

Stearns, P.N., 1994. *American cool: constructing a twentieth-century emotional style*. New York: New York University Press.

Swedish Research Council, 2004. *Ethical review of research involving humans* [online]. Available from: www.vr.se/

Theodosius, C., 2008. *Emotional labour in health care: the unmanaged heart of nursing*. London: Routledge.

Wettergren, Å., 2013. *Emotionssociologi* [The sociology of emotions]. Malmö: Gleerups.

Wharton, A.S., 1999. The psychosocial consequences of emotional labor. *The Annals of the American Academy of Political and Social Science*, 561 (1), 158–176.

Wharton, A.S., 2009. The sociology of emotional labor. *Annual Review of Sociology*, 147–165.

Wibeck, V., 2000. *Fokusgrupper. Om fokuserade intervjuer som undersökningsmetod* [Focus groups. About focused interviews as survey method]. Lund: Stundentlitteratur.

Zammuner, V.L., Lotto, L., and Galli, C., 2003. Regulation of emotions in the helping professions: nature, antecedents and consequences. *Australian e-Journal for the Advancement of Mental Health*, 2 (1), 1–13.

Zapf, D., 2002. Emotion work and psychological well-being. *Human Resource Management Review*, 12 (2), 237–268.

Zapf, D., *et al.*, 1999. Emotion work as a source of stress: the concept and development of an instrument. *European Journal of Work and Organizational Psychology*, 8 (3), 371–400.

Zoghbi-Manrique-de-Lara, P., 2012. Reconsidering the boundaries of the cyberloafing activity: the case of a university. *Behaviour & Information Technology*, 31 (5), 469–479.

# Frontstage and backstage emotion management in civil resistance

Majken Jul Sørensen and Andrew Rigby

**ABSTRACT**

Civil resistance requires significant forms of emotion management by activists. In this paper, we distinguish between the different foci of emotion management carried out frontstage and backstage – the frontstage focus is typically oriented to influencing the emotions of onlookers, opponents and other targets, the backstage focus is typically concerned with managing the emotions of the activists themselves in preparation for their frontstage performances. Of course, in any particular resistance activity the two dimensions of emotion management interact more or less continuously. Activists need to continually engage in impression-management to ensure they are maintaining their display of the appropriate emotions intended to evoke the desired emotional response in the targets of their performance.

## 1. Introduction

On 1 December 1955, Rosa Parks ignored the instructions from the driver of a public bus in Montgomery Alabama and refused to relinquish her seat to a white passenger. This act of defiance, and the subsequent Montgomery Bus Boycott became global symbols of the US civil rights movement. One of the key factors that enabled Parks to act as the catalyst for the launching of the bus boycott campaign was the manner in which she presented herself as a respectable private citizen who had simply had her fill of submitting to the racial segregation practices of the southern states of the USA. In truth she was a committed nonviolent activist who had just completed a programme at the Highlander Folk School in Tennessee in which nonviolent civil resistance had been one of the topics for discussion and study (Horton and Freire 1990, p. xxiv). Drawing on Erving Goffman's (1959) famous notion of frontstage–backstage and the presentation of self, we can say that in order for Parks to present herself frontstage on the bus, she rehearsed and prepared backstage with others in order to generate the desired emotional response from the people who heard about her action.

Parks became an international icon of civil resistance when she refused to move from her seat. Most definitions of civil or civilian resistance emphasise that it is a mode of challenging opponents (who are not averse to using violence) by civilians relying on the sustained use of methods that are predominantly nonviolent, unarmed or 'non-military' in nature, in pursuit of goals that are widely shared within the society (Semelin 1993, Roberts 2009, Schock 2013). The main focus of civil resistance studies has been the manner in which repressive regimes have been challenged, with a particular emphasis on the strategies and tactics adopted in order to undermine the 'pillars of support' upon which all regimes depend. Such studies have tended towards what might be characterised as a cognitive bias, in the sense that they focus on beliefs and assumptions of actors but neglect their emotions and moods, which remain 'seen but unnoticed' as background features (Goodwin and Pfaff 2001, p. 283).

There has been something of a surge in publications on civil resistance in recent years. (See for instance Ackerman and Kruegler 1994, Ackerman and DuVall 2000, Sharp 2005, Clark 2009, Carter 2012.) Much of this work draws on the original contribution of Gene Sharp who began publishing on nonviolent resistance in the 1950s and whose study, *The Politics of Nonviolent Action* (Sharp 1973) remains a keynote work in the field. More recently the work of Chenoweth and Stephan (2011) has documented that over the past century nonviolent forms of resistance to oppressive regimes have been more likely to succeed than violent forms of insurrection and armed struggle, a fact that they attributed primarily to the higher rates of popular participation possible in nonviolent struggles compared with violent ones.

Several important areas of civil resistance have been relatively under-researched, one of them is the emotional dynamic which is involved. In this article, we seek to address this gap by exploring the role emotions play in the different activities associated with civil resistance. In developing our analysis we shall draw upon what Ron Eyerman has termed performance theory, which 'gives central place to emotions as both actors and audiences must be moved if the performance is to be successful' (Eyerman 2005, p. 41). We start by reviewing the existing literature on social movements, civil resistance and emotions and placing it in the context of Goffman's theatre metaphor and the sociology of emotions. We then explore the divisions of labour with regard to emotion management – the frontstage activities that focus on influencing the emotions of others, and the backstage activities that tend to focus primarily on managing the emotions of the activists themselves. Although the terms frontstage and backstage might seem to indicate the two types of emotion management take place in different locations, in the lived experience of civil resistance the ideal-typical boundaries between frontstage and backstage can become permeable – as when police invade backstage spaces or when activists prioritise the control of their own emotions whilst enacting a contentious drama frontstage.

In order to illustrate the significance of the backstage–frontstage divisions of labour in emotion management, we draw on illustrative material from a range of examples of civil resistance and from the testimonies of civil resistance activists from different parts of the world who came together for an international symposium on 'Nonviolent movements and the barrier of fear' held at Coventry University, UK in April 2012.[1]

Too often, studies of protest and related confrontational actions focus on the frontstage performances with less attention paid to the backstage preparations. Therefore, in developing our framework, we have drawn on illustrative material from primary and secondary sources which have focused on the preparation and organisation of resistance rather than the confrontational performances themselves. In analysing the available material we adopted the standard grounded theory approach of iteration, repeatedly moving in and out of the data, reflecting on the insights thereby derived and refining our conceptual framework and working hypotheses accordingly.

## 2. Dramaturgy and emotions in social movements and civil resistance

Most sociological approaches to the study of emotions acknowledge that biology and physiology play an important role in how people feel and express emotions, but they nevertheless focus on the *social* aspect of feelings. In western societies, we often think of emotions in very individualistic terms. Emotions are experienced by individuals, but they are socially constructed and people can work on their feelings in order to change how they themselves as well as people around them feel (Turner and Stets 2005, Chapter 1, Fields *et al.* 2007, p. 156). Thus, we can also think of emotions as phenomena which can be socially constructed and de-constructed. Just as we learn through interaction with other people when it is appropriate to respond with fear and anger, together with others we can also learn new ways to respond emotionally to particular types of situations. However commonplace such observations might appear to sociologists of emotions, they are rarely brought under the analytical spotlight by everyday actors in the social world. Most people engaged in social interaction – including civil resistance – experience their feelings as 'natural' and seldom reflect on the fact that their emotions and the modes in which they are expressed are significantly influenced by cultural norms about what feelings are appropriate for particular types of situations (Jasper 1997, pp. 109–112, Fields *et al.* 2007, p. 156).

In sociological approaches to emotions Goffman's dramaturgical model has a central place. The metaphor of theatre that he developed in *The Presentation of Self in Everyday Life* (1959) was used to analyse social interaction in face-to-face situations in daily encounters. Extending this metaphor, Goffman introduced concepts such as performance, setting, on-stage, backstage, audience and script to understand the processes by which people made sense of the social situations. Analysing political conflicts in terms of drama and theatre is not unusual, and authors have developed the metaphor further (Martin 2013, Rigby 2014). Jenkins (2008) has pointed out that although Goffman rarely wrote explicitly about power, his observations can also contribute to insights beyond everyday life. Thus, we find his metaphors highly useful in when it comes to the power dynamics of face-to-face interaction in civil resistance.

Despite the growing interest in the emotional dimensions of social and political life, the field has remained relatively under-developed by comparison with other analytical frameworks for studying social movements and collective action (Jasper 2011).[2] Helena Flam was one of the first to explore the significance of emotions in collective action (Flam 1990), but James Jasper has been the most prominent author on the subject of emotions and social movements. His book *The Art of Moral Protest: Culture, Biography, and Creativity in Social Movements* (Jasper 1997) was an important work when it came to giving emotions the place they deserve in the study of protest. Critical of the structural approaches that had dominated the field of social movement research in the previous decades, he showed how emotions cannot be separated from the cognitive and moral elements which motivate people to become active and stay involved. Passion is central when people speak about their activism, and moral shocks are an important motivational factor for initial recruitment (Jasper 1997, pp. 103–108). Jasper also recognised the significance of emotions other than fear and anger as drivers of protest: the compassion for those who need help, the joy of being with like-minded people, and pride in one's group and identity (Jasper 1997, p. 114).

Jasper also co-edited *Passionate Politics: Emotions and Social Movements* together with Goodwin and Poletta (Goodwin *et al.* 2001b) where they explored the interaction between emotions and cognitive processes in the context of social movements. As they wrote at the time: 'Little cognitive processing is required to fear a lunging shadow, whereas quite a lot is needed before one fears a garbage dump or the policies of the World Trade Organization' (Goodwin *et al.* 2001a, p. 13).

Adding to the complexity of including emotions in the analysis of political movements is the heterogeneity of what we label as emotions. The short-term shock and alarm we can feel when a dog lunges at us differs considerably from the longer term and enduring emotions that we can feel when we think about our friends and family. Thus, writing about fear under the Pinochet dictatorship, the Chilean sociologist Manuel Antonio Garretón referred to two types of fear: the fear of the quite specific and identifiable threat – 'the dog that bites', and the generalised fear of the unknown – 'the darkened room' where something bad might be waiting for you (Garreton 1992, p. 14).

An additional challenge for those seeking to develop an understanding of the emotional dynamics of oppositional movements is the reluctance of some activists to acknowledge the importance of the emotions that drive them. In many cultures emotions are seen as contrary to rationality. Thus, in his study of an animal rights group in the USA Julian Groves examined the manner in which the movement embraced a scientific, philosophical outlook rather than one of compassion because such feelings were seen as unprofessional and 'overly-emotional'. As one of the women activists explained, 'We need to project a professional, well-educated, rational, non-emotional image in order to get our point across' (Groves 2001, p. 217).

## 3. Frontstage – aiming to influence the emotions of others

Applying Goffman's theatre metaphor of the distinction between backstage and frontstage when it comes to civil resistance, the most visible forms of civil resistance occur frontstage, such as Rosa Parks' refusal to vacate her seat on the bus. These are public performances carried out by activists who are generally seeking to present an emotional reframing of reality that can 'touch' and move target groups and publics. Often such activities involve some degree of confrontation with opponents, frequently with the aim of provoking particular feelings (anger, shame, indignation, anxiety, disgust) amongst onlookers and witnesses. For example, certain oppositional performances involving forms of confrontation with agents of the regime are intended to present the activists as the innocent victims of an unjust and repressive regime, the aim being thereby to cause feelings of moral outrage and distress amongst bystanders and others. As Ron Eyerman has pointed out:

> Social movement is a form of acting in public. Movements are political performances which involve representation in dramatic form, as they engage emotions inside and outside their bounds while attempting to communicate their message. Such performance is always public, as it requires an audience which is addressed. (Eyerman 2005, p. 43)

In presenting their political performances activists typically seek to embody and communicate a particular narrative that links the action to a broader and higher order of significance, and thereby amplify the emotional experience and its meaning for participants and audiences alike (Eyerman 2005, p. 46). As Joshua Ralston has commented, 'The best protests are those with deep symbolic resonance. They involve action that stirs the imagination and thereby exposes the incongruity and injustice of the present day' (Ralston 2013). Central to this process is the manner in which the public performances of protest encapsulate and communicate in dramatic fashion a particular narrative or 'morality play' that arouses appropriate emotional responses in the targets. A common narrative is that of the underdog going up against seemingly insurmountable odds – like David confronting Goliath, where the courageous and apparently weaker party challenges a seemingly more powerful opponent and, despite what appears to be a huge asymmetry in their weaponry, the creativity and the integrity of the challenger prevails (Ganz 2004).

One of the most famous instances of civil resistance was the campaign organised by Mohandas K. Gandhi against the British Salt Tax in India in 1930. The campaign was decisive in changing the relationship between Britain and India because it 'transformed the feeling in the country from one of pessimism to revolution' (Weber 1997, p. 538). The salt tax affected all Indians whatever their class, caste, religion or gender. As such the targeting of this particular tax was an inspirational means of involving large swathes of the population in the struggle and to dramatise the injustice of British colonial rule. The carefully prepared campaign began with the Salt March to the coast where Gandhi in an act of civil disobedience picked up salt from the sea and sparked a campaign where millions of Indians started to illegally produce salt.

Gandhi thought that it was possible to convert the British people when they saw how much the Indians were willing to suffer for their freedom. Before he broke the law, he wrote a long letter to Lord Irwin, the highest British official in India, explaining why he thought British rule was a curse and appealing to Lord Irwin's heart to grant India freedom (Letter to Lord Irwin, 2 March 1930, quoted in Gandhi 1971, vol. 43, pp. 2–8). The tone of Gandhi's letter was polite and friendly, an expression of Gandhi's refusal to hate and consider the British 'opponents' as 'enemies'. Irwin, who was a devout Christian, personally had respect and admiration for Gandhi (Weber 1997, p. 468), and Gandhi's plans created a severe dilemma for the British regarding how to treat his lawbreaking. Not arresting him would be interpreted as a sign of weakness and allow him to continue to lead the struggle, while an arrest would create severe unrest among the Indian masses.[3] In the end, Gandhi was arrested when he announced new plans for escalating the struggle which included a raid on the Dharasana saltworks.

Elite responses, such as Lord Irwin's, are essential in understanding the dynamics of civil resistance, but civil resisters also encounter opposition on the ground, in the form of state employees and others charged with halting the activities of the activists. In civil resistance the possibility of shifting the loyalty of those who are enforcing the status quo has been identified as a key element of success (Chenoweth and Stephan 2011). For this to happen it is important that soldiers and police do not fear for their own safety, which is why the emphasis on maintaining nonviolent discipline plays an important role in many movements. Soldiers and police officers who fear that angry demonstrators might attack them are less likely to defect or disobey orders to shoot and kill.

One way to undermine the loyalty of those charged with defending the status quo can be by reminding them of the links they share with the protestors. In West Papua, the nonviolent struggle for independence from Indonesia has embraced the value of West Papuan identity and its cultural symbols (MacLeod 2015). At the conference in Coventry, an activist from West Papua explained how cultural expressions reminding the police of their shared indigenous Papuan identity can be more powerful than political argumentation:

> It is very clear in West Papua that when we are demonstrating the opponent is the police and the military – sometimes some of them are our relatives. And the way to make them sympathise … if we talk about the political things it does not work because they are just doing their job and they get paid for their loyalty. The best thing we can do is sing songs about our identity, about our homeland, West Papua our motherland – and those people they are affected by this. You touch their emotions underneath the uniform. (Coventry 2012)

This 'touching the emotions beneath the uniform' can be attempted using different emotional resources. For example, in certain contexts the use of humour has created the opportunity for creative encounters with security forces. In her studies of humorous political stunts Sørensen has shown how they can be used to present alternative versions of dominant discourses by means of a variety of techniques that can transcend the usual logic of protest, with activists frequently reporting their impression that tensions with security officials had been defused and that the people wearing the uniforms had gained new insights and understandings (Sørensen 2016b). Moreover, in certain circumstances humour can 'disarm' authority-figures. Uniforms and other symbols of authority are only effective when people respect them. If their reaction is one of mirth, then the claims to authority are undermined.

As noted above, the maintenance of a nonviolent demeanour and discipline is deemed by many advocates of civil resistance to be crucial in any attempt to sway the emotions of immediate opponents and bystanders. It is seen as a core element of the morality play activists attempt to enact in order to illustrate the value and the integrity of their cause as contrasted with the violence and illegitimacy of their opponents and the defenders of the established order. An illustration of the complex dynamic that can take place in such encounters between activists, security personnel and third-party bystanders is the instance of the attempt to halt the operations of the Dharansana saltworks as part of the India freedom struggle. Despite the nonviolence of the protestors seeking to bring operations to a halt, the guards charged with repelling them continued to use all the violent means they deemed necessary in order to keep the plant operating. In other words, they would appear to have been unmoved by the suffering they inflicted on the activists, thereby calling into question the credibility of Gandhi's conviction that the way to touch the heart of the opponent was through a preparedness to suffer (Weber 1993). But, the brutal action of the guards was witnessed by onlookers, including an American journalist, Web Miller, who wrote a vivid piece describing the scenes he had witnessed. The British tried to cover up what had happened by preventing Miller from sending his text by cable, but it was subsequently published by 1350 newspapers around the world (Martin 2007).

Research on civil resistance has shown that so-called third parties can play an important role, but not explored the role of emotions. Through the concept of 'political jiu-jitsu', Sharp provided a metaphor to illustrate how powerful opponents can be thrown off-balance by nonviolent action when their brutality against activists catches the attention of third parties. Developing Sharp's analysis, Brian Martin has examined the ways in which the risk of 'backfire' can be minimised by perpetrators, whilst also identifying those processes whereby activists can enhance the likelihood of backfire occurring (Martin 2007). One of his examples was the case of the action at the Dharasana saltworks. Several of Martin's findings regarding backfire are relevant when it comes to attempts to manage other people's emotions frontstage. Thus, in the case of the action at the Dharansana saltworks, first of all the injustice has to be exposed. If no one knows that it has happened, they cannot react, which is why the British were so eager to prevent Miller's story from getting out. Secondly, when the information is communicated it is important that it is framed in such a manner as to evoke the kinds of emotional responses in the target audiences – disgust, shame, moral outrage – such that the recipients are moved to 'make an issue' of the reports which thereby become amplified as matters of public concern.

## 4. Backstage – the management of activists' emotions

To carry off the frontstage performances presented above requires not just the manipulation of emotion-evoking symbolism, but also a significant level of emotional self-management on the part of the activists. That is, they must control the public manifestation of their feelings in order to sustain the outward emotional display deemed necessary to evoke the desired emotional responses from their target groups (Goodwin and Pfaff 2001, p. 284). Such a level of emotion management requires training and nurturing (and practising) for it to be effective. As with any public performance rehearsals usually take place backstage – the sphere of civil resistance that does not usually involve direct confrontations with oppositional groups. We have identified three dimensions of the emotion management activities that typically take place 'behind the scenes'. (i) The creation of 'safe spaces'; (ii) The creation and reproduction of cultures of resistance; and (iii) The empowerment of potential constituencies of support through community organising.

### *4.1. Creating safe spaces*

Movement activists need safe spaces to which they can retreat in order to take a break from frontstage activities. These are places which are usually important for the personal well-being of the activists, but also places for bonding within the group and for addressing such emotions as fear and despondency. Safe spaces can be places where activists live together in community, but this is by no means necessary, as long as it is a physical place where people can come together 'off-stage'. In many struggles, such as East Germany in the late 1980s and the US civil rights movement, churches played a particularly important role as safe spaces or sanctuaries (Goodwin and Pfaff 2001). A similar function was performed by mosques during the first Palestinian intifada (Al Saafin 1996).

When psychologists have studied emotions, they have traditionally focused on how to overcome negative emotions that lead to depression, anxiety and aggression. It is only in recent years that positive emotions like joy, hope, amusement, inspiration and love have received the same degree of attention as psychologists have begun to study what it takes to enable people to flourish and thrive (Fredrickson 2011, Seligman 2011). In the study of social movements there was not the same bias towards studying negative emotions, but within movements themselves the same cannot be said. Barker, Martin and Zournazi have pointed out that while some activist groups have been very aware of the importance of the emotional well-being of activists, in many others people have been left to deal with emotions on their own. When emotions are viewed instrumentally as a mean to an end (*Any emotion which makes you a better activist is a good emotion!*) they are usually considered private matters (Barker *et al.* 2008, p. 425). In contrast, within certain movements the emotional health of members can be a key concern insofar as their well-being is considered to be an integral dimension of the prefiguration of the desired society (Barker *et al.* 2008). An obvious place to work on this type of emotion management in civil resistance is in the safe spaces.

For example, Israeli activists associated with an anti-militarist movement adopted the practice of occasional 'retreats' where activists could meet in a safe space. As one of their number explained:

> These safe spaces create containment and an environment for shared learning and have great importance in providing support and a climate for reflection and rejuvenation. They are also spaces where you can strategize and provide analysis. In addition, this is where you can come together and just see who survived. The physical meeting can give great comfort and strength so we are able to regroup and continue. … At first it was the creation of a space where women, such as myself, could learn about activism, feminist methodology, our role as women within Israeli society, and also learn from the examples of other strong activist movements like those in South Africa. Later we created safe spaces, for instance, for youth. Places where they can get together and explore new concepts, and learn together about anything starting from conscription or global economy or gender equality. These groups are really important because often young people are either not able or not allowed to explore their thoughts about these issues at home or at school, and look for other settings. (Coventry 2012)

This Israeli activist focused on safe spaces primarily as a place for cognitive-oriented reflection and learning, but safe spaces can also be places where stories that nurture hope can be shared. Marshall Ganz has emphasised the significance of stories as a source of inspiration and motivation from which important lessons can be learned. He quotes the twelfth century Jewish scholar Moses Maimonides who argued that 'hope is belief in the plausibility of the possible' as opposed to the 'necessity of the probable'. He continues:

> While it is always *probable* that Goliath will win, it is also true that sometimes David wins, a sense of the *possible* that we experience in our own lives as well. Hope emerges from this sense of possibility, freeing us from the shackles of probability. (Ganz 2016)

An illustration of this phenomenon – the generation of hope derived from the narratives of others – was provided by the Israeli peace activist quoted above as she reflected on her experiences at a symposium held in Coventry:

> I want to reflect on the power of the personal narratives of the speakers whom we heard yesterday. Each story shared what is possible, not just what may seem impossible, and this gave me many new insights and ideas.

### 4.2. Creating and sustaining cultures of resistance

The safe spaces are important for activists' emotional well-being, but they are also spaces within which cultures of resistance can be created and sustained. It is within such spaces that existing practices and cultural symbols can be explored and adapted so as to make them meaningful in the context of resistance. It is also within such spaces that new symbols and rituals of resistance can be created (Sørensen and Vinthagen 2012). The richness of such creative activity was evidenced by a Palestinian contributor to the Coventry symposium:

> To overcome fear you need a culture of resistance. In culture you have language, religion, customs and traditions, values and ideals – then we have the literature. Then we have the arts … and within these we have the popular folkloric arts – and this is where the culture of resistance is to be found. Dancing, folk-singing, design and embroidery – all that. You cannot shoot a song … All this cultural resistance is about rootedness – because they want to uproot us. (Coventry 2012)

Other cultural activities can fulfil a similar role of strengthening feelings of solidarity. Humour can be an important factor in creating and sustaining cultures of resistance. Having a good laugh together contributes to feelings of solidarity. In democratic contexts, activists express how playfulness and the possibility of expressing oneself in creative ways is life-affirming, and creates new energy which can counter burnout. In authoritarian regimes, such as in Serbia under the rule of Slobodan Milosevic in the late 1990s, activists viewed humour as a means of overcoming both fear and apathy (Sørensen 2016b, pp. 92–102).

Jasper has emphasised how rituals such as dance and songs can create a sense of belonging and reinforce loyalty between people engaged in contentious socio-political activities (Jasper 1997, Chapter 8).

One activity which is especially important within the safe spaces is organising mass meetings. When people are physically assembled together and share a focus of attention, they can experience a level of group solidarity that can generate such a level of 'emotional energy' that they become 'pumped up with enthusiasm and confidence' (Collins 2001, p. 28).

In the US civil rights movement music during the meetings played an important role, particularly in relation to the emotional management of fear and the sense of isolation that could be so debilitating. As Payne remarked, 'The music operated as a kind of litany against fear. Mass meetings offered a context in which the mystique of fear could be chipped away. … Much of the humour at mass meetings was an attack on fear' (Payne 2007, p. 262). Indeed, according to Payne, the emotional experience of participating in mass meetings and engaging in the singing and feeling the communal solidarity embodied and symbolised by the music could have a transformational impact on people. He records:

> Mixtures of the sacred and the profane, the mass meetings could be a very powerful social ritual. They attracted people to the movement and then helped them develop a sense of involvement and solidarity. By ritually acting out new definitions of their individual and collective selves, people helped make those selves become real. Informed and challenged by speakers, pumped up by the singing and the laughter and the sense of community, many of those who only meant to go once out of curiosity left that first meeting thinking they might come once more, just to see. (Payne 2007, p. 263)

When it comes to creating and sustaining cultures of resistance, the Brazilian landless worker's movement *Movimento dos Trabalhadores Sem Terra* (MST) provides an especially interesting example. It has been one of the largest social movements in Latin America and the struggle for land and dignity for impoverished landless workers has continued for over 30 years. Within MST, the practice of *Mistica* has played an important role in strengthening members' emotional identification with the movement. The term has been used in different ways and cannot easily be translated to English. One way it has been used is to refer to a specific type of performance in which members participate. John L. Hammond has described one such a performance that he witnessed:

> The meeting began with a mística. In the middle of the large room, performers pantomimed various ills of urban life: robbery, begging, a homeless couple with a baby (played by a real live baby). A crowd stormed the performance area and drove out the evils; they unfurled on the floor a very large MST flag (bright red, with a circle in the center showing a map of Brazil and a farm couple, the man holding a raised machete)-MSTv2. A young person recited a poem alluding to poverty in Brazil and hope in the midst of that poverty. Then all chanted 'This country is ours', and invited the audience to stand up and join them in marching around the flag in a circle. There was singing and poetry, but no dialogue; the enactment was carried out in silence. (Hammond 2014, p. 373)

Although the attitudes towards these performances are currently undergoing changes, especially among the younger members, they have been extremely important throughout the history of MST (Flynn 2013). They have been used for a variety of purposes – to commemorate those who died during the struggle for land but also as 'educational performances' identifying the causes of people's poverty, ignorance and social ills (Flynn 2013, p. 170). The *mistica* performances at internal meetings have a formal and an informal dimension. They are not scripted and have a spontaneous quality, but at the same time there are accepted guidelines as to how *mistica* should be performed and they are rehearsed beforehand (Issa 2007, p. 130).

With its roots in the tradition of liberation theology, the term *mistica* has also been applied in a broader sense to the symbols representing MST (the flags and apparel with the logo of MST) and to the worldview that underlies the movement (Flynn 2013, p. 173). Daniela Issa portrayed this dimension as '… the more abstract, emotional element, strengthened in collectivity, which can be described as the feeling of empowerment, love and solidarity that serves as a mobilizing force by inspiring self-sacrifice, humility, and courage' (Issa 2007, p. 125). From this description, it is clear how significant the practice has been in the reproduction of those emotions and sense of identity that have been vital to the life and strength of the movement. Thus, observers of the movement have reported members' affirmations that the performances and associated ritual helped them manage their emotions – cope with fear in the face of violent repression and overcome feelings of despair and hopelessness (Issa 2007, p. 129, Flynn 2013, pp. 174–178). In her study, Issa reported one informant who expressed this very clearly:

> Mística moves us, it's everything, dedication. We're not in the MST for a salary or promotion. As a militant, there's an increase in responsibility, not in salary, so it's the mística that moves us to become a militant. It moves us to cry, to joke around. The militant does not live without mística. It comes from within, your hope of a dream, of constructing … (Issa 2007, p. 130)

### 4.3. Community organising

In the literature on civil resistance most attention has been given to actions which are clearly frontstage dramas. However, much important work is also going on backstage in the form of community organising. Gandhi believed there should be two integral dimensions to any campaign to transform systems of oppression and injustice. There was the frontstage resistance, such as the Salt March, but there was also what he called the 'constructive programme'. The purpose of this programme was to create alternatives to the systems and practices within Indian society that needed change, such as untouchability and repression of women. Gandhi considered the constructive programme to be significant as a means of social reform and addressing social ills within Indian society, far more important than the confrontations with the British. He also considered involvement in the constructive programme as the context within which people might develop the capacity and the confidence to exercise control over their own lives. It was this 'inner freedom' that he considered to be a necessary precondition for national freedom or *swaraj*. Thirdly, he saw the constructive work within the villages as a prime means whereby people could develop the self-discipline and emotional control necessary for them to engage in nonviolent confrontational resistance without resorting to violence (Overy 1982, p. 110).[4]

# RESISTANCE AND EMOTIONS

One of Gandhi's ongoing concerns was the propensity to violence of those engaged in confrontational struggle that was intended to be nonviolent (Mantena 2012). Eventually he concluded that any attempt to launch a large-scale civil disobedience campaign would be doomed to deteriorate into violent confrontations unless the bulk of the participants had been trained and disciplined by their involvement in different forms of constructive action. For Gandhi civil resistance was a nonviolent alternative to armed struggle, and just as engagement in armed revolt required training, so it was with civil resistance – and the training ground for developing the discipline and commitment necessary for sustained large-scale civil resistance was the backstage sphere of constructive work. As Gandhi wrote in 1945, '… when Civil Disobedience is itself devised for the attainment of Independence, previous preparation is necessary … Civil Disobedience in terms of Independence without the cooperation of the millions by way of constructive effort is mere bravado and worse than useless' (Gandhi 1945, p. 35). Constructive work at village level also played another significant role as a 'safe space' for activists, a sanctuary where they could withdraw from the frontstage struggle in order to recuperate, recharge their batteries, avoid 'burn-out' (Chandra 1989, p. 510).

Community organising has also played an important role in other struggles. In his study of this tradition within the Southern US civil rights movement Charles Payne returned again and again to the manner in which the young activists from the Student Non-violent Coordinating Committee tapped into pre-existing community activist networks. According to Payne, what made this possible was the time spent by the young incomers and the local people getting to know each other and establishing a basic trust and mutual respect. He noted:

> The SNCC workers were seen as having the usual human failings, but the bottom line for many of the local people was that they also had virtues of courage, character, and commitment that more than compensated. … By demonstrating that they could live up to the values that the community respected, organizers legitimated themselves and their program. (Payne 2007, pp. 241–243)

As a consequence of the personal relationships created, awareness of the emotional attributes of the activists spread through the local community networks, a process Payne described taking place in Greenwood, Mississippi:

> The first factor in the transformation of Black Greenwood has to be the sheer courage and persistence of the young organisers, awakening a like response in some local residents, the more so as the organizers became deeply rooted into the Black community. The Sam Block the police roughed up in July 1962 was, in most eyes, at best a foolhardy young stranger. The Sam Block they arrested in February 1963 was someone who had patiently earned the respect and admiration of a great many people. (Payne 2007, pp. 175–176)

A South African anti-apartheid activist recalled how important community-empowerment was in the overall struggle:

> We learned a lot from the Philippines in the 1970's and the way they organised and drew on their example in terms of building up localised communities and genuinely empowering people at the local level so they could take control of their communities. And that was phenomenal in terms of prefiguring – prefiguring the society to come. People dealing with problems, actually taking control at that level of their life (like problems with sewerage) which I think was an amazing aspect of that struggle, it was not all about confrontation and violence. It was creating spaces within which people could exercise control of aspects of ordinary day to day life. (Coventry 2012)

These different examples show the integrated relationship between community organising and emotions. Through involvement in backstage activities which appear mundane but are essential for survival and fulfilment of basic needs, activists can reinforce their commitment and build trust and loyalty with the wider community they are seeking to empower and mobilise.

## 5. Transcending backstage and frontstage

Above we have presented an ideal-typical distinction between frontstage and backstage as they relate to emotion management in civil resistance. However, the division lines can be blurred and the backstage/frontstage dichotomy collapses. This happens when the safe spaces backstage become frontstage, and on those occasions when activists are required to focus on their own emotion management in public.

### 5.1. Invasions of the backstage

There are occasions when the backstage becomes the frontstage – such as when what was considered a safe space backstage is 'invaded'. This happens for instance when the police enter places where the activists are meeting and preparing their frontstage performances. When such an intrusion occurs, the backstage becomes frontstage. An example of such an occurrence happened in 1958 when civil rights activist Jamila Jones went to the Highlander Folk School for nonviolent activist training. Whilst she was there it was raided by the police, who shut off all the lights in the building. She found the strength to sing out into the darkness, adding a new verse, 'We are not afraid', to the anthem 'We Shall Overcome'. She recalled later:

> And we got louder and louder with singing that verse, until one of the policemen came and he said to me, 'If you have to sing', and he was actually shaking, 'do you have to sing so loud?' And I could not believe it. Here these people had all the guns, the billy clubs, the power, we thought. And he was asking me, with a shake, if I would not sing so loud. And it was that time that I really understood the power of our music. (Civil Rights History Project n.d)

A similar story from the civil rights movement is included in the book *Passionate Politics*:

> [During] a freedom meeting in a rural church near Albany [Georgia] the sheriff and his deputies suddenly crashed into the church, and the people were struck with fear. The sheriff strutted around the church and made his point clear: 'We don't wanna hear no talk 'bout registerin' to vote in this county ...' But while he was speaking, the congregation began to hum 'We'll Never Turn Back' softly. As the sheriff moved to the rear of the church and shouted, 'There won't be no Freedom Riders round here...' the congregation commenced to sing, still softly. Then the singing became stronger and louder and some sister began to moan till you could hardly hear the sheriff over the singing and moaning. The sheriff did not know what to do. He seemed to be afraid to tell the people to shut up. Finally, he and his men just turned their backs and stomped out. Those beautiful people sang the sheriff right out of their church! That was some powerful music. (Young 1996, p. 183, quoted in Goodwin and Pfaff 2001, pp. 291–292)

In both these cases, the activists responded to the threat posed by the invasion of their backstage space with displays of emotional defiance sufficiently powerful to frustrate the attempts by their opponents to intimidate them into submission. Of course there are many possible reasons why the activists were able to summon up the courage and resolve to face up to the intruders, but perhaps one particularly significant factor is that in both cases the

## RESISTANCE AND EMOTIONS

police invaded what the activists considered to be 'their space', and as such they reacted with the resources they had to hand, the power of song that communicated their determination not to submit to such attempts at intimidation.

### 5.2. Permeability between front- and backstage

Another blurring between frontstage and backstage takes place every time activists are performing their action frontstage, but where their own emotion management still takes a great deal of attention.

A South African activist recalled the fear she and other women felt as they led a funeral procession for one of the many victims of police violence during the height of the struggle in the townships against the apartheid regime. They had decided that the women should lead the procession in the hopes that this would minimise the danger of violent confrontations between the township youths and the state security forces. They found that singing together helped manage the fear they all felt:

> I think what enabled women to overcome their fear in that situation was singing. I don't need to explain how that worked in South Africa as a means of overcoming fear. And there was a strong sense of joy which enabled people to overcome their fear about immediate police action. (Coventry 2012)

An activist from Zimbabwe also shared her story about how dancing helped overcome their fear during protest marches directed at the Mugabe regime:

> When we started the demonstrations I used to get extremely irritated for the first couple of years because people were always dancing on the demonstrations ... I could take the singing but not the dancing. Let's be serious here ... So whenever they danced I would watch them closely, and then I realised that in dancing – for that moment in the demonstration, the person feels complete and has that freedom to enjoy. They don't feel threatened, they are in solidarity with the others and so they can dance. (Coventry 2012)

In our analysis we have distinguished between the different foci of emotion management carried out frontstage and backstage – the frontstage focus, typically oriented to influencing the emotions of onlookers, opponents and other targets, the backstage focus, typically concerned with managing the emotions of the activists themselves in preparation for their frontstage performances. But in both the illustrations from southern Africa cited here the women resorted to singing and dancing as a means of managing their own emotions (primarily that of fear) whilst engaging in frontstage performances of contestation and protest. In other words, in the midst of a frontstage performance they were engaged in the backstage activity of managing their own emotions. This phenomenon should not surprise us inasmuch as any encounter requires ongoing impression-management in order to deal with any potential threats to the interaction process, and in this regard civil resistance is no different from normal everyday interaction.

## 6. Conclusion

Drawing on the seminal work of Erving Goffman, we adopted the ideal-type distinction between frontstage and backstage as a heuristic device that would enable us to explore the different types of emotion management taking place in the process of civil resistance. The model has proven useful as a way to identify the two ideal types of emotion management

# RESISTANCE AND EMOTIONS

taking place in the different spheres. Typical frontstage performances are aimed at evoking particular types of emotions in target audiences, opponents, bystanders and third parties. Backstage performances are typically focused on activists managing their own emotions in preparation for frontstage public performances. Of course, like Goffman, we have used the distinction between frontstage and backstage as a heuristic metaphor and not as a designation of separate physical spaces. Thus, whilst we have emphasised the different prime focus of emotion management in the two symbolic spheres, in any particular resistance activity the two dimensions of emotion management interact more or less continuously. Activists need to continually monitor their performances to ensure they are maintaining their display of the appropriate emotions that will evoke the desires emotional response in the intended targets of their performance. For experienced activists such performances can become 'second nature', seemingly requiring little in the way of conscious self-management of their emotions. As one experienced Palestinian activist responded when one of the authors asked him how he coped with fear in the face of Israeli occupation troops, 'Oh, you get used to it!'. But for the less experienced there is a felt need for ongoing management of their emotional display, and frequently they will turn to the more experienced for help in facing the challenge during the course of a frontstage performance. In such situations frontstage and backstage performances are taking place simultaneously within the same physical space.

Despite the inevitable counterexamples that can be identified whenever one proposes ideal-typical distinctions between phenomena, we believe that our framework possesses sufficient heuristic worth to justify further analysis of the emotional dimensions of civil resistance against injustice and oppression that we have begun to explore in this article. In particular we would suggest two fruitful areas of enquiry.

(1) Exploring the dynamic interaction between the different types of emotional self-management pursued by civil resisters whilst engaged in public performances of contestation and the emotional and cognitive responses of different target groups and audiences. In what circumstances can the projection of a non-threatening demeanour on the part of activists result in a 'change of heart' on the part of those targeted by the action? In the contemporary era when social and electronic media mean that international actors can be touched by protest actions taking place on the other side of the globe, what lessons can we learn regarding the significant ways cultural differences can impact on the efficacy of different types of emotion management intended to touch the hearts (and minds) of different targets?

(2) Exploring the relationship between constructive forms of civil resistance and the emotional responses of target groups, including bystanders and third parties that constitute potential constituencies of support. There is anecdotal evidence that people are touched more by 'dramatic encounters' that have the power of simple morality tales in which good is challenged by evil than by the less dramatic (and photogenic) instances of constructing alternative institutions and ways of life that are intended – over time – to undermine the dominant order.

## Notes

1. The international symposium was held at Coventry University 10–13 April 2012. More than 40 academics, researchers and activists from over 20 countries participated. The discussions

and work-groups were held under 'Chatham House rules': participants were free to share the information, but not the identity or affiliation of the speaker. The proceedings were recorded and transcriptions made available to the participants. We have retained the anonymity of all speakers, and therefore see no ethical problems in using the quotes from the symposium. See Rai (2012).

2. The growing awareness of the socio-political significance of emotions is evidenced by the establishment of the new research programme on the history of emotions at the Max Planck Institute for Human Development in Berlin. See https://www.history-of-emotions.mpg.de/en (Accessed 28 September 2016).

3. 'Dilemma actions' are significant in nonviolent resistance when they create 'response challenges' for authorities. For an exploration of this dimension of civilian resistance see Sørensen and Martin (2014).

4. For a discussion of how Gandhi's ideas regarding the constructive programme relates to the field of resistance studies and studies of prefigurative politics, see Sørensen (2016a).

## Disclosure statement

No potential conflict of interest was reported by the authors.

## References

Ackerman, P. and DuVall, J., 2000. *A force more powerful: a century of nonviolent conflict.* New York: St. Martin's Press.

Ackerman, P. and Kruegler, C., 1994. *Strategic nonviolent conflict: the dynamics of people power in the twentieth century.* Westport, CT: Praeger.

Al Saafin, A., 1996. *Political communication under occupation: Palestinian techniques of socio-political mobilisation under the Israeli occupation.* Unpublished PhD thesis. University of Bradford.

Barker, C., Martin, B., and Zournazi, M., 2008. Emotional self-management for activists. *Reflective Practice*, 9 (4), 423–435.

Carter, A., 2012. *People power and political change: key issues and concepts.* Abingdon: Routledge.

Chandra, B., 1989. *India's struggle for independence 1857–1947.* Harmondsworth: Penguin.

Chenoweth, E. and Stephan, M.J., 2011. *Why civil resistance works: the strategic logic of nonviolent conflict.* New York: Columbia University Press.

Civil Rights History Project, n.d. Music in the civil rights movement [online]. Available from: https://www.loc.gov/collections/civil-rights-history-project/articles-and-essays/music-in-the-civil-rights-movement/ [Accessed 27 Oct 2016].

Clark, H., ed., 2009. *People power: unarmed resistance and global solidarity.* London: Pluto Press.

Collins, R., 2001. Social movements and the focus of emotional attention. *In*: J. Goodwin, J.M. Jasper, and F. Polletta, eds. *Passionate politics.* Chicago, IL: University of Chicago Press, 27–44.

# RESISTANCE AND EMOTIONS

Eyerman, R., 2005. How social movements move: emotions and social movements. *In*: H. Flam and D. King, eds. *Emotions and social movements*. London: Routledge, 41–56.

Fields, J., Copp, M., and Kleinman, S., 2007. Symbolic interactionism, inequality, and emotions. *In*: J.E. Stets and J.H. Turner, eds. *Handbook of the sociology of emotions*. New York: Springer, 155–178.

Flam, H., 1990. Emotional 'man': I. The emotional 'man' and the problem of collective action. *International Sociology*, 5 (1), 39–56.

Flynn, A., 2013. Mística, myself and I: beyond cultural politics in Brazil's landless workers' movement. *Critique of Anthropology*, 33, 168–192.

Fredrickson, B., 2011. *Positivity: groundbreaking research to release your inner optimist and thrive*. London: Oneworld.

Gandhi, M.K., 1945. *Constructive programme: its meaning and place*. Ahmedabad: Navajivan.

Gandhi, M.K., 1971. *Collected works of Mahatma Gandhi volume forty-three*. New Delhi: Publications Division, Ministry of Information and Broadcasting.

Ganz, M., 2004. Why David sometimes wins: strategic capacity in social movements. *In*: J. Goodwin and J. Jasper, eds. *Rethinking social movements: structure, meaning and emotion*. Lanham, MD: Rowman and Littlefield, 177–198.

Ganz, M., 2016. *Organizing: people, power & change notes* [online] Available from: http://projects.iq.harvard.edu/files/ganzorganizing/files/what_is_public_narrative.pdf [Accessed 10 Jan 2017].

Garreton, M.A., 1992. Fear in military regimes. *In*: J.E. Corradi, P.W. Fagen, and M.A. Garretón, eds. *Fear at the edge: state terror and resistance in Latin America*. Berkeley: University of California Press, 14.

Goffman, E., 1959. *The presentation of self in everyday life*. Garden City, NY: Doubleday.

Goodwin, J., Jasper, J.M., and Polletta, F., 2001a. Introduction: why emotions matter. *In*: J. Goodwin, J.M. Jasper, and F. Polletta, eds. *Passionate politics*. Chicago, IL: University of Chicago Press, 1–24.

Goodwin, J., Jasper, J.M., and Polletta, F., eds., 2001b. *Passionate politics: emotions and social movements*. Chicago, IL: University of Chicago Press.

Goodwin, J. and Pfaff, S., 2001. Emotion work in high-risk social movements: managing fear in the us and east german civil rights movements. *In*: J. Goodwin, J.M. Jasper, and F. Polletta, eds. *Passionate politics*. Chicago, IL: University of Chicago Press, 282–302.

Groves, J.M., 2001. Animal rights and the politics of emotion: folk constructions of emotion in the amimal rights movement. *In*: J. Goodwin, J.M. Jasper, and F. Polletta, eds. *Passionate politics*. Chicago, IL: University of Chicago Press, 212–230.

Hammond, J.L., 2014. Mística, meaning and popular education in the Brazilian landless workers movement. *Interface: A Journal for and about Social Movements*, 6 (1), 372–391.

Horton, M. and Freire, P., 1990. *We make the road by walking: conversations on education and social change*. Philadelphia, PA: Temple University Press.

Issa, D., 2007. Praxis of empowerment. *Latin American Perspectives*, 34, 124–138.

Jasper, J.M., 1997. *The art of moral protest*. Chicago, IL: University of Chicago Press.

Jasper, J.M., 2011. Emotions and social movements: twenty years of theory and research. *Annual Review of Sociology*, 37 (1), 285–303.

Jenkins, R., 2008. Erving Goffman: a major theorist of power? *Journal of Power*, 1 (2), 157–168.

MacLeod, J., 2015. *Merdeka and the morning star: civil resistance in West Papua*. St Lucia: University of Queensland Press.

Mantena, K., 2012. Another realism: the politics of Gandhian nonviolence. *American Political Science Review*, 106 (2), 455–470.

Martin, B., 2007. *Justice ignited: the dynamics of backfire*. Lanham, MD: Rowman & Littlefield.

Martin, D.D., 2013. The drama of dissent: police, protesters and political impressions management. *In*: C. Edgley, ed. *The drama of social life: a dramaturgical handbook*. Surrey: Routledge, 116–130.

Overy, B., 1982. *Gandhi as a political organiser: an analysis of local and national campaigns in India, 1915–1922*. Unpublished doctoral thesis. University of Bradford, UK.

Payne, C.M., 2007. *I've got the light of freedom: the organizing tradition and the Mississippi freedom struggle*. Berkeley: University of California Press.

Rai, M., 2012. Feel the fear and do it anyway. *Peace News*, July–August , Issue no. 2547-8. Available from: http://peacenews.info/node/6865/feel-fear-and-do-it-anyway [Accessed 10 Feb 2017].

Ralston, J., 2013. Prophetic protest: Palestinian settlement and the witness of Bab al-Shams. *Religion and Ethics*, 6 February.

Rigby, A., 2014. Sea-dogs for peace: an exploration of nonviolent maritime interventions for peace and justice. *Peace & Change*, 39 (2), 242–269.

Roberts, A., 2009. Introduction. *In*: A. Roberts and T. Garton Ash, eds. *Civil resistance and power politics: the experience of non-violent action from Gandhi to the present*. Oxford: Oxford University Press, 1–24.

Schock, K., 2013. The practice and study of civil resistance. *Journal of Peace Research*, 50 (3), 277–290.

Seligman, M.E.P., 2011. *Flourish: a visionary new understanding of happiness and well-being*. New York: Free Press.

Semelin, J., 1993. *Unarmed against Hitler: civilian resistance in Europe, 1939–1943*. Westport, CT: Praeger.

Sharp, G., 1973. *The politics of nonviolent action*. Boston, MA: P. Sargent.

Sharp, G., 2005. *Waging nonviolent struggle, 20th century practice and 21th century potential*. Boston, MA: Extending Horizon Books.

Sørensen, M.J., 2016a. Constructive resistance: conceptualising and mapping the terrain. *Journal of Resistance Studies*, 2 (1), 49–78.

Sørensen, M.J., 2016b. *Humour in political activism*. New York: Palgrave Macmillan.

Sørensen, M.J. and Martin, B., 2014. The dilemma action: analysis of an activist technique. *Peace and Change*, 39 (1), 73–100.

Sørensen, M.J. and Vinthagen, S., 2012. Nonviolent resistance and culture. *Peace & Change*, 37 (3), 444–470.

Turner, J.H. and Stets, J.E., 2005. *The sociology of emotions*. Cambridge, UK: Cambridge University Press.

Weber, T., 1993. "The marchers simply walked forward until struck down": nonviolent suffering and conversion. *Peace & Change*, 18 (3), 267–289.

Weber, T., 1997. *On the Salt March: the historiography of Gandhi's march to Dandi*. New Delhi: HarperCollins Publishers India.

# Campaigning for cooperatives as resistance to neoliberal capitalism

Kristin Wiksell ⑩

**ABSTRACT**

This article investigates the eventual performance of critical resistance to neoliberal capitalism in the discourse of a marketing campaign that promotes the organisational form of cooperatives. Through discourse analysis, this article shows that the performed resistance activity in the campaign discourse is non-critical resistance since the dominant discourse of neoliberal capitalism is reproduced. The analysis shows that affective and economic articulations are intertwined in resistance through the discursive promotion of cooperation. The article contributes to understandings of cooperation as potential resistance to neoliberal capitalism, and highlights the risk of resistance simultaneously reproducing the power of dominant discourses.

## 1. Introduction

Capitalism with a conscience. (Cooperatives for a better world 2016)[1]

This article investigates the eventual performance of critical resistance to neoliberal capitalism in the discourse of a marketing campaign that promotes the organisational form of cooperatives (co-ops). The analysis will show that affective and economic articulations are intertwined in the discursive promotion of cooperation as a means to resist neoliberal capitalism by creating an affective 'we' and constructing subjects differently. The overarching risk of performing resistance that simultaneously reproduces the power of dominant discourses is investigated through the theoretical concept of critical resistance (Hoy 2004). In doing this, the article contributes to research on resistance (cf. Scott 1985, Bayat 2000, Lilja and Vinthagen 2014, Odysseos *et al.* 2016), and fills a gap in the understandings of how a discursive promotion of cooperation can entail resistance to the dominance of neoliberal capitalist discourse.

The capitalist goal of profit accumulation has persisted as a dominating principle in the global economy in spite of the critique directed against it over the decades (Boltanski and Chiapello 1999/2007). Key characteristics of modern capitalism such as rationality, capital accounting, freedom of the market, wage-labour, competition, and commodification (Marx 1867/2013, Weber 1927/2007, Paulsen 2010), have become intertwined with a globalised neoliberalism that constitutes subjects as free, autonomous and self-interested Homo Economicus – asking *what's in it for me?* – through discourses of markets, entrepreneurship, rationality and self-confidence (Harvey 2005, Foucault 2008, Hamann 2009, Brown 2015, Peters 2016, Springer 2016b, Türken *et al.* 2016). The idea of neoliberalism, 'as the latest incarnation of capitalism, [...] is made flesh through the very power that we assign it through our discursive participation in its routines and rituals, and importantly, through the performances we enact' (Springer 2016b, p. 1). From a Foucauldian perspective on discourse (for example 1982, 2008), further developed by Butler (1993), neoliberal capitalism can be understood as a performatively discursive, materialising process of 'top-down and bottom-up (re)production through continually (re)articulated citational chains' (Springer 2010, p. 931). Different implementations of neoliberalisation are being performed through human activity (Springer 2016b), which means that there are possibilities to perform differently and challenge the dominance of neoliberal capitalism.

Boltanski and Chiapello (1999/2007) argue that for capitalism to be reproduced, it needs to be morally justified in a way that motivates people's engagement in capitalist practices. One example is how the semantic construction of social entrepreneurship 'neutralize the self-seeking aspects of entrepreneurialism' (Holborow 2015, p. 79) and pre-empts the critique that business is only about greed. Reber (2012), following Illouz (2007), points out that affective dimensions such as empathy and care for others legitimise capitalism – capitalism is justified as a homeostatic system, that when in balance, is most beneficial for all. The entanglement of economic reasons and affect in the discourse of neoliberal capitalism denotes that resistance against its dominance should take both aspects into account in order to entail effective emancipation. However, the domination of neoliberal capitalism has constituted certain challenges regarding the prospect of resistance (Hamann 2009). Since freedom and autonomy are part of a neoliberal discourse, subjects are, in a way, already produced as free to act, which implies that no particular freedom constraints motivate resistance. This sought freedom could therefore be the freedom that has already been produced by neoliberalism (Hoy 2004), which means that there is a continuous risk that resistance activities might be co-opted by the power of domination so that it supports rather than stifles that which is being resisted (Foucault 1977). Accordingly, for the cooperative movement to perform effective resistance to neoliberal capitalism, it has to resist rather than reinforce the productive power of the neoliberal, capitalist discourse itself, or in other words, avoid performatively reiterating it (Butler 1993). The present understanding of resistance that is not co-opted by oppressive forces is drawn from the concept of critical resistance, defined by Hoy (2004), as emancipatory resistance to domination (cf. Haugaard 2012).

The organisational form of co-ops has the potential to resist the dominance of neoliberal capitalism since the cooperative ideals of 'human solidarity, economic democracy and collective endeavour [...] challenge neoliberalism directly' (Satgar 2007, p. 73). Co-ops are employee-governed, member-owned organisations that emphasise social values and member benefits rather than profit maximisation. Worker co-ops include shared ownership and control where labour rents capital rather than the other way around, and the decision-making principle is often 'one member, one vote' (Spear 2004). General values of self-help, self-responsibility, democracy, equality, equity, and solidarity guide co-ops around the globe, which were adopted in 1995 by the International Co-operative Alliance (ICA 2016c), originated from the first modern co-op in Rochdale, England in 1844. Furthermore, ICA (2016c) outlines seven organisational principles that should guide co-ops, such as voluntary and open membership, cooperation among co-ops, and concern for community. These values and principles come from a social rather than economic-rational sphere, compared with neoliberal self-interest and the capitalist goal of profit accumulation, thus offering a potential to resist neoliberal capitalist discourse through the promotion of cooperation. In Springer's words, 'our community, our cooperation, and our care for one another are all loathsome to neoliberalism' (2016a, p. 289). However, the introductory quote 'Capitalism with a conscience', from a marketing campaign aimed at the promotion of co-ops, indicates that the campaign promotes a form of social change that transforms rather than obstructs neoliberal capitalism.

This article aims to explore the eventual performance of critical resistance to the dominant discourse of neoliberal capitalism in the discursive promotion of cooperation. Specifically, the article investigates how the cooperative alternative is being constructed through discursive articulations of affect and economic-rational reasoning in relation to neoliberal capitalist discourse. Through discourse analysis of the marketing campaign 'Building a better world now', which was initiated in 2015 by ICA (2016a) to promote the cooperative identity, this article shows that the performed resistance activity in the marketing campaign should be understood as non-critical resistance since the dominant discourse of neoliberal capitalism is being reproduced throughout the campaign. The article contributes to research on cooperation as resistance, by showing how cooperation is constructed and promoted through discursive articulations of affect and economic reasons that challenge and reproduce neoliberal capitalist discourses. In this way, the article emphasises the importance of studying the critical aspects of resistance and including affect in the analysis of discursive resistance to neoliberal capitalism.

## 2. Materials and methods

The present study consists of a discourse analysis of the construction of co-ops in relation to neoliberal capitalism in the global marketing campaign 'Building a better world now', which was initiated on 11 November 2015 by ICA (2016a). ICA launched the campaign with the explicit aim of promoting the cooperative identity and increase the global influence of the cooperative sector. The campaign, which is linked to ICA (2016b) main website, entails marketing material published online on the campaign's internet website (buildingabetterworldnow.coop (ICA 2016a), presently cooperativesforabetterworld.coop (Cooperatives for a Better World 2017)). The campaign, initially piloted in four countries across the globe, is intended to be customisable – engaged co-operators can help spread the message in their communities – and targets people with or without previous engagement in co-ops. The analysed material was collected in the summer of 2016 and consists of publicly available PowerPoint presentations.[2] The first (1), most extensive presentation details the motivation plan for the campaign, intended to promote engagement in the campaign. The second (2) presentation focuses on change through the outlining of an 'action plan' for spreading the cooperative movement. The third (3) presentation consists of just one vertical lengthy slide that describes the plan and possible impact of the enhancement of increased scope of the campaign. The fourth (4) presentation concerns 'the cooperative identity' and entails statements about who (we as) co-ops are, collectively and uniquely. All presentations have a uniform graphic design and are mostly text-based. Some pictures are included, for example one showing a clock, as are a few authentic photographs: one example depicts hands holding pencils around a table, but none include faces.

The methodology, inspired by the Discourse Theory (DT) of Laclau and Mouffe (2008), is based on the assumption that the radical contingency of discourse makes attempts to discursively fix political meaning. Dominant discourses of seemingly fixed structures that exclude other meanings can be challenged (Torfing 1999). The analysed marketing campaign is thus understood as a social arena for possible critical resistance to the dominance of neoliberal capitalism through attempts to shape meaning differently. The present study follows the interpretation of DT's practical applicability by Winther Jørgensen and Phillips (2000), specifically, on how discursive structures are formed through meaning-shaping articulations that relate signs to each other. The analysis consists of the structuring and deconstruction of the different logic of the collected material through the search for the operational concepts *signs* and *nodal points,* and how they are situated in relation to each other. *Signs* are the building parts of the discourse, the dot-points in the web of meaningful differences that constitute a discursive structure. A sign is essentially without content but creates meaning in an articulation when it is placed in a structure of similarity and difference. Signs can entail certain functions in different discursive formations, *nodal points* are one example. Nodal points are privileged signs that function as a kind of centre of a discourse so that other signs then receive meaning in relation to these. The establishment of nodal points is the result of articulatory practices that shape meaning (Torfing 1999, Winther Jørgensen and Phillips 2000). In practice, the discourse analysis was conducted by coding central recurring signs and then investigating how those privileged signs are combined with other signs that give them meaning. These first steps led to the reconstruction of the relatedness between privileged signs and nodal points in an attempt to recreate and analyse the meaning-shaping articulations of the text. The focus is on whether and how co-ops are being articulated – particularly through articulations of affect and economic-rational reason, in a way that challenge or reproduce neoliberal capitalist discourse in the search for possible critical resistance within the campaign discourse.

## 3. Previous research on cooperatives as resistance

Research on co-ops has not focused on resistance to any large extent, and research on resistance has scarcely dealt with the empirical case of co-ops, but there are some exceptions. Satgar (2007) writes that co-ops stand apart from the relations of production that push capitalism. By representing an alternative to individual gain and primitive accumulation affiliated with neoliberal capitalism, the cooperative ideals of 'human solidarity, economic democracy and collective endeavour […] challenge neoliberalism directly' (Satgar 2007, p. 73). Puusa *et al.* (2013) also indicate that the cooperative ideals offer resistance, based on a study of economics students' descriptive accounts of what co-ops are. They show that co-ops are largely constructed through critical comparison with other types of businesses, by emphasising social rather than economic values, but reflect a dual nature. Co-ops should still be profitable in order to last, and the humanistic, cooperative values might be undermined if profit and growth becomes increasingly important (Puusa *et al.* 2013). Larger co-ops risk becoming similar to hierarchically governed organisations (Spear 2004). Even if cooperative ideals contrast with neoliberal capitalism, this stresses that co-ops do not necessarily entail resistance to neoliberal capitalism in practice.

Cooperation as resistance to neoliberal capitalism can be understood through the concept of 'self-governmental resistance' (Pahnke 2015), referring to the oppositional performance of social movements as institutionalisation of resistance by building a new order. Pahnke (2015) shows how self-governing agricultural production in the form of co-ops is a productive kind of resistance that takes control of policy implementation and design, challenging both state power and neoliberal discourse. However, such institutionalisation creates rules and procedures that both enable and constrain the resistance activity into a certain structure with less flexibility to counter different attempts of dominance. Self-governance also entails entrepreneurship, included in neoliberal discourse (Holborow 2015, Türken *et al.* 2016), which indicates that resistance to neoliberal capitalism through cooperation is feeble in some areas but might reproduce it in others.

Governmental regulations and policies as well as neoliberal capitalist discourse can entail aggravating circumstances for co-ops regarding both organisation principles and how subjects act and think (Evans 2007). Satgar writes that there are neoliberal attempts to restrain the resistance potential of co-ops by 'appropriating cooperatives into the globally competitive market, commodifying their ownership structure, reducing the developmental role for strategic state support and introducing typical managerial prerogatives', which 'closes off the possibilities for an alternative logic of accumulation based on human needs' (2007, p. 70). Hierarchical ideals in the surrounding society can also be challenging for democracy in co-ops – lack of knowledge about how to practise democracy may bring forth hierarchies within co-ops, since members might be more familiar with such order-structures (Varman and Chakrabarti 2004). Varman and Chakrabarti (2004) suggest education in democracy within co-ops in order to enhance members' 'democratic consciousness', which is arguably an attempt to resist the productive power of neoliberal discourse through an alternative way of shaping cooperative individuals. The official adoption of cooperative values by ICA (2016c) represents another way in which the movement responds to the risk of being co-opted by neoliberal capitalism, and Satgar (2007) suggests the creation of a strong regional, national and global alliance between the cooperative and labour movements that demands exception from the implementation of capitalist principles. However, other aspects of neoliberal capitalism might simultaneously be reproduced. The cooperative movement thus faces a challenge to advance from the shallow protection of co-ops' ideology against global neoliberalisation into a powerful counter-hegemonic struggle that is not merely defensive (Evans 2007).

The feebleness of co-ops as resistance is emphasised by Whyman (2012) who shows a historical, close association between cooperation and mainstream economics, despite the widespread understanding that neoclassical economists ignore co-ops in economic theory (Whyman 2012). That co-ops are not something completely different but instead included in mainstream economic theory might be an argument against the resistance potential of cooperation. White and Williams (2012) touch upon this last notion in arguing that non-capitalist practices such as cooperation and reciprocity are in fact embedded confidently in the present, but to focus on and construct cooperation as a presently occurring and viable alternative can be a way to perform resistance in itself, that is, by discursively reiterating articulations of desired futures instead of reproducing the idea of undesired neoliberal capitalism (Butler 1993, Springer 2016b). Similarly, by performing differently from the reiterated values of neoliberal capitalism in everyday life as a form of 'constructive resistance' (Sørensen 2016), neoliberal capitalism can be challenged without overt protest

(Springer 2016a). The construction of co-ops as such everyday resistance can be described through the notion of anarchy, understood as mutual aid and cooperation through voluntary association (Springer 2016a). Anarchy offers a way to oppose neoliberal capitalism in practice by performing joint, embodied community control without hierarchical authority (Rothschild and Whitt 1986, Springer 2016a, White and Williams 2016). The potential to perform resistance against neoliberal capitalism through a 'prefigurative politics' of anarchist cooperation is strongly emphasised by Springer, in a paper with the significant title 'Fuck neoliberalism':

> We can start living into other possible worlds through a renewed commitment to the practices of mutual aid, fellowship, reciprocity, and non-hierarchical forms of organization that reconvene democracy in its etymological sense of *power* to the *people*. (Springer 2016a, p. 289, emphasis in original)

Previous research on co-ops and resistance brings forth the conclusion that the cooperative movement can offer resistance against neoliberal capitalism in some respects, for example through the cooperative ideals (Satgar 2007) and anarchist mutual aid (Springer 2016a), but faces challenges in performing resistance that is critical enough to escape co-optation by neoliberal capitalism. Research on such critical resistance in relation to co-ops is required, as well as research that takes a discursive–affective approach to the promotion of cooperation as potential resistance to neoliberal capitalism, which the present discourse analysis contributes to.

## 4. Critical resistance

Resistance has been conceptualised in different ways, but there is agreement that resistance refers to an action that relies on some kind of constraint and a possibility of opposing this 'something else' (Hollander and Einwohner 2004). In this article, the relation between constrain and opposition is understood through the concept of performativity, developed by Butler (1988, 1993). Discursive regimes and material structures have a history which functions as a 'constitutive constraint', by both enabling and impeding the becoming of subjects, and those subjects' performances. Although such constraint 'does not foreclose the possibility of agency, it does locate agency as a reiterative or rearticulatory practice, immanent to power' (Butler 1993, p. 15), with the consequence that historical and material structures are easily reproduced. According to this view, opposition can be described as a shift in the reiteration of norms that breaks away from the normative constraints of discourse and materiality, regardless of whether the 'shift' is intended or not. Resistance can thus be discursively and bodily performed by 'acting differently' (Scott 1985, Butler 1988, 1993, 2015, Glass and Rose-Redwood 2014). The potential opposition to neoliberal capitalism analysed in this article is the discursive articulation of the marketing campaign 'Building a better world now' (ICA 2016a). In order to investigate if resistance that escapes reiteration is being performed through the campaign, I turn to the notion of *critical resistance* defined by Hoy (2004), in particular his readings of Foucault on power and resistance.

According to Foucault, power is not only repressive domination in a top-bottom relationship, but power 'produces things, it induces pleasure, forms of knowledge, produces discourse' (1980, p. 119). Power does not belong to individual subjects, rather discourse has the power to produce subjects and the appropriate actions for certain subject positions. A central part of how power functions is the ability to make itself true through normalisation processes (Foucault 1977, p. 183). Subjects' disciplinary conformity to a norm incorporates disciplinary power in subjects' self-control, neutralises discourses, and hides the workings of power. Power functions more effectively the more normalised it is – subjects might not identify the possibility of resisting the prevailing order if power is hidden. What seems to be resistance might strengthen rather than subvert domination by hiding its spreading normalisation, which means that resistance is co-opted by the dominating power. Resistance in such cases since does not entail an effective threat. This is where critical resistance enters the picture (Hoy 2004, p. 83). By adding 'critical' to resistance, Hoy means to distinguish it from the type of resistance performed by domination in order to resist emancipatory efforts. Critical resistance is thus defined as *emancipatory resistance to domination* (Hoy 2004, p. 2). Reactionary resistance performed without critique may lack the emancipatory potential of social change and maintain the status quo, since 'utopian imaginings of freedom may not be aware of the extent to which they presuppose the patterns of oppression that they are resisting' (2004, p. 3). Resistance relates to social constraints understood in the structure that produces the constraints, which means that resistance is meaningful only where these constraints are practised and may run the risk of preserving them. Hoy draws upon Nietzsche (1959 cited Hoy 2004, p. 1) who argues that it is constraints of freedom in a social structure that drive the motivation for resistance, but the conscious understanding of freedom might conceal deeper motivations, such as a self-denial of not being free or powerful enough to create own values. This is why neoliberal discourse, in producing subjects as free, autonomous individuals, is especially challenging for the potential of critical resistance – the sought freedom might be the type of freedom that has already been produced by neoliberalism. For resistance to be critical with regard to this risk, it should take the full contingency of social reality into account. No truth is true forever and neither should resistance insist on it being so – that might reproduce prevailing power relations.

Critical resistance with the potential to effectively change the prevailing order questions both domination and the oppressed subject positions. One way to perform critical resistance, according to Hoy's (2004, p. 84) interpretation of Foucault (1997), is to co-opt the domination's own strategies of co-optation; i.e. to use the power's own mechanisms in order to undermine and subvert domination. For example, if science and scientific arguments are used by domination to resist emancipatory effort, critical resistance can be performed by doing the same but differently, and produce scientific results that strengthen its own case. 'Reverse discourse' is another example of such overt resistance, i.e. to use the dominating discourse in a new context and ascribing new meaning to it (Foucault 1988 cited in Hoy 2004, p. 86). The process of desubjectification or desubjugation is also a way to perform critical resistance, related to freedom and the possibility to act differently. Since the power of discourses produces subjects and fixes their positions, desubjectification refers to the questioning of subjects' own understanding of themselves. Desubjectification is the resistance of the discursive production of who people are, of their constructed social identities (Hoy 2004, p. 87).

In the case of the dominance of neoliberal capitalism, critical resistance can be to avoid reproducing discourses of entrepreneurship and rationality as well as the construction of subjects as calculating, self-interested Homo Economicus. Cohen (2004) uses the concept 'politics of deviance' to refer to a way of life that cannot be explained, understood, or valued through the dominating discourse, unable to receive accountability within the logic of, for example, neoliberal discourse. To avoid being explicable according to the values of the dominant discourse is thus a form of critical resistance (Hoy 2004, Cacho 2012). In conclusion, critical resistance concerns emancipatory resistance to domination that resists being co-opted by the power of domination and resists the power's productive force of subjectification, without reproducing the dominant discourses of power. The significance of analysing resistance activities from a perspective of critical resistance is given by the overarching risk that resistance maintains the status quo of the social context in which it is being performed. The critical resistance approach to the analysis of the campaign promoting cooperation is complemented with an acknowledgement of the intertwinement of reason and affect in justificatory discourses – it holds for neoliberal capitalism, and is therefore important to take into account when analysing resistance to the same.

## 5. Discursive articulations of affect

Boltanski and Chiapello (1999/2007) argue that capitalism needs to be morally justified in order to be reproduced by acting subjects. Emotional justifications of neoliberal capitalism have been brought to light through the 'affective turn', which is increasingly emphasised in research in different areas (Clough and Halley 2007, McElhinny 2010, Sointu 2016). Reber (2012), following the works of Illouz (2007), arrives at an explanation of affect as the free-market episteme that increasingly overshadows rationality as justificatory logic in present globalised capitalism. Although reason has been articulated as the dominant organisational principle of capitalism, exemplified by the strict calculations of Fordism and Taylorism, the self-legitimising discourse of capitalism was originally 'based on the moral balance of homeostatic health and well-being' (Reber 2012, p. 77). Moral sentiments of empathy and sympathy are included in the notion of capitalism as a homeostatic flow that is most beneficial for all. Reber emphasises that affect-as-episteme can be understood as 'a tool of social domination as well as a tool of liberational contestation' (2012, p. 92), pointing to several cases where capitalism has been opposed through a 'protest discourse [that] features empathy as a guiding logic of the action and objectives' (2012, p. 90). The entanglement of reason and affect in the discourse of capitalism points to the importance of studying critical resistance against neoliberal capitalism by taking both aspects into account.

The discursive aspects of affect induce a perspective on feelings as textual and social affect, existing in the encounters between subjects and in relation to signs (Ahmed 2004b, 2014, Richard and Rudnyckyj 2009, McElhinny 2010). A view on affect as movement between subjects and signs can contribute to an understanding of how the discursive articulations in the present campaign discourse might affectively appeal to the connecting of people both to each other and to certain textual representations. Ahmed (2004a) outlines a view where 'movement between signs converts into affect' (Ahmed 2004a, p. 120). Affect circulates between bodies and signs through relationships of difference and adherence, which either bind or separate subjects and objects depending on how words are articulated. 'Emotions' in such affective economies accumulate over time, and 'work by sticking figures together (adherence), a sticking that creates the very effect of a collective' (Ahmed 2004a, p. 119). Affect surfaces specific individuals by moving between them and forming boundaries that shape collectives and exclude others by, for example, continuously constructing a discursive 'we' that appeal to certain subjects (Ahmed 2004b). Repeated formations of solidarity and care in descriptions of co-ops can accumulate love between appealed subjects and the sign 'cooperative', and repeated formations of a collective 'we' can entail the accumulation of affect between people of the cooperative movement. This collective is simultaneously differentiated from uninvolved outsiders. In the case of resisting neoliberal capitalism by promoting co-ops, those who are associated with neoliberal capitalism are possibly excluded from the collective 'we' of the cooperative movement, which can work as an engine for the accumulation of negative affect in relation to capitalism and its associated subjects.

When it comes to critical resistance, it is important to acknowledge the affective dimension. If affect is being circulated in the same way as the dominating discourse moves signs, it indicates that domination might be reproduced. Since subjects are in a way already produced as free in neoliberal discourse (Hamann 2009), it also implies an autonomy regarding affect. Affect circulating between subjects through their participation in a neoliberal capitalism system (Reber 2012) enables individuals to act emphatically but at a distance, without forming collectives. This implies that critical resistance to neoliberal capitalism that escapes the production of neoliberal subjects regarding affect ought to articulate adherence to a specific collective rather than affect through individual autonomy. By taking the discursive, circulating–accumulating aspects of affect into account in the analysis of potential resistance in the present marketing campaign, it can further understanding of the challenges faced by the discursive performance of critical resistance to neoliberal capitalism (D'Aoust 2014).

## 6. Analysis: campaigning for cooperatives

This article examines if and how an emancipatory, critical resistance (Hoy 2004) to the domination of neoliberal capitalism is being discursively performed in a global marketing campaign, 'Building a better world now' (ICA 2016a), aimed at spreading the cooperative identity. The analysis recreates the discursive structure of the campaign, thematised into three parts of how resistance to neoliberal capitalism is mainly being performed; i.e. through articulations (1) of co-ops as a loving 'we', (2) of co-ops as better than 'conventional corporations', and (3) of the goal to achieve economic growth. The final discussion concludes that the performed resistance of the campaign does not entail *critical* resistance.

### 6.1. Cooperatives as a loving 'we'

The sign 'cooperative' is the most recurrent one in the campaign's marketing material and emerges as an important key signifier. It might function as a nodal point, but comes forth as the sign that needs to be filled with meaning. Co-ops are, for instance, explicitly associated with long lists of adjectives in the fourth (4) PowerPoint presentation, which forms a description about what co-ops are. Several slides begin with the headline '*Who we are*' and ends with '*We are a cooperative*', and the content in between consists of descriptive articulations, such as the following:

> We are family.
>
> We offer value.
>
> We are people helping people.

The meaning of co-ops is articulated through similarities between the sign 'cooperative' and the positively displayed adjectives. Similar articulations are produced in other parts of the campaign. In the second PowerPoint presentation (2), several slides show an image of

## RESISTANCE AND EMOTIONS

clusters of words in different size, where the largest, centred sign 'cooperate' is surrounded by signs such as 'vision', 'community', 'help' and 'together'.

These examples reflect a general pattern in the campaign discourse – the representation of positive affect concerning the sign 'co-operative'. The continuous sticking together of the sign 'co-operative' with positive adjectives, such as 'value', create the impression of co-ops as positively valuable, which may – if circulated through repetition – contribute to the accumulation of positive affect in relation to co-ops as a representation (Ahmed 2004a). In this way, resistance is performed by representing an alternative to neoliberal capitalism as positive and attempting the circulation of loving affect regarding the figuration.

Furthermore, articulations of positive assemblies of people through signs such as 'family', 'together', and 'everybody' are being connected to co-ops in the examples. If such a narrative is circulated, it can generate the effect that a group, a 'we', is being formed. The wording 'We are people helping people' depicts the members of the 'we' as caring for others, which articulates the collective as a loving one. According to Ahmed (2004b), feelings can become generated by narratives, which in this case can accumulate feelings of collectiveness among the people who are appealed to by the articulated 'we'. It may bring them closer to each other and be interpreted as an affective appeal to love between the group members, and since the formation of a 'we' differentiates that collective from 'them' who are excluded, it may accumulate distant affect or potentially hate in relation to 'them' (Ahmed 2004b). This indicates that affect is involved in the performed resistance of the campaign through the representation of a positive collective, which might, on the one hand, motivate members of co-ops to feel more strongly for each other and enhance their wish to promote the movement and circulate positive affect in relation to it, while on the other hand, it might motivate non-members' to join the movement – i.e. if they do not feel excluded and further distanced by the strong articulation of a 'we'.

The representations of togetherness can further entail resistance through a shift in the reproduction of subjects (Butler 1993). The campaign discourse represents the 'we' as consisting of subjects that aid and support each other, acting collectively, and driven by social, emphatic values in a way that challenges the neoliberal discourse of autonomous and self-interested subjects. The narrative of caring affect can thus be understood as the production of a different kind of subjectification (Foucault 1982), however, it cannot be understood as critical resistance through desubjectification since the shift only entails some aspects. The cooperative subject is still produced as an entrepreneur that strives for business, although collectively and with social aims (see Holborow 2015 on social entrepreneurship). The following quotes from different parts in the fourth (4) presentation exemplifies how this is being articulated in the campaign:

Cooperatives working together and supporting other cooperatives creates more business.

Together we are strong!

The two quotes articulate that togetherness can contribute to aspects that are outlined as beneficial for co-ops (support, more business, strength). The non-co-operators are articulated as a threat that the cooperative movement can fight together, as indicated by the use of the sign 'strong'. The articulations of co-ops as a loving and caring collective that feels for others is here combined with economic-rational arguments of how to create business, which reproduces dominant values of a neoliberal capitalist discourse. This points to the conclusion that resistance, albeit non-critical, is being performed throughout the campaign.

The centrality of entrepreneurship and economic business is present in the campaign discourse in several ways as shown in the next section.

### *6.2. Cooperatives in relation to conventional corporations*

In the campaign discourse, the sign 'cooperative' is predominantly differentiated from 'conventional corporations' – the most common articulation of difference in the material. In the first (1) PowerPoint presentation are the signs 'corporation' and 'cooperative' differentiated in a comparative chart that lists what corporations and co-ops count in their internal economics, such as quarterly returns vis-à-vis sustainable returns. The meaning of the sign 'cooperative' is continuously being explained in relation to corporations, not the other way around, which is exemplified by the above-mentioned listing of descriptive adjectives concerning co-ops. One example from the third (3) PowerPoint presentation shows this relationship:

> Once a consumer understands a cooperative they are 78% more likely to choose a cooperative business over a conventional business.

The quote indicates that consumers in general are knowledgeable about conventional businesses, often articulated as corporations in the campaign. The association of corporations with the sign 'conventional' suggests that its meaning does not need further explanation. This makes 'corporation' function as a nodal point in the campaign discourse, and signs such as 'cooperative' receive meaning in relation to this nodal point. The centrality of 'conventional corporations' implies that the campaign discourse is affected by and possibly reproduces neoliberal capitalism. Lack of knowledge about cooperation is simultaneously articulated as the main obstacle for the cooperative movement and presented as an explanation for why co-ops are not more prevalent. Although the campaign states that co-ops are widespread in America (presentation one (1)), the prevalence is significantly lower when compared with corporations. The following examples from two slides in the first (1) presentation show how the articulated explanation also constructs co-ops as better than conventional corporations:

> When we asked people about cooperatives, we were surprised to find out how little they knew.

> More awareness increases the amount of customers choosing cooperatives.

Knowledge about cooperation is presented as low, and 'more awareness' is articulated as positive for the cooperative movement. The articulation insinuates that co-ops are better – if people understand how co-ops work, they are obviously positive about them. The low prevalence that might function as an argument against co-ops – why are they not more common if they are so good? – is discursively turned into an argument in favour of co-ops. Lack of knowledge is articulated as a problem that increased knowledge can solve, which legitimises the activity of the marketing campaign.

The nodal point 'corporation' is rarely associated with other descriptive signs in the material collected, but there are some articulations of similarity that produce a certain understanding of the sign; for example, the attachments to the signs 'stock value' and 'profit' in the comparative chart in the first (1) presentation, mentioned above. The meaning of 'conventional corporation' is also produced as equal to the present global economy, which is exemplified by a line in the first (1) PowerPoint presentation:

> The world we live in is dominated by the conventional corporation.

# RESISTANCE AND EMOTIONS

By articulating corporations as dominant in the world, the sign 'world' relates to the same meanings as 'corporation'. The current position of the world is in turn associated with economic inequality, which a text in the first (1) presentation exemplifies:

> 1% of the world's population holds over 50% of its wealth.

The world, and therefore also 'conventional corporations', is associated with statistics of global inequality. Corporations are articulated as causing economic inequalities in the world, and inequalities are produced as an effect of the dominance of conventional corporations. Since co-ops are differentiated from 'corporations', these articulations shape the meaning of both – co-ops are indirectly represented as offering the solution of equality. This is further strengthened by the association of co-ops with comparative adjectives such as 'better' and 'superior' throughout the campaign. One example is the name of the whole campaign, 'Building a better world now', which articulates the direction of the difference: co-ops are better than corporations. This indicates that resistance is performed through the identification of a problem, global inequalities, and the articulation of an idealised utopia of global equality. Co-ops and cooperative subjects are articulated as those that can create equality and the campaign discourse thereby articulates what kind of social change that is called for. Those who speak against cooperation are indirectly constituted as speaking in favour of inequality and individual, monetary greed, in contrast to empathy and care represented as cooperative ideals. There is no mention of the 'emotionality' of capitalist discourse and the justifying notion of being most beneficial for all (Reber 2012). The articulation of corporations and the global capitalist economy as undesirable can be understood as an attempt to 'stick' negative affect to 'corporations' and 'capitalism', which if repeated might accumulate feelings of hate to those representations (Ahmed 2004a).

Another example of the relationship between co-ops and corporations are the headlines in a set of slides in the first (1) PowerPoint presentation:

> What if the world's largest corporations were cooperatives?

> Understanding our current position is imperative in charting our future.

The headlines suggest a rethinking of the presently dominant economy towards a cooperative one. The content below consists of calculations of how much income the employees in global organisations like Apple and Walmart would receive if they were co-ops, in an attempt to reformulate what to do with the profits. The cooperative alternative is promoted by advocating distribution among the employees, instead of capital accumulation for more or less external owners. The resistance activity is thereby partly performed through criticism of economic actions (profit distribution and private ownership) of corporate organisations, and the cooperative model is promoted as an alternative way to act. The campaign thus produces both economic-rational and affective arguments as resistance to neoliberal capitalism. The campaign discourse produces subjects not only as emphatic and supportive, but also as economic calculators that adhere to arguments of (economic) benefits that are accountable according to neoliberal capitalism – the employees would take part of the profit and potentially earn more money if the above-mentioned global organisations were co-ops. This points to a reproduction of the neoliberal, capitalist discourse within the marketing campaign. The same notion concerns the continuous presentation of 'cooperative' as a 'business model' which articulates doing business as a way of organising action that holds for both co-ops and corporations. Neoliberal, capitalist discourse is not challenged in this respect; business and entrepreneurship are reproduced as central values.

In the articulated differentiation between corporations and co-ops, co-ops are associated with other values in some ways, but signs such as profit, income and business – commensurable with neoliberal capitalism – are associated with both corporations and co-ops. The performed resistance of the campaign is thereby accountable in a neoliberal discourse even if the primary goal of capital accumulation is circumvented, which indicates that the performed resistance is not critical (Hoy 2004). The campaign discourse cannot be understood as emancipatory resistance to the domination of neoliberal capitalism since its logic is simultaneously reproduced to some extent. The following section further points to this conclusion through the analysis of how the promoted change is articulated in the campaign discourse.

### 6.3. *Cooperatives aiming for economic growth*

The sign 'building', included in the campaign name 'Building a better world now', is one of the most frequent signs in the campaign discourse since the campaign title occurs in several PowerPoint slides. In slides where it is not used, other signs that refer to some form of transformative movement are prevalent, such as 'create', 'action', 'change', 'engage', 'increase', 'growth', etc. One example is the text from a slide in the first (1) presentation:

> Our Vision of 2020: Create a Movement.
>
> Our unified vision compels us to move forward and shift momentum.

The sign 'create' is here combined with 'move forward', which articulates the aim of the campaign – change from the present condition to something prospectively different. Signs of action and change are throughout the campaign associated with descriptions of motives and possible impacts; here the 'vision' is articulated as a sought future (a movement in 2020) that 'compels us' to act toward that vision. In other examples the present condition is outlined as a reason for action; for instance, the above-mentioned articulation of undesirable world inequality as caused by capitalism. The signs 'growth' and 'increase', frequently occurring in the campaign discourse, are associated with both economic increase and the number of cooperative businesses and people engaged in co-ops, and shape the kind of change that is called for. One example from the second (2) PowerPoint presentation shows how 'growth' is associated with organisational size and economic success:

> The cooperatives that exist today are already making a big impact on their communities. Helping these cooperatives grow and become more successful can shift the momentum of the world economy.

The sign 'growth' here is associated with existing co-ops and more success. Growth is thereby articulated as something positive, as a legitimate goal of the campaign and a means to achieving social change. The following wording from the second (2) presentation exemplifies the positive articulations of 'growth' and 'increase':

> Everybody Wins: Increased Exposure & Growth Benefits all Cooperatives.
>
> As our movement gains visibility and consumer understanding the potential for new cooperatives and larger existing cooperatives increases.

Positive words like 'wins' and 'benefits' are used together with 'growth' and 'increase', filling the latter signs as desirable. This coincides with neoliberal discourse, where the repeated use of words such as 'growth', 'wealth', and 'output' reinforces the way in which well-being for societies and individuals is being conceived, i.e. through economic market exchange (Massey 2013, Holborow 2015). Similarly, the neoliberal construction 'social entrepreneurship', that places social projects within the entrepreneurial idea, is resting on 'confidence in the ability of existing institutions and business mind-sets to actually deliver inclusiveness and empowerment' (Holborow 2015, p. 84). The articulations of action and change in the present campaign discourse are for example paralleled in the slogan of a recent neoliberal project of social entrepreneurship in Ireland: 'Think Big, Act Now, Change Ireland' (Holborow 2015, p. 80).

In the present campaign, the idealised (social) change and the aim of the resistance activity is articulated as a growing cooperative movement and enhanced cooperative sector in the economic sphere. It is implied in the example above that growth should be sought by 'everybody'. The formulation 'everybody wins' refers to all cooperative organisations, but the meaning can be extended to involve all people engaged in co-ops as well as those without previous engagement. To join the cooperative movement is articulated as an emphatic, loving alternative that is beneficial in both an affective and rational-economic sense. The articulation 'beneficial for everyone' is paralleled in the legitimation of neoliberal capitalism (Illouz 2007, Reber 2012). No-one is by definition excluded from the open, free market (but no specific subject is included either), but regarding cooperation, the enjoyment of benefits requires membership in co-ops. The 'everyone' is thus more restrictive in the campaign than in free-market legitimisations of neoliberal capitalism, and affect is being circulated through adherence to a specific collective, thus challenging the articulation of affect through individual autonomy in neoliberal capitalism. Whether the cooperative economy is aimed to encompass everyone in the global economy is not explicated in the campaign, but the campaign's call for growth indicates that more people are invited to join the movement.

The sought growth that is outlined in an economic sense is paralleled with the centrality of income throughout the campaign discourse. One example from a set of slides in the first (1) PowerPoint presentation that shows the widespread unawareness of co-ops presents income range as the only descriptor of personal identity:

'I have never heard of a co-operative before.'

Income $26,000–$50,000

The example indicates that money is a central value in the campaign discourse. Earning income is articulated as an important value, which is also reflected in the above-mentioned slides where corporations were rewritten as co-ops regarding profit distribution. Equality and democracy are thus connected to economic democracy and equality – articulations of inequality in ownership, income, and wealth are being related to the problematic, present global economy. Co-ops are articulated as a solution to economic injustices, which means that the value of money is explicated not only in the problem but also in the solution. This indicates that the marketing campaign reproduces a capitalist, neoliberal discourse where money is a privileged value that rational individuals consider when deciding how to act. However, a solitary goal of capitalist profit accumulation is challenged by the promotion of social benefits in the cooperative alternative. The emphasis on social values entails resistance, as the analysis above has shown, but the discourse in the collected material simultaneously reproduces neoliberal logic which stifles the critical, emancipatory effect.

## 7. Concluding discussion: campaigning for cooperatives as non-critical resistance

A neoliberal capitalism with discourses of rationality, entrepreneurship and autonomy that produces individuals as free Homo Economicus is challenging for the prospect of resistance and has persisted in dominating the global economy in spite of the critique directed against it (Boltanski and Chiapello 1999/2007, Hamann 2009). For the cooperative movement to perform effective resistance to neoliberal capitalism, it has to resist rather than reinforce the productive power of the neoliberal, capitalist discourse itself (Foucault 1977, Hoy 2004). The present analysis of the marketing campaign 'Building a better world now' (ICA 2016a) shows that resistance to the domination of neoliberal capitalism is performed in some respects – through articulations of co-ops as a loving 'we', through comparison with conventional corporations, and by the articulated aim for (economic) growth – but neoliberal, capitalist discourse is simultaneously reproduced. This section discusses the conclusion that the resistance activity of the campaign discourse is not to be understood as critical resistance in the way that is conceptualised by Hoy (2004); i.e. as emancipatory resistance to domination that resists being co-opted by the power of domination.

The campaign discourse performs resistance to neoliberal capitalism through continuous association of the sign 'cooperative' with positive adjectives, which may – if circulated through repetition – contribute to the accumulation of positive affect in relation to the representation of co-ops (Ahmed 2004a), and is combined with articulations that may generate negative affect regarding 'conventional corporations' by representing them as the cause of global inequalities. Articulations of the cooperative movement as a supportive collective that emphasises social values entail a narrative that may appeal to certain subjects and generate effects by associating them more closely and further circulate positive affect. Such an accumulation of affect might resist neoliberal capitalism by empowering an alternative to its dominance, but does not necessarily entail critical resistance (Hoy 2004). Although the campaign discourse produces a somewhat different subjectification (Foucault 1982), from the individual autonomy of self-interested Homo Economicus (Hamann 2009, Brown 2015) to the collective autonomy of supporting, caring co-operators, the idea of rational entrepreneurs that seek individual (economic) gain is being reproduced. Despite the collective member benefits can each co-operator ask, *what's in it for me?* The answer is outlined as participation in a loving community as well as monetary benefits – social and economic ideals are emphasised and co-ops offer both. The utilitarian argument of neoliberal capitalism as emphatic and most beneficial for most people (Boltanski and Chiapello 1999/2007, Illouz 2007, Reber 2012) is met with a similar narrative in the campaign discourse that promotes cooperation – it is not critically different.

Hoy (2004) outlines that critical resistance should entail emancipation from the power of productive discourses without being co-opted by the power of domination. The cooperative movement has the potential to strive for emancipation from neoliberal capitalism (Satgar 2007, Pahnke 2015); however, the cooperative alternative is described as a business model and economic values of profit and growth are continuously emphasised, which are aspects that are commensurable with neoliberal capitalism (Boltanski and Chiapello 1999/2007, Holborow 2015). Co-ops are articulated as another way of doing business and distributing profit through emphasis on equality and care for others, but the outlining of economic values as privileged does not significantly deviate from the sense-making of neoliberal capitalism. This indicates that the resistance activity in the campaign is co-opted by the power of dominating economic discourse and must therefore be understood as an uncritical form of resistance. The article's initial quote 'Capitalism with a conscience', from the campaign website (buildingabetterworldnow.coop, (ICA 2016a)) is a direct example of this. The sign 'capitalism' is articulated as compatible with a cooperative economy and the performed resistance does not explicitly deviate from a capitalist agenda. It is possible that the use of the word 'capitalism' together with the sign 'conscience' here could be understood as resistance through 'reverse discourse', by filling the sign with a different meaning (Hoy 2004), but since a neoliberal, capitalist discourse is present in the campaign – for example, by reproducing the value of economic gain – it is more probable that the quote reflects a normalisation of the dominant power of capitalism.

Resistance to neoliberal capitalism through the campaign discourse precludes certain assumptions about social reality. This can be understood as an example of the circumstance where resistance is related to social constraints that are understood in the structure that produces these constraints, and is therefore only meaningful in contexts where these constraints are practised (Hoy 2004, p. 2). The articulated resistance is concerned with work, income, entrepreneurship and business, aspects that are central for the characteristics of neoliberal capitalism as well. The campaign discourse concerns a change in performing business, and offers affective and economic arguments for why cooperation is a 'better' alternative. The campaign calls for collective, entrepreneurial business that aims for member benefits and social values on cooperative markets as resistance to neoliberal capitalism, associated with autonomous performances of entrepreneurial business that aims for profit accumulation on competitive markets. The social reality is assumed to be an economic one. The economic sphere is articulated as a societal context in which the pursuit for social ideals can be conducted (see Holborow 2015 on social entrepreneurship), indicating a continuous subjectification in the shape of Homo Economicus (Brown 2015, Peters 2016). Whether resistance to neoliberal capitalism is most effectively performed in the same context as domination is a possible case for future research – the present article indicates that critical resistance to the productive power of neoliberal, capitalist discourse is challenging.

It might be a resistance strategy to follow the logic of the dominant discourse in order to make the performance explicable according to its rules and values, but such a move should, in the present case, not be conceptualised as *critical* resistance. This campaign is not a politics of deviance (Cohen 2004), not a sidestepping of the dominant values of the discourse – rather, it is a way to construct co-ops as not so deviant after all, in accordance with Whyman's (2012) attempt to include co-ops in mainstream economic history. Instead of critical resistance to neoliberalism, for example by co-opting domination's own strategy to resist emancipatory efforts (Hoy 2004), this particular campaign reproduces, normalises and neutralises its logic and social practices. Since the core value of profit accumulation is challenged, discursive articulations of cooperation offer some potential for critical resistance, on condition that it manages to resist adaptation to neoliberal logic (Satgar 2007). The challenge for the performance of resistance to neoliberal capitalism is how the latter dominates not only the practices of organisations, but also how subjects are being disciplinarily produced as already free to act. Neoliberal logic transcends economic capitalism and there is a constant risk of reproducing it, which indicates that critical resistance to its domination should take several levels into account in order to be emancipatory enough. To conclude, resistance is performed through the campaign discourse, but it is an uncritical one.

This article shows, in line with previous research (e.g. Satgar 2007, Pahnke 2015), that co-ops offer a potential to perform resistance to neoliberal capitalism, but adds insight to the difficulties faced by the performance of critical resistance that does not simultaneously reproduce the power of dominant discourse (Hoy 2004). This article strengthens the understanding that co-ops are, to a large extent, constructed in comparison with and through criticism of other business models (Puusa *et al.* 2013), and that affect and economic-rational reasoning are intertwined in economic discourses (Illouz 2007, Reber 2012). Previous research on cooperation as resistance is, however, scarce and further research could shed light on the challenges and possibilities of resisting the values of neoliberal capitalism. The study presented in this article is not an exhaustive account of the discursive construction of co-ops as resistance, or of the cooperative movement's social practice of resistance to the domination of neoliberal capitalism. Rather, it is an argument for the potential of performing such resistance, and an acknowledgement of the challenges faced by emancipatory resistance to domination. Furthermore, the article shows how discursive articulations of affect can be a central element in the performance of resistance, and how resistance can be useful in understanding the intertwining of social and economic ideals in discourses. More research on this subject is hereby called for. Resistance Studies is a growing academic field and the possible contributions of turning the scientific gaze towards cooperation and neoliberal capitalism is demonstrated in this article.

## Notes

1. The quote, retrieved in June 2016, comes from a headline on the website buildingabetterworldnow.coop (ICA 2016a), now cooperativesforabetterworld.coop, managed by Cooperatives for a Better World (2017), initiated by the International Co-operative Alliance in 2015.
2. The campaign has grown since the materials analysed were collected. It presently (January 2017) consists of an extensive website with marketing materials such as videos and statistics, accessible from the internet domain cooperativesforabetterworld.coop (Cooperatives for a Better World 2017), previously buildingabetterworldnow.coop (ICA 2016a).

## Disclosure statement

No potential conflict of interest was reported by the author.

## ORCID

*Kristin Wiksell* http://orcid.org/0000-0002-7641-2744

## References

Ahmed, S., 2004a. Affective economies. *Social Text 79*, 22 (2), 117–139.

Ahmed, S., 2004b. Collective feelings. *Theory, Culture & Society*, 21 (2), 25–42.

Ahmed, S., 2014. *The cultural politics of emotion*. Edinburgh: Edinburgh University Press.

Bayat, A., 2000. From 'dangerous classes' to 'quiet rebels': politics of the urban subaltern in the Global South. *International Sociology*, 15 (3), 533–557.

Boltanski, L. and Chiapello, E., 1999/2007. *The new spirit of capitalism*. London: Verso.

Brown, W., 2015. *Undoing the demos: neoliberalism's stealth revolution*. New York: Zone Books.

Butler, J., 1988. Performative acts and gender constitution: an essay in phenomenology and feminist theory. *Theatre Journal*, 40 (4), 519–531.

Butler, J., 1993. *Bodies that matter: on the discursive limits of 'sex'*. New York: Routledge.

Butler, J., 2015. *Notes toward a performative theory of assembly*. Cambridge, MA: Harvard University Press.

Cacho, L.M., 2012. *Social death: racialized rightlessness and the criminalization of the unprotected*. New York: NYU Press.

Clough, P.T. and Halley, J., 2007. *The affective turn: theorizing the social*. Durham, NC: Duke University Press.

Cohen, C.J., 2004. Deviance as resistance: a new research agenda for the study of black politics. *Du Bois Review*, 1 (1), 27–45.

Cooperatives for a Better World, 2017. *Cooperatives for a Better World* [online]. Available from: https://cooperativesforabetterworld.coop/ [Accessed 10 February 2017].

D'Aoust, A., 2014. Ties that bind? Engaging emotions, governmentality and neoliberalism: introduction to the special issue. *Global Society*, 28 (3), 267–276.

Evans, W.T., 2007. Counter-hegemony at work: resistance, contradiction and emergent culture inside a worker-occupied hotel. *Berkeley Journal of Sociology*, 51 (globalization & social change), 33–68.

Foucault, M., 1977. *Discipline and punish: the birth of the prison*. London: Penguin Books.

Foucault, M., 1980. *Power/knowledge*. Brighton: Harvester Press.

Foucault, M., 1982. The subject and power. *In*: H.L. Dreyfus, P. Rabinow, and M. Foucault, eds. *Beyond structuralism and hermeneutics*. Chicago, IL: University of Chicago, 208–226.

Foucault, M., 1988. *The history of sexuality, volume 1: introduction*. New York: Vintage.

Foucault, M., 1997. *Ethics: subjectivity and truth*. New York: New Press.

Foucault, M., 2008. *The birth of biopolitics: lectures at the Collège de France, 1978–1979*. New York: Palgrave Macmillan.

Glass, M.R. and Rose-Redwood, R., 2014. *Performativity, politics, and the production of social space*. New York: Routledge.

Hamann, T.H., 2009. Neoliberalism, governmentality, and ethics. *Foucault Studies*, 6, 37–59.

Harvey, D., 2005. *A brief history of neoliberalism*. Oxford: Oxford University Press.

Haugaard, M., 2012. Rethinking the four dimensions of power. *Journal of Political Power*, 5 (1), 35–54.

Holborow, M., 2015. *Language and neoliberalism*. New York: Routledge.

Hollander, J.A. and Einwohner, R.L., 2004. *Conceptualizing resistance. Sociological forum*, 19 (4), 533–554.

Hoy, D.C., 2004. *Critical resistance: from poststructuralism to post-critique*. Cambridge, MA: MIT Press.

ICA, 2016a. *Building a better world now* [online]. Cooperatives for a better world. Available from: http://buildingabetterworldnow.coop/ [Accessed 10 June 2016].

ICA, 2016b. *International Co-operative Alliance* [online]. International Co-operative Alliance. Available from: http://ica.coop/ [Accessed 10 June 2016].

ICA, 2016c. *What is a co-operative?* [online]. International Co-operative Alliance. Available from: http://ica.coop/en/what-co-operative/ [Accessed 10 June 2016].

Illouz, E., 2007. *Cold intimacies: the making of emotional capitalism*. Cambridge: Polity Press.

Laclau, E. and Mouffe, C., 2008. *Hegemonin: Den socialistiska strategin*. Göteborg/Stockholm: Glänta/Vertigo.

Lilja, M. and Vinthagen, S., 2014. Sovereign power, disciplinary power and biopower: resisting what power with what resistance? *Journal of Political Power*, 7 (1), 107–126.

## RESISTANCE AND EMOTIONS

Marx, K., 1867/2013. *Capital: a critical analysis of capitalist production*. Ware: Wordsworth Editions.

Massey, D., 2013. Vocabularies of the economy. *Soundings*, 54, 9–22.

McElhinny, B., 2010. The audacity of affect: gender, race, and history in linguistic accounts of legitimacy and belonging. *Annual Review of Anthropology*, 39 (1), 309–328.

Nietzsche, F., 1959. *The portable Nietzsche*. London: Penguin.

Odysseos, L., Death, C., and Malmvig, H., 2016. Interrogating Michel Foucault's counter-conduct: theorising the subjects and practices of resistance in global politics. *Global Society*, 30 (2), 151–156.

Pahnke, A., 2015. Institutionalizing economies of opposition: explaining and evaluating the success of the MST's cooperatives and agroecological repeasantization. *The Journal of Peasant Studies*, 42 (6), 1087–1107.

Paulsen, R., 2010. *Arbetssamhället: Hur arbetet överlevde teknologin*. Malmö: Gleerups.

Peters, M.A., 2016. Education, neoliberalism, and human capital: *Homo economicus* as 'entrepreneur of himself'. *In*: S. Springer, K. Birch, and J. MacLeavy, eds. *The handbook of neoliberalism*. New York: Routledge, 297–307.

Puusa, A., Mönkkönen, K., and Varis, A., 2013. Mission lost? Dilemmatic dual nature of co-operatives. *Journal of Co-operative Organization and Management*, 1 (1), 6–14.

Reber, D., 2012. Headless capitalism: affect as free-market episteme. *differences*, 23 (1), 62–100.

Richard, A. and Rudnyckyj, D., 2009. Economies of affect. *The Journal of the Royal Anthropological Institute*, 15 (1), 57–77.

Rothschild, J. and Whitt, J.A., 1986. *The cooperative workplace: potentials and dilemmas of organizational democracy and participation*. Cambridge: Cambridge University Press.

Satgar, V., 2007. Cooperative development and labour solidarity: a neo-Gramscian perspective on the global struggle against neoliberalization. *LABOUR, Capital and Society*, 40 (1/2), 56–79.

Scott, J.C., 1985. *Weapons of the weak: everyday forms of peasant resistance*. New Haven, CT: Yale University Press.

Sointu, E., 2016. Discourse, affect and affliction. *The Sociological Review*, 64 (2), 312–328.

Sørensen, M.J., 2016. Constructive resistance: conceptualising and mapping the terrain. *Journal of Resistance Studies*, 2 (1), 49–78.

Spear, R., 2004. Governance in democratic member-based organisations. *Annals of Public and Cooperative Economics*, 75 (1), 33–60.

Springer, S., 2010. Neoliberal discursive formations: on the contours of subjectivation, good governance, and symbolic violence in posttransitional Cambodia. *Environment and Planning D: Society and Space*, 28, 931–950.

Springer, S., 2016a. Fuck neoliberalism. *ACME: And International Journal for Critical Geographies*, 15 (2), 285–292.

Springer, S., 2016b. *The discourse of neoliberalism: an anatomy of a powerful idea*. London: Rowman and Littlefield International.

Torfing, J., 1999. *New theories of discourse: Laclau, Mouffe and Žižek*. Oxford: Blackwell.

Türken, S., *et al.*, 2016. Making sense of neoliberal subjectivity: a discourse analysis of media language on self-development. *Globalizations*, 13 (1), 32–46.

Varman, R. and Chakrabarti, M., 2004. Contradictions of democracy in a workers' cooperative. *Organization Studies*, 25 (2), 183–208.

Weber, M., 1927/2007. *General economic history*. New York: Cosmo Classics.

White, R.J. and Williams, C.C., 2012. The pervasive nature of heterodox economic spaces at a time of neoliberal crisis: towards a 'postneoliberal' anarchist future. *Antipode*, 44 (5), 1625–1644.

White, R.J. and Williams, C.C., 2016. Everyday contestations to neoliberalism: valuing and harnessing alternative work practices in a neoliberal society. *In*: S. Springer, K. Birch, and J. MacLeavy, eds. *The handbook of neoliberalism*. New York: Routledge, 603–612.

Whyman, P.B., 2012. Co-operative principles and the evolution of the 'dismal science': the historical interaction between co-operative and mainstream economics. *Business History*, 54 (6), 833–854.

Winther Jørgensen, M. and Phillips, L., 2000. *Diskursanalys som teori och metod*. Lund: Studentlitteratur.

# Concluding remarks

Mona Lilja, Mikael Baaz, Satu Heikkinen and Annika Jonsson

In this final chapter, we will further elaborate on the 'politics of emotions' by returning to the five analytical themes that were outlined in the Introduction section of this book. The themes analytically highlight some aspects of the assemblage of resistance and emotions, and could serve as a point of departure for future research on understanding the complex relationship between the two. In these concluding remarks, we will also elaborate further on self-making in relation to resistance and emotions. Different practices of *constructing a resisting 'me'* appear in all the categories discussed and thus run as a common thread throughout the text.

As argued in the introduction, *emotions translate into motivations and various resisting practices*. Emotions appears to be an engine of resistance by removing the effects of disciplinary technologies, creating non-governable subjects and entangling in 'moral shocks', which motivates people 'to do something' (Goodwin *et al.* 2001). Emotions contribute to how we construct objects of love or hate, processes that are not dependent on whether the thing is good or bad, but on whether it seems agreeable or hurtful to us or others (Ahmed 2004; Lilja 2017b). While issues, political institutions and/or their practices are attributed emotional values (such as hate or frustration), this sometimes forms the very basis for political activities. Frustration, sadness and anger, which arise in relation to objects and practices, could be seen as circulating, moving between individuals as well as between individuals and signs; sometimes they also translate into actions (Goodwin *et al.* 2001). According to Hemmings (2005, 2014), however, emotions should not only be seen as a 'rescue' from the deterministic aspects of power. Emotions are not always emancipatory, but also disciplinary – they discipline bodies and shape realities.

Moreover, emotions are also important in the embodying of different activist subject positions or 'figurations', thereby contributing to various resisting practices. Or in other words, emotions are often at play in the construction of resistance identities and positions. Critically interrogating the emotional components of different identity positions and the embodying of these positions, enable a richer understanding of those who identify themselves as resisters. These emotional components may of course alter with time and, by this, create interesting identity trajectories of resistance.

'Techniques of the self' involves the practices through which individuals inhabit subject positions and transform existing subjectivities (Foucault 1998). Diaries, confessions, therapy, diet, daily training schedules and so on are practices that might provide another narrative of who one is and reveal one's attempts to reconstruct habits and abilities (Foucault 1988a; Burkitt 2002). We would like to argue that these processes embrace various emotional reflections. Assumed, reflected and rejected discourses and practices of punishments and rewards, all entangle in different emotions and contribute to processes of embodying (or not) certain positions.

Emotions as an engine of resistance tangentially interact with other fields and aspects, such as space. The loss of land, visiting memorial places or inheriting land are all practices connected with space, which invoke different emotions (King 2010; Robins 2014). These emotions emerge in the nexus between the particular/individual and more general discourses about land. Dominant discourses of land evoke emotions as people practice, navigate, relate, resist to, or assume these discourses (cf. Lang 2003). In addition, occasionally there are temporal aspects of 'emotional' resistance. As suggested in the Introduction, fear is an emotion experienced in the face of something that threatens us in the future. According to Heidegger (1962, p. 180), fear relates 'as something that threatens us, is not yet within striking distance, but it is coming close'. Fear, then, moves between the present and the future; between the immediate experience and potential hurt, and makes us resist potential dangers (Ahmed 2004).

Also, emotions, such as rage or compassion, are, in different ways, entangled in time. On some occasions, representations of violence, poverty or other forms of local and global inequalities have made people on one side of the globe rise with moral outrage against actions and events that have happened on the other side of the globe. This outrage is not grounded in physical proximity but in solidarity, which emerges across space and time. Images can make suffering at a distance seem very close, while distancing what is proximate (Butler 2015, pp. 100, 103). The violent images preserve traumatic experiences of what has happened 'there', so that it also seems to have happened 'here'. Still, what happens 'here' now – as we watch the image – happened 'there' before (in previous times when the image was taken). Still, the 'time-lagged' images impact on our comprehension of reality and ourselves in relation to others 'now' and encourage resistance.

In addition, emotions create memories, which might nourish resistance. When we laugh, or cry at something, we will remember it. Thus, emotions are a part of remembering and inform what moments we keep alive and later knit together in complex stories of, among other things, the subject's 'place' in relation to power and the corresponding performances of resistance.

Finally, we should also connect the emotional aspects of resistance to 'proxy resistance'. Active listening, reflexivity and empathy enable individuals and groups to explore the vulnerability of others, which, in turn, enable proxy resistance. Understanding others through an exploration of emotion opens up possibilities for attention as well as spaces for resistance and a transformation of the divide between 'us' and 'them'.

# RESISTANCE AND EMOTIONS

Emotions not only translate into motivations and various resisting practices, but *management of emotions can also be seen as a form of resistance.* To manage emotions, how we convey emotions to others, can be understood as powerful forms of resistance. Several chapters in this book explore resistance through Arlie R. Hochschild's theories of emotional labour (1983). Managing emotions, through conscious attempts of manoeuvring emotional expressions or reactions, should be understood as resistance practices that mirror different forms of power. Resistance here is expressed through emotions, which are managed in order to create different effects. Disguising ones 'real' emotions might be a powerful act of dissent. However, this does not mean that to 'fake' emotions does not have real implications. The distinction between the 'real' and the 'fake' is one that is difficult to establish given that bodily experiences of 'faking' inform resisting subjectivities (Lilja 2017a).

Moreover, emotional management as resistance is also connected with space. Hochschild points out that physical settings, such as mass graves or demonstrations, evoke different emotions and should, thus, be seen as a part of our emotion management. As we decide which settings to visit or which to avoid, we are managing our emotions. Demonstrations might be spaces where emotions are generated and circulate. Thus, if we decide to visit demonstrations this could be seen as emotional management with consequences for resistance. In political actions, such as demonstrations, emotions not only circulate but also find a clear direction with a sender (the assembly) and a receiver.

Not only could managing emotions be seen as resistance, but also can *non-conformity with, and non-management in accordance with, emotional rule.* As subjects, we constantly 'read' and 'decode' discursive rules, and conform and regulate our behaviours to norms. Non-conformity to emotion rules could be investigated as a form of resistance. Butler (1995, p. 236), for example, argues that there are textual movements in the works of Foucault when freedom from the normalising oppression is pictured as the return of the body to a non-normalisable wildness. Sudden unrelated outbreaks of laughing, uncontrolled, dislocated and expressed sexual desire or undesired silence create 'inappropriate' resistance. To not manage one's emotions in line with disciplinary technologies could shake the cultural order as well as challenge norms and different disciplinary 'truth-regimes' (Ackroyd and Thompson 1999; Rasmussen 2004; Lindqvist and Olsson 2017).

The non-normalised, non-disciplined movements of resisting bodies disrupt the normality of public spaces, thus shaking up and unsettling orders where: 'the body (could be) regarded as a source of interference in, and a danger to, the operations of reason' (Grosz 1994, p. 5; Lilja 2017b). Emotions make masses move in a direction against others, against political institutions and their embodied figurations. The intensity of the emotions that are directed towards concrete bodies or state institutions could be frightening for the receivers of the emotions.

*Emotions also create communities (of resistance).* Emotions makes people stick to resistance movements and to others who are aligned with the movement. Thus, emotions are performative – they do things, they direct bodies and create practices. Emotions are at the very core of loyalties, attachments, humour and bonds (see e.g. Scheff 1990 on social ties and Goodwin *et al.* 2001 on social movements). Coalitions are formed through affective commitments, by recognising solidarity with others who are like-minded, and by affective

131

meetings that generate communities of belonging, social movements or 'circulating resistance' (such as the #metoo campaign) (Foy *et al.* 2014). The latter form of resistance, 'circulating resistance', interestingly, displays how not only power, but also resistance, can be transmitted in more of a net-like organisation that involves intensities, signs, and the recognition of signs, as well as different emotions. Resistance inspires, provokes, generates and encourages, as well as sometimes discouraging, resistance while strengthening power.

When demonstrating, protesting and resisting bodies must be viewed and their vocalised sounds must be heard in order to create emotions, agency and communities of belonging. Or in Butler's words: 'the body must enter the visual and audible field . . . if those bodies on the line are not registered elsewhere, there is no global response, and also, no global form of ethical recognition and connection, and so something of the reality of the event is lost' (Butler 2015, p. 86). This indicates that visual representations must be further included into our political analyses in order to understand emotions such as outrage and solidarity; there are no purely linguistic speech acts that can be separated and distinguished from bodily acts.

People do not only emotionally connect around the globe. Carolyn Dinshaw (2007), for example, displays how organisations also draw on emotional encounters with people of the past to strengthen their communities. By dissolving the border between them and us, and feeling their vulnerability, we might connect affectively with the inhabitants of the past (such as feminist now, who sometimes build their politics on memories of the struggles of the suffragettes). The possibility of forming communities across time reveals the temporal aspect of forming networks, communities of belonging or social movements (Dinshaw 2007, p. 178).

Finally, and perhaps most interestingly, *some forms of emotional, devoted resistance could be displayed as a non-oppositional resistance.* Stephen J. Ball and Antonio Olmedo (2012) argue that resistance sometimes arise as subjects care for themselves. Drawing on Foucault, resistance might then be the result of a 'care for the self' (Foucault 1988). The feeling of 'I don't want to be/live like this' may spark off resistance, which distinguishes itself from larger social or political movements. Also, larger resistance movements might be formulated without the 'opposition' being a crucial property of its appearance. Enthusiasm and devotion for 'alternative' or 'prefigurative' practices, which challenge the existing social order (i.e. 'constructive resistance') sometimes prevail as emotional forms of resistance that are played out without actively by being in opposition to the 'other(s)'.

The above text provides a conceptual and theoretical reflection on the messy relationship between resistance and emotions. Emotions have been embraced as both collective and circulating as well as subjective reflections that spring from the social context (Cf. Clough and Halley 2007; Koivunen 2010; Braidotti 2011). Thus, hate, desire or love are emotions embedded in social contexts that create the possibility for us to communicate, share and circulate emotions, while still having an individual attachment to them. Experiencing emotions is a social practice that is influenced by dominant discourses as well as by common practices of emotional management still emotions are also subjective experiences. 'Particular' emotions provide material for extra-discursive experiences, serving as a point of departure for resistance and the negotiation of various discourses.

The collective and individual character of emotions impact on how emotions are entangled in the embodying of different positions. 'Moral shocks', make people subjects who

# RESISTANCE AND EMOTIONS

'do something'. Emotions are also important in the embodying of different activist subject positions and are at play in the construction of resistance identities. Emotions create memories, which we might use in our diaries, in our stories about ourselves and which, sometimes, nourish resist ance. Also, how we identify in relation to others is informed by emotions, such as empathy, loyalty, solidarity and by affective meetings, that generate communities of belonging and an 'us'. In addition, emotional encounters with people in the past or future bodies-to-become, strengthen the communities of today and how we identify as parts of larger groups and communities (Dinshaw 2007).

## References

Ackroyd, S. and Thompson, P. 1999. *Organizational misbehaviour*. London: Sage.

Ahmed, S. 2004. Affective economies. *Social Text*, 22 (2), 117–139.

Ball, S.J. and Olmedo, A. 2012. Care of the self, resistance and subjectivity under neoliberal governmentalities. *Critical Studies in Education*, 54 (1), 85–96.

Braidotti, R. 2011. *Nomadic subjects: embodiment and sexual difference in contemporary feminist theory*. 2nd ed. New York: Columbia University Press.

Burkitt, I. 2002. Technologies of the self: habitus and capacities. *Journal for the Theory of Social Behaviour*, 32 (2), 219–237.

Butler, J. 1995. Subjection, resistance, resignification. In J. Rajchman, ed. *The identity in question*. New York: Routledge, 229–250.

Butler, J. 2015. *Notes toward a performative theory of assembly*. Cambridge, MA: Harvard University Press.

Clough, P.T. and Halley, J. 2007. *The affective turn: theorizing the social*. Durham, NC: Duke University Press.

Dinshaw, C. 2007. Temporalities. In P. Strohm, ed. *Middle English, Oxford twenty-first century approaches to literature*. Oxford: Oxford University Press, 107–123.

Foucault, M. 1988. Technologies of the self. In L.H. Martin, H. Gutman and P.H. Hutton, eds. *Technologies of the self: a seminar with Michel Foucault*. Amherst: The University of Massachusetts Press, 16–50.

Foy, S., Freeland, R., Miles, A., Rogers, K.B. and Smith-Lovin, L. 2014. Emotions and affect as source, outcome and resistance to inequality. In J. McLeod, E. Lawler and M. Schwalbe, eds. *Handbook of the social psychology of inequality*. Dordrecht: Springer, 295–324.

Goodwin, J., Jasper, J.M. and Polletta, F. 2001. *Passionate politics: emotions and social movements*. Chicago, IL: The University of Chicago Press.

Grosz, E. 1994. *Volatile bodies: towards a corporeal feminism*. Bloomington, IN: Indiana University Press.

Heidegger, M. 1962. *Being and time*, translated by J. Macquarrie and E. Robinson. London: SCM Press.

Hemmings, C. 2005. Invoking affect: cultural theory and the ontological turn. *Cultural Studies*, 19 (5), 548–567.

Hemmings, C. 2014. The materials of reparation. *Feminist Theory*, 15 (1), 27–30.

Hochschild, A.R. 1983. *The managed heart. Commercialization of human feeling*. Berkeley/Los Angeles/London: University of California Press.

King, A. 2010. The Afghan War and 'postmodern' memory: commemoration and the dead of Helmand. *The British Journal of Sociology*, 61 (1), 1–25.

Koivunen, A. 2010. An affective turn? Reimagining the subject of feminist theory. In M. Liljeström and S. Paasonen, eds. *Working with affect in feminist readings: disturbing differences*. New York: Routledge, 8–28.

Lang, L.J. 2003. *Working with men to end gender-based violence: lessons for the South Asian context*. Unpublished manuscript. New Delhi, India.

# RESISTANCE AND EMOTIONS

Lilja, M. 2017a. Layer-cake figurations and hide-and-show resistance in Cambodia. *Feminist Review*, 117 (1), 131–147.

Lilja, M. 2017b. Dangerous bodies, matter and emotions: public assemblies and embodied resistance. *Journal of Political Power*, 10 (3), 342–352.

Lindqvist, M. and Olsson, E. 2017. Everyday resistance in psychiatry through harbouring strategies. *Journal of Political Power*, 10 (2), 200–218.

Rasmussen, B. 2004. Between endless needs and limited resources: the gendered construction of a greedy organization. *Gender, Work & Organization*, 11 (5), 506–525.

Robins, S. 2014. Constructing meaning from disappearance: local memorialisation of the missing in Nepal. *Journal of Conflict and Violence*, 8 (1), 104–118.

Scheff, T.J. 1990. *Microsociology: discourse, emotion and social structure*. Chicago: Chicago University Press.

# Index

*Note*: Page numbers followed by "n" refer to endnotes.

acceleration 43, 49, 51
Adam, B. 42
administrative online systems 40, 41; 'approaching the system' 52; digital 42; effectiveness of 55; emailing 49–50; emotions and resistance 44–6; materialities 54; material-semiotic situation 45; negative approach reactions 51; new public management 41–2; 'resistance by escape' 48; respondent experienced 48–9; Rosa, H. 43, 44, 49; scripts, concept of 44; shadow system 52–3; stressful experiences 49–50; technology 42–4, 46; temporality and acceleration 42–3; time, concept of 42–4; time-consuming online systems 51; transparency 47; universities 43–4
affect-as-episteme 117
affective turn 62
Ahmed, Sara 25, 34, 45, 47, 119
anarchy, notion of 115
anti-militarist movement 100
antinormativity, in queer theory 24, 26–7
'approaching the system' 52
Arendt, Hannah 53
*Art of Moral Protest: Culture, Biography, and Creativity in Social Movements, The* (Jasper) 95
*Art of Social Theory, The* (Swedberg) 9
Arvidson, Markus 4
authoritarian regimes 101
autonomy 12–13, 16, 19
Axelsson, Jonas 4

back stage deep acting 69–70
Ball, S. J. 132
Barbalet, Jack 25–6
bathroom, emotional harbouring work 83, 87; comfort of emptiness 85–6; crying and anger 84; cyberloafing and self-talking 85; as deep backstage 83–5; 'emotional void' 84; withdrawal to 86
Beck, R. 14

Berceli, D. 59
Bergman, A. 9
Bêrivan 65–6
Billingsley, A. 3
biopolitical temporal strategy 42
Bloch, C. 50
Boltanski, L. 27, 111, 117
Bolton, S. C. 75, 77–8
Boyd, C. 75
Bratt, Ingvar 17
British colonial rule 97
British Salt Tax in India (1930) 97
buffer group, concept of 80
'Building a better world now' (ICA campaign) 126n1, 126n2; aim 112; corporations and co-ops 120–2; economic growth 122–3; non-critical resistance 124–6; powerpoint presentation 112; resistance to neoliberal capitalism 124; togetherness, representations of 118–20; transformative movement 122–3
bureaucracy 25, 53
*Business Ethics Quarterly* 8
Butler, J. 26, 111, 132

capitalism 111; with conscience 112, 125; self-legitimising discourse 117; *see also* neoliberal capitalism
'care for self' 132
Chakrabarti, M. 114
'Chatham House rules' 106n1
Chenoweth, E. 94
Chiapello, E. 27, 111, 117
'circulating resistance' 132
civil disobedience 103
civil resistance: advocates 98; backstage activities 99–105; constructive forms 106; dynamics of 97; face-to-face interaction 95; frontstage performances 96–9; Gandhi, Mohandas K. 97, 102–3; nonviolent 93, 94; Parks, Rosa 93; publications on 94; research on 98; social movements and 95–6; studies 94; *see also* emotion management

# INDEX

coalitions 131
Cohen, C. J. 116
Communist Party of Italy 25
communities of resistance 131
computer-based administrative systems 40, 41
Connor, J. 10, 11
constructive programme 102, 107n4
cooperatives and neoliberal capitalism 110; affect-as-episteme 117; anarchy, notion of 115; campaign discourse *see* 'Building a better world now' (ICA campaign); constrain and opposition 115; cooperation as resistance 113–15; cooperative movement 114, 115, 124; critical resistance 115–17; democratic consciousness 114; desubjectification 116; discourse theory 113; discursive–affective approach 115; discursive articulations of affect 117–18, 126; dominant discourses 110–12; feebleness 114; Foucauldian perspective 111, 115; International Co-operative Alliance 111–12; modern capitalism, characteristics of 110; 'politics of deviance' 116; profit accumulation 110; promotion of cooperation 110, 112; reverse discourse 116; self-governmental resistance 114; signs and nodal points 113
corporations and cooperatives 120–2, 124
Coventry symposium 100
Cowburn, J. 74, 76
critical resistance 125; cooperatives and neoliberal capitalism 115–17; eventual performance of 110, 112
cultural activities, of resistance 100–2
cyberloafing 84–5

Dahl, U. 4
deep acting, Hochschild's concept of 60, 64, 70, 71
Deleuze, Gilles 27
'deliberate absence' 83
Delta Airlines 63, 64, 68
'democratic consciousness' 114
desubjectification/desubjugation 116
digital administrative online systems 42, 51, 55
Dinshaw, C. 49, 132
discourse theory (DT) 113
discursive articulations of affect 112, 117–18, 126
Doucet, L. 51, 52
dramaturgical model 95

economic growth, cooperatives for 122–3
Edkins, J. 47
educational performances 102
Einwohner, R.L. 15
emailing 49–50
emancipatory resistance 111, 116, 117
emotional competence 24
emotional coping strategies 77
emotional/emotive dissonance 76, 80

emotional gifts 86–7
emotional labour 3, 64; effects 77; emotion work and 75–6, 78; healthcare workers 80; mental healthcare and psychiatry 74
emotional recovery 86–7
emotional regimes 25, 26
emotional resistance 60, 66–7, 69
emotional turn 62, 70
'emotional void' 84
emotion-evoking symbolism 99
emotion management 64, 68, 71, 75, 131; Bolton's typology 77, 78; community organising 102–4; cultures of resistance 100–2; employees and 78; foci of 105; invasion of backstage 104–5; in psychotherapeutic work 76; 'safe spaces' creation 99–100, 104; strategies 77–8
emotion rules: display rules and 76, 88, 89n1; non-conformity to 131
emotion–theoretical framework 80–1
emotion work 64, 68, 70, 74; in buffer group 80; emotional labour and 75–6, 78; harbouring work and resistance 80–1; individual work 76; organising 75; philanthropic management 78; presentation management 78; surface-acting 76, 89n2; *see also* harbouring work
enunciative modalities 24, 27–8
Equality Ombudsman 28
*Everyday Peasant Resistance: Hidden Transcripts* (Scott) 63
everyday resistance 63, 79, 82
*Exit, Voice and Loyalty* study 11, 12
experiencing emotions 132
Eyerman, Ron 94, 96

face-to-face interaction, in civil resistance 95
Fairclough, Norman 17
'fake' and 'real' emotions 131
family resemblance 9, 12–13, 19
fear, notion of 47, 130
Felder, Don 16
Flam, Helena 95
Foucault, M. 1, 26–8; on autonomy 13; enunciative modalities 24; norm-critical subject 35; norms as means of power 37; panoptical scheme 34; perspective on discourse 111; power and resistance 115; resistance 132; self-discipline and 12, 17; self-surveillance 30; subject of discourse 33; 'the care of the self' 8
Freyermuth, Gundolf S. 13
frontstage–backstage emotion management 93–5, 104–5
front stage surface acting 68–9

Gandhi, Mohandas K. 97
Ganz, Marshall 100
Garretón, Manuel Antonio 96
Gerring, John 41
Gillberg, G. 18

# INDEX

Goffman, Erving 60, 68, 81, 88, 93, 95, 96, 105
Goodwin, J. 59, 61, 62, 69, 96
Gothenburg Energy (2010) 15
Gould, Deborah B. 62
greedy organisations 86–7
Groves, Julian 96
'Gülçin' 59, 67–70
Gülen, Fethullah 59

Hammond, John L. 101
harbouring work: concept of 74, 80; 'deliberate absence' 83; emotional recovery and gifts 86–7; emotion work and resistance 80–1; ethical issues 82; focus group interviews 81; greedy organisations 86–7; management of 76; new public management 82; selection of interviewees 82; in somatic healthcare 76; *see also* bathroom, emotional harbouring work
Haugaard, M. 12
healthcare workers 89n3; emotional labour 80; issues for 76–7; somatic and psychiatric care 76
'heavy emotional lifting' 87
Heidegger, M. 3, 47, 130
Hemmings, C. 3, 129
hidden emotional resistance 60, 63, 68–71
hidden transcripts 63, 70
Hirschman, A.O. 11, 12
Hobbins, J. 16
Hochschild, A.R. 44, 60, 62, 63–4, 68, 71, 75, 76, 78, 80, 131
Hodson, R. 78
Hollander, J.A. 15
Hoy, D. C. 124
Huzell, H. 79

ICA *see* International Co-operative Alliance
Illouz, E. 111
'inappropriate' emotions 4
individualistic tendency 8
International Co-operative Alliance (ICA) 111–12
involuntary self-loyalty 11, 17–18
irrational resistance 20n6
Issa, Daniela 102
Ivarsson, Lars 16

Jansson, A. 44
Jasper, J.M. 59, 61, 62, 69, 95, 96, 101
Jenkins, R. 95
Jones, Jamila 104
*Journal of Business Ethics* 8

'Karlskoga-spirit' 17
Karlsson, J. C. 9, 15, 79, 83, 86
Kendall, Gavin 27
Kirchhoff, J.W. 15
knowledge gap 2
Koefoed, Minoo 3
Kurdi-Der 61

Kurdish guerrillas 60, 64–5
Kurdish martyrs 65, 66

Laclau, E. 113
land, discourses of 130
Langmann, Elisabeth 35, 36
layering, concept of 10
LGBTQ organisations 28
Lim, V. K. 85
Lindqvist, Mona 3
linear time, concept of 47
LO 28
loyalty 4; Chinese definition of 11, 15; concept 8–9, 11; Connor, J. 10, 11; dichotomy 12; Japan and China 11; layered reality 10–11; Raz, J. 11; and resistance 14; *see also* self-loyalty

Maimonides, Moses 100
*Managed Heart: Commercialization of Human Feelings, The* 62, 63
Mann, S. 74, 76
Månsson, Niclas 35, 36
MAPER 61
Martin, Brian 98
Martinsson, Lena 26
martyrdom 60, 64–6
memorial places 3, 130
memories, emotions and 133
method acting approach 64
MEYA-DER 66
Meyrowitz, J. 81, 84, 88
militant biographies 66
Miller, Web 98, 99
Milosevic, Slobodan 101
*mistica* performances 102
Montgomery Bus Boycott 93
'moral shocks' 129, 132–3
Mouffe, C. 113
*Movimento dos Trabalhadores Sem Terra* (MST) 101

neoliberal capitalism 4, 110–11; domination 111, 112; emotional justifications 117; *see also* cooperatives and neoliberal capitalism
new public management (NPM) 41–2, 82, 87
non-critical resistance 4, 124–6
'non-emotional' expressions 3
non-oppositional resistance 4, 132
nonviolent civil resistance 94
nonviolent confrontational resistance 102
non-work: and deliberate absence 83; Paulsen's notion 79
norm-critical initiatives, in Sweden 38n2
norm-critical pedagogy 23–5
norm-critical subject 29, 31–2; emotional distance 37; inhabitants 33; self-surveying 29–32; (un) settled subject 32–4; target groups 34–6
norm critique 23, 25, 30; as discourse 24, 29, 30, 32, 36; levelled at norms 29; means to varying

# INDEX

ends 32; overcoming of negative emotions 31; panoptical scheme and 37; queer resistance and 36; series of methods 31; social resistance movements and 24

Northern Kurdistan 59, 70; Kurdish movement in 60; martyrdom 60, 64–6; martyr's ceremony 66–8; research methodologies 61; resistance movement in 3

Nowotny, Helga 14

NPM *see* new public management

Olmedo, A. 132

Olsson, E. 3, 80, 81; and Bolton's perspective 77; harbouring work, concept of 74, 80, 81

one-way communication 54

online administrative systems *see* administrative online systems

online travel expense system 52

organisational misbehaviour 15, 79

organisational resistance 78

Orhan, M. 65, 66

Pahnke, A. 114

Parks, Rosa 93, 96

Partîya Karkerên Kurdistanê (Kurdistan's Workers' Party) (PKK) 58, 65

*Passionate Politics: Emotions and Social Movements* (Jasper) 96, 104

Paulsen, R. 79

Payne, Charles 103

performance theory 94

philanthropic management 78

Phillips, L. 113

political argumentation, in Indonesia 98

'political jiu-jitsu', concept of 98

political movements 96

political socialisation 65

'politics of emotions' 129

*Politics of Nonviolent Action, The* (Sharp) 94

Polletta, F. 96

Pratt, M.G. 51, 52

prefix 'self' 8–9

presentation management 78

*Presentation of self in everyday life, The* (Goffman) 63, 95

*prima facie* 10, 15

'proxy resistance' 130

psychiatry 88; new public management in 87; official discourse 86

public emotional resistance 60, 68–9, 71

public transcript 68

queer emotions 25

*Queer feminist agenda* (Rosenberg) 25

queer resistance 23, 26, 37; critique at norms 24; in Gothenburg 25

queer theory 23, 25; antinormativity 26–7; norm critique 36

radical political activism 15

Ralston, Joshua 97

rational/irrational resistance 20n6

Raz, J. 11

reactionary resistance 116

'real' and 'fake' emotions 131

Reber, D. 117

'resistance by escape' 48

'reverse discourse' 116

RFSL Ungdom 24, 28, 29

Rigby, Andrew 4

Rosa, H. 7, 13, 43, 44, 49; 'deceleration as ideology' 14; 'forced self-thematising' 18; theoretical framework 18

Rosenberg, Tiina 25

Rose, Nikolas 13

'safe space' backstage 99–100, 104

Salt March 102

Satgar, V. 114

Scott, J.C. 1, 44, 52, 60, 62–4, 68–9, 71, 79

Scott, S.V. 43, 53

scripts, concept of 44

self-binding strategy 15–16

self-discipline 3, 12–13, 55

self-governmental resistance 114

self-loyalty 4; social accelerations; 'altered face' 10; characteristics 16; concept 8–9, 13; definition 11; emergence of 8; and family resemblance 12–13; Foucault, M. 8, 12–13, 17; involuntary strategy 17–18; layered reality 10; methodological approach 9–10; motivates resistance 15; Simmel, Georg 9–11, 14, 19; theorising method 9; voluntary strategy 14–17; *see also* loyalty

self-realisation process 18

self-reflection, norm critique and 35

self-surveillance 30, 36, 37

self-talking 85, 88

Sennett, R. 14

shadow system 52–3

Sharp, Gene 94

Simmel, Georg 9–11, 14, 19, 34

Smith, P. 74

social accelerations 7; centrality of 13; concept of 14; dimensions in 14; 'playing the game' 17–18; Rosa, Hartmut 7, 13–14; voluntary self-loyalty as resistance 14–17

social entrepreneurship 111, 123

Social Movement Research 61

social movements: and civil resistance 95–6; emotions of rationality and 24–6, 34, 59; in Sweden 24

*Sociology of Emotions* 61, 62

sociology, Simmel's notion of 19

Sørensen, Majken Jul 4

sovereign power, concept of 1

# INDEX

Stanislavski, Constantin 64
Stephan, M. J. 94
Stern, Maria 47
stressful experiences 49–50
surface acting emotion work 60, 64, 76, 89n2
Swedberg, Richard 7–9, 12, 13, 19
Swedish Agency for Youth and Civil Society 28
Swedish Lutheran Church 23

target groups, norm-critical work and 34–6
*tazîye* 65, 66–7, 70, 71
technical acceleration 14
'techniques of self' 130
Tema Likabehandling 28
temporal and affective resistance 41
temporal changes 43
temporality 42–3
theatre, as metaphor 81
Theodosius, C. 74
Tibetan–Chinese conflict 60
time, concept of 42–3
time-consuming online systems 51, 52
time-consuming technical systems 53
'time-space' compression 43
'tolerance perspective' 30
travel expenses system 48
Turkish–Kurdish conflict 58, 64

Ulysses, self-binding strategy 15–16
Ungdomsstyrelsen 24, 28
university spaces 40, 42, 43–4, 47, 50, 54, 55
Urry, J. 49, 50
US civil rights movement 93, 99, 101, 103, 104

Varman, R. 114
virtual technologies 44
voluntary self-loyalty 11, 14–17

Wagner, E.L. , 43
Wasshede, Cathrin 25
Weber, T. 53
West Papuan identity 97–8
Wettergren, Å. 44
whistle-blowing 16
White, R. J. 114
Whyman, P. B. 114
Wickham, Gary 27
Wiksell, Kristin 4
Williams, C. C. 114
Winther Jørgensen, M. 113
Wittgenstein, L. 9–10, 13, 19
workplace emotion, management strategies 77–8
    *see also* harbouring work

Zakiye Alkan 65–6